What people say about Day–Signs

"Every so often a book of originality and penetrating intelligence appears on the astrological scene and marks the beginning of a fresh area of inquiry. Bruce Scofield's Day–Signs is such a book. The author has reconstructed the astrology of Aztec and Maya civilizations and, for the first time, made it pertinent to the modern world. Here you will find a "new" typology of personality based on the twenty Mesoamerican day–signs which capture the range and complexity of human emotion and behavior. Scofield's delineations of the day–signs are like x–rays that cut to the basic issues confronting the human personality. Once you test these Native American techniques in your chart interpretations, you will find yourself returning to this book again and again. Anyone who counsels clients or seeks self–understanding will find much of value here."

Anthony Louis, M.D. psychiatrist and author of Horary Astrology: The History and Practice of Astro–Divination, The Art of Forecasting Using Solar Returns, and Tarot Beyond the Basics: Gain a Deeper Understanding of the Meanings Behind the Cards.

"Bruce Scofield's Day–Signs presents and ancient wisdom in a fresh, original way. Check it out and test it for yourself. It may not clear up your pimples or get you dates, but it offers to the serious student a unique and scholarly approach to the study of the relationship between heaven and Earth."

Michael Lutin, author of Made In Heaven: The Astrology of Relationships Ideal and Real, Childhood Rising, and Saturn Signs.

"Astrologers have long had an interest in the ancient roots of their subject; the cultures of Egypt, Mesopotamia, India and China. Unknown to many, and much closer to home, the cultures of Ancient Mexico and Central America created an astrology that reached unimaginable levels of sophistication and complexity. In this book, Scofield reveals for the first time, and in a practical way, the myth and meaning behind Aztec and Maya astrology. Day–Signs, which updates the knowledge of an ancient culture, is a useful tool that can give deep insights into personality and added meaning to personal destiny."

Steve Cozzi, author of Planets in Locality, and Generations and the Outer Planet Cycles.

Day-Signs

Native American Astrology
from Ancient Mexico

Bruce Scofield

The Wessex Astrologer

Published in 2017 by
The Wessex Astrologer Ltd,
4A Woodside Road
Bournemouth
BH5 2AZ
www.wessexastrologer.com

© Bruce Scofield 2017

Bruce Scofield asserts the moral right to be recognised as
the author of this work.

Cover Design by Jonathan Taylor

A catalogue record for this book is available at The British Library

ISBN 9781910531198

Previously published by One Reed Publications 9780962803109

No part of this book may be reproduced or used in any form or by any
means without the written permission of the publisher. A reviewer may
quote brief passages.

Bruce Scofield began a lifelong study of astrology in 1967 and since the mid 1970s has been an astrological consultant specializing in psychological analysis, relationships and electional astrology. He is the author of, or contributor to, many books and a large number of articles on astrology and other topics. He has served on the education committee of the National Center for Geocosmic Research (NCGR) since 1979 as both member and director, presently serving as president of the Professional Astrologers Alliance (PAA), has Level 4 certification from NCGR–PAA, professional certification from American Federation of Astrologers and holds an M.A. in history and a Ph.D. in geosciences. Since 2000 he has taught science at the University of Massachusetts and astrology–related courses for Kepler College. His website www.onereed.com contains information on Mesoamerican astrology and other topics.

Contents

Preface	ix
Introduction	xii
Part I: The 260–Day Astrological Calendar	**1**
Chapter 1: Ancient Calendars and the Conquest of Time	1
Chapter 2: The Restoration of The Astrological Calendar	13
Chapter 3: Using Day–Sign Astrology	25
Part II: Delineations of the Day–Signs	**37**
Introduction	37
Crocodile	41
Wind	48
House	55
Lizard	61
Serpent	67
Death	73
Deer	80
Rabbit	86
Water	92
Dog	98
Monkey	103
Grass	108
Reed	114
Ocelot	120
Eagle	126
Vulture	132
Earthquake	138
Knife	144

Rain	150
Flower	156

The 13–Day Periods   163

Part III: Ephemeris of the Day–Signs   171

References   211

Aztec Day–Sign Glyphs

Maya Day–Sign Glyphs

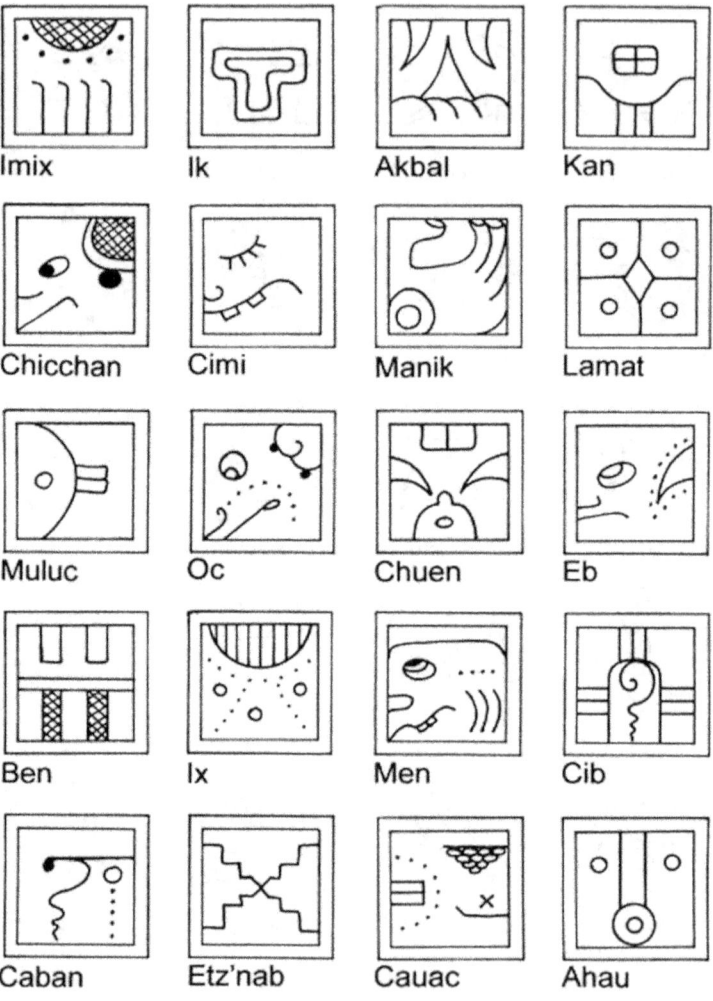

Preface

Prior to the Spanish Conquest, a distinctive Native–American astrological tradition existed and flourished in ancient Mesoamerica, today's Mexico and northern Central America. At the core of this tradition were 20 named days that cycled 13 times forming a count of 260 days that resonates with numerous astronomical cycles. Like Western astrology, Mesoamerican astrology is used as a structure and guide to the timing of collective rituals and a means of forecasting and interpreting events. It is also a system of personality classification and in this sense a way of self–knowledge.

The 260–day astrological calendar with its 20 day–signs is unique to the high Native–American cultures, including that of the Maya, Toltec, Zapotec and Aztec, of Mesoamerica. For millennia it served the people of this region, giving structure and meaning to civilized life. The Spanish Conquest stopped its use in all but the most remote areas where remnants of it are still carried on by an oral tradition. Today, most astronomers and archaeologists regard it as a strange and curious relic of the ancient Mesoamericans, not as something worth restoring.

During the 1980s I tried in various ways to piece together the few strands of information about the calendar and its components. Using historical documents, reports from the oral traditions, the ideas of other modern writers on the subject, techniques that explore the imagery of the subconscious, and plain common sense, I slowly uncovered what I believe to be some of the key concepts associated with the rich symbolism of the 20 named days. Reports and summaries of my investigations appear in three books, including this one, and a computer program.

The results of a series of psychic–archaeology experiments done in 1986 were published in 1988 by Llewellyn Publications as *The Aztec Circle of Destiny*. Angela Cordova was co–author. In this popular work (actually a tool–kit that comes with tarot–like cards and rune–like chips) both the astrological and divinatory aspects of the 260–day astrological calendar are presented and individual meanings of the 20 days, from both historical sources and ideas generated by the experiments, are listed. In 1991 the first edition of this book, *Day–Signs: Native American Astrology from Mexico* was published. The delineations of the signs are a marked advance over previous publications, including *The Aztec Circle of Destiny*. A print run of 3,000 copies was sold over about ten years. In 1993 a far more technical summary of Mesoamerican astrology was published – *Signs of Time: A Reconstruction of Mesoamerican Astrology*. In this work the major astrological practices of the ancient Mesoamerican civilizations, including the use of the 260–day calendar, are examined in detail and discussed. About this same time the delineations published in 1991 for the day–signs were incorporated into a software package published by Astrolabe, Inc., called *Aztec Astro–Report*. This was a relatively sophisticated calculation and text–writing program for IBM compatible computers. A no–frills version of the program, called *Aztec Astrology* was also made available at a lower cost. The program was written by Barry Orr, the text by myself. This software was expanded several times since that time and is now sold by Astrolabe under the name *Mayan Life Path Astrology*. Over a decade later I assembled a selection of articles I had written on Mesoamerican astrology and collaborated with Barry Orr on *How to Practice Mayan Astrology* which was published in 2007. Unique in this book is a daily table of day–signs and other factors in Mesoamerican astrology.

Day–Signs: Native American Astrology from Mexico concentrates only on the 260–day calendar as a personality matrix built on natural cycles. I have tried to present the material clearly and simply and with an emphasis on practice, not theory. The delineations of the day–signs are, to my knowledge, far more detailed than anything published previously and, I believe, they open up a new human typology for astrologers, psychologists and others who work with human nature. The success of these delineations is evidenced by the number of times I have been plagiarized by other writers. In some cases, authors using a completely different calendar correlation have published delineations that were clearly taken from my work.

The West has much to learn from the Native–American tradition. In this book I share my own personal discovery of one aspect of their cultural and cosmic perspective. I wish to thank Barry Orr for his masterful computer programing without which the present work might have taken much longer to complete. For the first edition, July 1989, George

Young provided valuable technical advice and hands–on help with the production of the manuscript. Steve Cozzi and Diana Rosenberg also deserve recognition for their keen insights, suggestions and interest in the material. For the second edition, July 2012, feedback from numerous people has motivated me to get the book back into print.

Introduction

This book contains the first practical delineations of the 20 *tonalli* or day–signs, the lost astrology of Pre–Columbian Mexico. Using the tables at the end of the book, you will be able to determine the signs that ruled the day you were born. A turn to the description of your day–sign, and the 13–day period within which you were born, will lead you through a deep psychological tour of your motivations, behaviors, relationship patterns and personal quirks. In short, this book is a guide to one of the world's most powerful methods of personality delineation and self–knowledge ever created.

How to Use this Book

Before you read Chapters 1 to 3, you should turn to the tables at the end of the book and determine your day–sign, and the sign ruling the 13–day period in effect on the day of your birth. Most people will be influenced by two different signs. In some respects, this is similar to Western astrology where each person has both a Sun–sign and a Moon–sign.

The detailed instructions for using the ephemeris on page 171 will help you navigate the ephemeris. Table I lists the 13–day periods. The sign, always numbered 1, that precedes your birthday is your 13–day period sign. If your birthday is one of the dates listed in Table I, then you are influenced by only one sign, the one listed, and it is both your day–sign and your 13–day period sign. In most cases, however, you will need to turn to Table II to find out your actual day–sign. Find your 13–day period in Table II, and then using the month and day number of your 13–day period, count the days down to your birthday. The day–sign listed here is yours. (Note: Every day–sign is preceded by a number which shows its position within a 13–day period. The sign with the number 1 preceding it rules the next 13 days.)

Unfortunately, space did not permit an entire day–to–day listing of the day–signs, but the tables should allow you to locate day–signs without much difficulty. (A daily listing of day–signs is found in *How to Practice Mayan Astrology*.) But before getting deeply into the text, find your day–sign and take a look at the description below. If you find it appropriate, turn to the chapter devoted to that sign and read about it in more detail. Then, you may wish to read chapters 1 to 3 to learn more about the nature of ancient Mexican astrology and how the delineations of the signs were arrived at.

The Twenty Day–Signs of Ancient Mexico

Crocodile: Energetic, creative and initiating. Protective and dominating in a parental way. Sensitive and private.
Challenge: To become free from feelings of rejection, often from parents.
Solution: Found a business or create a home.

Wind: Communicative, mental, agile, clever and multifaceted. Idealistic and romantic. Fashion conscious or artistic.
Challenge: Fears about responsibility, obligations, commitment and decision–making.
Solution: Education and learning to communicate accurately.

House: Powerful, logical, organized, deep, thoughtful and conservative. Good endurance, introspective.
Challenge: Mental rigidity and problems with sharing.
Solution: Become a builder of systems and establish secure foundations in whatever you do.

Lizard: Interested in leadership and performance. Active, dynamic and sexual. Influential, with high standards.
Challenge: To become a balanced individual, to mature sexually.
Solution: Engage in artistic or performance related activities and master the details.

Serpent: Strong–willed, extremist, powerful and charismatic. Has strong emotions and feelings that affect others powerfully.
Challenge: To experience powerful transformations consciously.
Solution: Learning to accept change as part of the learning process.
Death: Security conscious, materialistic, sacrificing and helpful. Interest and concern for the community and politics.

Challenge: Having faith, not being a victim.
Solution: Give meaning to life by making contributions to society.

Deer: Peaceful, generous, cooperative, artistic and inspiring. Also nomadic, outspoken and individualistic. Needs companionship.
Challenge: To handle the contradictory needs of personal freedom and relationship security.
Solution: To be comfortable with one's own individuality, no matter how strange it may be.

Rabbit: Energetic, busy, nervous, clever and playful. Intelligent, but somewhat paranoid. Likes to fight.
Challenge: Keeping oneself under control in order to finish things.
Solution: Learning to express feelings and avoidance of extremes and excesses.

Water: Emotional, imaginative, psychic, romantic and fantasy prone. Dominates others easily by projecting strong feelings.
Challenge: Self–control and responsibility issues.
Solution: Being consistent, persistent and intelligently responsive.

Dog: Cooperative, consistent, loyal and helpful. Good team player and joiner, but also good leader. Needs much variety in life.
Challenge: Emotional maturity and father–related/authority issues.
Solution: Acceptance of leadership when it is needed.

Monkey: Attention getting, artistic, clever and demonstrative. Multiple interests, communicative and very curious.
Challenge: To stay with one thing long enough to master it.
Solution: Many creative outlets and an active social life.

Grass: Relaxed, courteous, careful and useful. Also sensitive, touchy and easily hurt. Ambitious and hard-working.
Challenge: To avoid poisoning oneself by suppressing anger.
Solution: Expressing feelings and fostering purifying and healing actions.
Reed: Popular, knowledgeable, accomplished and competent. A fighter for principles, a crusader. Takes on challenges.

Challenge: To not be opinionated, to loosen up rigid attitudes.
Solution: Knowledge of human nature and development of good social skills.

Ocelot: Secretive, sensitive, intelligent and psychic. Concerned with religion or spirituality. Aggressive but avoids direct confrontations.
Challenge: Complex and entangled human relationships.
Solution: Education and the development of counseling skills.

Eagle: Independent, ambitious and escapist. Scientific, technically inclined, critical and exacting. Has unique ideas about life.
Challenge: Acceptance of unusual relationship patterns.
Solution: Cultivation of friendships that place a high value on personal freedom.

Vulture: Serious, deep, wise, realistic and pragmatic. Hardened to life, status conscious. Sometimes dominated by others. Has very high standards.
Challenge: To overcome self–consciousness and personal insecurities.
Solution: To excel in one's career and be comfortable with authority related issues.

Earthquake: Mentally active, rationalizing, clever but practical. Usually liberal and progressive. Often controversial. Strong convictions.
Challenge: To hold one's life together according to a plan.
Solution: To become more flexible and patient.

Knife: Practical, mechanically inclined, well–coordinated. Social, but struggles in close relationships. Compromising and self–sacrificing, but suppresses anger.
Challenge: Self–interest versus self–sacrifice.
Solution: Cooperation and sharing with others.

Rain: Youthful, restless, friendly and helpful. Multi–faceted, a good learner and teacher. Drawn to philosophy or religion. Concern for healing and purification.

Challenge: To become a healer of others.
Solution: Study under a master.

Flower: Loving, devoted, artistic, dreamy and romantic. Socially awkward but well–intentioned. Stubborn and uncompromising.
Challenge: Handling disappointments due to unrealistic expectations.
Solution: Be a good friend but keep life simple.

These twenty signs are the foundation on which much of ancient Mexican astrology stands. Each person is linked by birth to these signs that symbolize both personality patterns and, consequently, destiny. Like all forms of astrology, they can serve as a road map of life, a way of personal knowledge.

Part 1

The 260-Day Calendar

Chapter 1

Ancient Calendars and the Conquest of Time

According to our present knowledge, the earliest of the great ancient civilizations were those of the Near–East. At least five thousand years ago along the Nile, Egyptian high–culture began and flourished for several thousand years. Around the same time, along the Tigris and Euphrates, the Sumerians established a cultural pattern that was carried on by successive Semitic groups. The first flowering of these large, agriculture–based societies occurred around 3000 BCE or possibly earlier. Not much later than that, similar high–cultures came into being along the major rivers in India and China. By 2500 BCE the foundations of many Western and Eastern traditions that influence the world to this very day, had been laid.

In the Americas, archaeologists tell us that Amerindians in Mesoamerica, today's Mexico and northern Central American, were just beginning to domesticate corn and other crops around 3000 BCE. It wouldn't be until 1500 BCE or later that the first high–cultures flourished along the Gulf of Mexico and along the Pacific coast. If this is the case, then the New World was about 1500 years behind the Old, at least in terms of the fusion of complex social structures and cultural values into what is called civilization. When the Spanish landed in Mexico in the early 16th Century, they were stepping back in time. They met (and quickly destroyed) a civilization that was in many ways comparable to that of the Egyptians or the Babylonians.

Today we stand nearly 5000 years distant from ancient Egypt and Mesopotamia, but only 500 years distant from Ancient Mesoamerica. The cultures of the Old World have long since been eradicated or transformed. They continue to influence us primarily through our religion, the Judaeo–Christian tradition, and the values and attitudes these creeds promote. On the other hand, the New World cultures of Maya, Toltec, Zapotec, Mixtec and Aztec still survive intact in some ways. The cultural values and traditions of these people were rejected by the Spanish, but they did not die out entirely. Some native ideas and concepts survived by merging with Christianity. In remote areas, oral traditions have carried on the indigenous folklore, myths, philosophy and sky–knowledge. In Mexico, we come very close to the world of ancient civilizations, far closer than many realize.

Ancient civilizations were made possible through agriculture; hunting and nomadic groups could not afford to become too large, as there simply wouldn't be enough food to go around. With domesticated grains, food could not only be stored for long periods of time, it could allow for rapid population growth and even feed those not directly engaged in agriculture. For the first time in history, a reliable and abundant food supply could sustain workers building pyramids or artists painting books or murals. But this was true only if nature cooperated.

Of immediate concern to all ancient agricultural civilizations was the weather. Crops had to be planted at just the right time for proper and abundant growth. If the planting season was missed by a week or two, a year's worth of food would be lost. Obviously, knowledge of the weather patterns and the seasonal changes was vital to survival. This situation forced early civilizations to come up with reliable calendars that linked the movements of the Sun and Moon with the seasons and weather patterns on earth. The creation of a calendar was a development of profound consequence, a first step toward control, prediction, and ultimately, science.

Calendars, Astronomy and Astrology

A calendar is a way of counting time, and time has traditionally been based on recurring astronomical cycles such as the rotation of the Earth. In creating or developing a calendar, knowledge of the sky is a prerequisite. The most basic time–keeping unit is the day, a unit of time that is part dark and part light. The change of dark to light, or the reverse, can be used as a starting point and successions of days can then be counted. But a count of days has to begin somewhere. There has to be a wider perspective against which the count takes on meaning and value. There have been two major solutions to this problem. The first is to begin the count at a determinable date in the lunar cycle.

The Moon and Sun conjoin once a month, about every 29 days at the New Moon. During this period the Moon is seen to grow larger until the Full Moon is reached. During the second half of the cycle the Moon decreases in size. Early hunting and herding societies noticed that mammalian fertility cycles, including those of humans, seemed to be closely related to the length of the lunar cycle. (This observation may constitute the "discovery" of astrology.) In part due to its prominence in the sky, and in part because it seemed to be linked to the rhythms of fertility, the counting of days relative to the lunar cycle was adapted by some early societies, usually those who were carrying on a herding tradition of some sort. The counting of "Moons" was common also to many nomadic groups including North American Indian tribes.

One of the problems with a lunar cycle calendar is that it is not linked to the seasons and therefore presents problems for agriculturalists. In the ancient Near East, where the Semitic peoples had nomadic roots, the lunar calendar was established and maintained, but it required frequent adjustments to the solar calendar. Even today, lunar calendars are used by the Jewish and Islamic peoples who must periodically inject extra months in the year to keep it in synch with the seasons. The ancient Egyptians, on the other hand, early on developed a solar calendar. This calendar was later adopted by the Romans and was the forerunner of the one we use today. The fact that there are approximately twelve lunar cycles in one solar year prompted the division of the year into twelve months, or twelve signs. It should be apparent that the linkages between calendars, astronomy and astrology are quite deep.

Starting a count of days from a fixed point in the solar year is the basis of a solar calendar. From the casual observer's point of view, the Sun rises in the east and sets in the west. The astute observer will notice that the Sun generally rises and sets at differing places, its passage along the horizon reaching maximum distances north or south only two times a year at the solstices. At the winter solstice, the first day of winter, the Sun rises a good distance south of east for several days. The nights are long and the days are short at this time of year (in the Northern Hemisphere, of course). Gradually, at first, the Sun begins to rise further to the north, crossing the due east point on the first day of spring, the vernal equinox. On this day, the length of day and night are equal. During succeeding weeks, the Sun rises farther and farther to the north until it again slows down and rises in the same place for several days. This is the first day of summer, the summer solstice. Now, the Sun begins to retreat from this northernmost rising position, and at the beginning of autumn, it once again rises due east, this being the autumnal equinox. Finally, at the beginning of winter, the Sun once again rises where it did the year before, at its southernmost rising position.

The motion of the rising position of the Sun on the horizon is conveniently divisible into four stages that correspond with the seasons. The two solstices (solstice means Sun standstill) divide the year in half, and the two equinoxes bisect these half–years making four quarters, which is what we call the seasons. In ancient cultures, counts of days were usually begun at one of these points. In order to pin–point the exact day of a solstice or equinox, ancient skywatchers had to develop sophisticated observational techniques. The setting of posts or stones to use as sights, or the construction of special architectural structures was necessary for these measurements. Today, the science of archaeoastronomy concerns itself with the remains of early skywatching efforts.

The Calendars of Ancient Mesoamerica

Of all the early cultures and civilizations, those of ancient Mexico and Central America developed the most complex and sophisticated calendars. The Maya, in particular, created a network of calendrical rhythms that precisely dovetailed with each other at certain points in time. Some of these calendars were tied to the seasons, but others were not. The Maya were abstract numerologists and seekers of order, and in a sense, they were attempting to conquer time itself. By creating cycles that closely approximated natural cycles, but were also numerically workable, they were able to place their history and the fluctuations of individual experience into a fixed framework of time. Like Western scientists, they were obsessed with orderliness and control, but they expressed this drive on the intellectual, not material, level.

Like other early agricultural civilizations, the Maya, Aztecs and other Mesoamerican civilizations used a calendar that was tied to the seasons, and like the Egyptians, it contained 365 days. This is a close approximation to the actual 365.24 days of the year, but not close enough. After four years, this count of days would lag one day behind the actual seasonal year and periodic adjustments would become necessary. In the West, the custom of having leap years, where a day is added to February every four years, was established early on. One Mesoamerican solution to this problem was to make a 13-day adjustment every 52 years, which amounts to the same thing. The Maya let the calendar run on against the seasons for the full 1,461 years it takes the same day to come around again – always keeping close records on where things stood. The important point here is that the cultures and civilizations of Mesoamerica used a solar calendar, as did the Egyptians.

Western cultures divided the 365-day year into twelfths, forming the signs and the months. Month means "moon" (from the Latin, *mensis*) and its inclusion in the year was an attempt to join the lunar and solar cycles into one calendar. As we saw above, this only works in a rough sense because there are 12.4 lunar synodic cycles per 365.24 days. Nearly two weeks are left over. The Egyptians made this work better by adopting a month of 30 days which leaves only 5 extra days at the end of the year. During these "epagomenal" days, large-scale festivities were held, the precursors of our winter holiday season. In Mesoamerica, the 365-day year was divided into eighteen months of 20 days with the same 5 days left over. Here are two solutions to the same problem, either one being quite workable.

Calendars to Conquer Time

The Maya had other calendars, however, that make the early Western attempts in this area seem primitive. Working on an abstract numerological level, the Maya counted days in sets of 4, 13, 20 and 360. The 20-day unit, called the *uinal*, was a primary unit and was in some ways like the Western 7-day unit we call a week. Each day had a name, and when the cycle was complete, it repeated itself. Eighteen cycles of the 20 named-days took 360 days, a most workable number. This 360-day count was called a *tun* and it was the basic building block of longer periods of time. Twenty tuns (20 x 360 days = 7,200 days), called a *katun*, was considered extremely important in the social and political life of the community. This unit of time, just short of 20 years, closely approximates the cycle of Jupiter and Saturn, the largest planets in the solar system. Twenty Katuns (144,000 days or about 394 years) made a *baktun*. Thirteen baktuns formed a creation epoch of 5,200 tuns or approximately 5,125 years. This later period is called the Long Count.

There are two important points that need to be made here about Mayan calendrics. First, the creation epoch of 13 baktuns is accurately dated. According to ancient inscriptions, the present era began on August 12th, 3114 BCE and ended on December 21st, 2012. This is what the Harmonic Convergence was about in August of 1987. It was apparently a mass exercise to prepare for the last katun (20 year period) of the present Mayan creation epoch. Similar gatherings were held at the actual start of this katun in 1993 and of course at the end of the Long Count in 2012. What all this means, I'm not sure, but it is a rather remarkable thing to know the exact date that this ancient calendar ended. It is even more remarkable to see it happen in one's life–time.

The second point, and one very relevant for this book, is that during a creation cycle of 5,200 tuns, there are 260 katuns. The Maya grouped the katuns in bundles of 20 per baktun, but also in bundles of 13. The cycle of the 13 katuns, as it was known, was important enough to the Maya for them to have recorded it in a number of books written shortly after the Spanish conquest – these being the source of the Maya prophecies. This "Short Count" was seen as having a correlation with the rise and fall of kingdoms. Here, in both bundles, the interplay of the numbers 13 and 20 is seen. Thirteen baktuns, each containing 20 katuns, equals a creation cycle. And so does twenty occurrences of the cycle of the thirteen katuns. Here is the sacred astrological count of 260 writ large.

The 260–Day Calendar

It should be apparent by now that the subject of ancient Mesoamerican calendars is quite complex. In fact, there are many other rhythms of time discovered or created, and used by the ancient Maya that are well beyond the scope of this book. But instead of reaching for the limits, as Maya mathematicians and astronomer/astrologers did, let's now concentrate on the concern of this book, the cycle of 260 days. More detail on Mesoamerican astrology can be found in my books *Signs of Time* and *How to Practice Mayan Astrology*.

The 260-day cycle or count was called the *tonalpouhalli* (tow-nal-pawh-lee) by the Aztecs and the *tzolkin* (zol-keen) by the Maya. Modern researchers have referred to it as the "sacred calendar" or the "divinatory almanac", or other similar names. The importance of the 260-day cycle is shown by the fact that many of the surviving Aztec manuscripts, and most of those of the Maya, contain almanac-like depictions of this cycle. The Aztec word for these books of fate is *tonalamatl* which means "book of days." Later native writings after the conquest also list the days, each one having a prognostication attached to it. In the 1980s artist and mythologist Jose Arguelles came up with an interesting name for the 260-day cycle – the "Harmonic Module." He elaborated at length on its numerological aesthetics in his creative but dense book *The Mayan Factor*. In the present work, it will from here on be referred to as the 260-day astrological calendar or, more simply, the 260-day calendar.

At the core of the 260-day astrological calendar are the 20 named days or day-signs, called *tonalli* by the Aztecs. These were days that had names, like our seven-day week, and had a constant place relative to each other. The earliest archaeological evidence for these named days is controversial but an origin of roughly 500 BCE is not impossible. Although the actual names of the days varied from one language group to another, basically the same themes were stressed in Maya, Toltec, Zapotec, Mixtec and Aztec languages. Today, the twenty named days are kept alive by daykeepers and divination experts among the more remote Maya communities in Mexico and Guatamala.

The twenty day-signs or named days are, of course, named in the indigenous languages of Mesoamerica. For reasons of accessibility to Westerners, I will be using in this book translations of the names for the days used by the Aztecs, the last of the great Mesoamerican cultures. Readers should keep in mind that there are a few discrepancies between Aztec, Maya, Zapotec and other versions of the names, though these will all be noted in the chapters on each named day. Below is a list of the days:

Crocodile	Serpent	Water	Reed	Earthquake
Wind	Death	Dog	Ocelot	Knife
House	Deer	Monkey	Eagle	Rain
Lizard	Rabbit	Grass	Vulture	Flower

The twenty named days are repeated thirteen times in the 260-day calendar. This is exactly like the baktuns and katun relationship described above. Further, the numbers from one to thirteen are counted twenty times against the twenty named days to yield twenty cycles of thirteen. Again, this is exactly like the twenty bundles of thirteen katuns used by the Maya. It is the interplay of the numbers 13 and 20 that make the 260-day period, strange numbers to Westerners more familiar with 7, 10 and 12.

The twenty named days traditionally begin with the day "Crocodile." At the start of the 260-day count, the number 1 would be attached to this day which would then be called 1-Crocodile. The next named day, "Wind", would become 2-Wind. Following this would be 3-House, 4-Lizard, 5-Serpent, 6-Death, 7-Deer, 8-Rabbit, 9-Water, 10-Dog, 11-Monkey, 12-Grass, 13-Reed. The next day, Ocelot, is not number 14, it becomes number 1 and the count of 13 begins again. So, from 1-Ocelot we go to 2-Eagle, 3-Vulture, 4-Earthquake, 5-Knife, 6-Rain, and 7-Flower. Now we are back to Crocodile again, the first of the days, but it is now 8-Crocodile. 9-Wind is next, then 10-House, 11-Lizard, 12-Serpent, 13-Death and then 1-Deer. After twenty 13-day cycles, a total of 260 days, 1-Crocodile comes up again.

What is unique about this 260-day interplay of named days and numbers is its astrological or divinatory properties. Both the ancient and modern Maya considered the rhythm of the days sacred and powerful. Being born on a particular day was of great importance as that day was said to stamp its characteristics on the newborn and seal its fate. This was, and is, a calendar with no agricultural purpose as it could not possibly be used to predict the seasons. It is more a magical calendar, or, in my opinion, quite possibly the embodiment of a great discovery about circadian cycles or biorhythms.

The Seven Day Planetary Week

A comparison of the 20 named days and our more familiar 7-day week is appropriate here. Our 7-day week, now used nearly world-wide, was used by the Babylonians and Jews. Its exact origins, place and period, are uncertain. Most likely, it was developed early on by Mesopotamian skywatchers and timekeepers for purposes very similar to those of the

20 named days. Later, it was adopted in a few places and then spread throughout the Mediterranean region during Greco–Roman times. For over 2,000 years the count of seven named days has remained constant. Even the Gregorian calendar adjustment in the 16th century did not disturb the regular sequence of days from Sunday to Saturday.

It appears that the 7–day week is an approximation of a quarter of a lunar cycle, and the seven days were named for the seven visible planets; this is apparent in the Romance languages. What most people don't know is that the days themselves are named for the planet that rules its first hour. The astrologers of ancient Mesopotamia divided the daylight and night–time hours into twelfths and they assigned rulership of each hour to a planet. As there are seven visible planets, every eighth hour the same planet would be "in charge", so to speak. The sequence of rulership was constant and is known as the Chaldean order, an order based on the apparent motions of the planets. The order began with Saturn, the slowest moving planet, and ended with the Moon, which moves through the sky most quickly. Since there were 24 hours in a day, the seven rulers of the hours would cycle three complete times with three left over. Counting from sunrise to sunrise, a different planet, and one four places ahead in the Chaldean order, would rule the first hour of each day. This planet would then give its name to that day. Below is the Chaldean order and the order of the week. Notice how the sequence of the weekdays follows the Chaldean order if you move ahead three places for each day.

Chaldean Order	**Planetary 7–Day Week Order**
Saturn	Saturday (Saturn)
Jupiter	Sunday (Sun)
Mars	Monday (Moon)
Sun	Tuesday (Mars)
Venus	Wednesday (Mercury)
Mercury	Thursday (Jupiter)
Moon	Friday (Venus)

Bringing the analogy between the Mesoamerican 20–day count and the Mesopotamian 7–day week a step further is the notion of its influence or control over everyday life. The 7–day planetary week was, and to some still is, believed to have an astrological influence over events and births. During the Middle Ages there was considerable interest in the fates of those born on a particular day of the week. Many of us today have heard the rhyme that describes the character of births on each day. "Monday's child is fair of face…etc." Actually, this makes good astrological sense since Monday is ruled by the Moon. Taking the comparison even further, we even have traditions that place an emphasis on a day and its number in the month. Most obvious is the fuss about Friday the 13th. While this may be a superstition based on the date of a major Christian event, it suggests that our thinking about time and dates is not really that different from what is being presented in this book. The big difference is that our culture has lost contact with the origins of our taken–for–granted calendar. We have rejected its "magic."

The idea of counting time and its astrological or divinatory effects was also found in ancient China. In that culture the numbers ten and twelve took on great significance. The Ten Celestial Stems and the Twelve Terrestrial Branches cycled with each other until their lowest common denominator, 60, was reached. This pattern was imposed on both days and years, giving a 60–day and a 60–year cycle with astrological qualities. This is not unlike the ancient Mesoamericans who applied the 13 and 20–fold rhythm to both days and 20–year periods.

Why different cultures emphasized different cycles is not clear. In the Western cultures, the cycle of 7 days and the division of the year into 12 months became established early on. The importance of these numbers, which, as we have seen were undoubtedly derived from sky–knowledge, is reflected in their frequent appearance in the Bible. In China, the number 12 appears, but not just as a division of the year. A longer cycle of 12 years, today known as the Chinese Zodiac, is most likely based on the 12–year cycle of the planet Jupiter. The number ten does not seem to have any obvious connection to the motions in the sky. In Mesoamerica, 13 and 20 are pre–eminent among numbers. Interestingly, it takes the Sun about 13 days to travel the same distance as the Moon does in one day. Also, the cycle of Jupiter–Saturn conjunctions takes about 20 years. While these may not be the main reasons for choosing these numbers (finger and toe–counting were probably a factor also) they may have been of some consideration back in the days when the early inhabitants of Mesoamerica were seeking a numerical solution to the order of the universe. As we will see in the next section, there are some other reasons why the cycles of 13 and 20 days, and the 260–day astrological calendar itself came into being.

The Internal Structure of the 260–Day Astrological Calendar

Let's summarize what has been said so far about the 260-day astrological calendar of ancient Mesoamerica. First, it consists of 20 named days, or day-signs, that cycle in a consistent order. Second, a cycle of 13 numbered days runs concurrent with the cycle of 20 days. These two cycles meet on the same day only once in 260 days. Third, this calendar has nothing to do with the seasons. Fourth, it was used for divinatory or astrological purposes. It is also worth emphasizing that this calendar was the creation of Native American peoples and that its origins can be dated perhaps as far back as 500 BCE.

A number of reasons for the 260–day length of this calendar have been forwarded by the many archaeologists and astronomers who have done extensive research on the subject. One possible explanation is found in the cycle of the planet Venus which has morning and evening star phases of approximately 263 days. It is known that the ancient Mesoamerican skywatchers found Venus to be of particular interest and a number of architectural structures have been found aligned to its rising and setting points. These ancient astronomers knew that the Venus year of 584 days and the solar year of 365 days "meshed" every eight solar years. This means that five Venus years (5 x 584) equals eight solar years (8 x 365). Although the argument is beyond the scope of this book, it has been argued that the origin of the 260–day calendar lies hidden in the astronomical facts (along with some numerology) of this Venus–Sun relationship.

The 260–day calendar resonates with numerous astronomical cycles. There are 9 lunar cycles in 260 days and the Mars synodic cycle is 520 days, double 260, and this number also meshes with the cycle of eclipses. It's also true that the synodic cycle of Mercury, about 118 days, ties into the 260-day calendar in the ratio 9:4. Another interesting astronomical fact is that the Sun spends 105 days north of the zenith at the latitude of two early Maya centers where, it is speculated, much pioneer astronomical work was done in ancient times. If 105 is subtracted from 365, then the Sun spends 260 days of the year south of the zenith at this latitude. It may be that the unit of 260 days was found to be neatly linked to so many astronomical phenomena that it served as a master counting tool of sorts.

Finally, there is the testimony of the people who still use the calendar. They say that it represents the length of human gestation. In other words, conception and birth would occur on the same date in the calendar, 260 days apart. There might be something to this explanation if the Moon is brought in. It is well known that mammalian fertility cycles are usually a multiple or division of the lunar cycle. There are, however, several lunar cycles ranging from the 27.3 day sidereal cycle to the 29.5 day synodical (Sun and Moon) cycle. But 260 days divided by 9 yields a cycle of 28.88 days, not too far off the average of the various lunar cycles.

Whatever the reasons for its origins, the 260–day calendar contains within itself a complex and fascinating interplay of number. Its interplay with the solar year of 365 days and their convergence every 52 years, and with that of the 584–day Venus year every 104 years is even more remarkable. The creation of this elaborate web of day–counts with their relations to astronomical cycles, and also to pure number, was perhaps the crowning intellectual achievement of ancient Mesoamerica.

While astronomers and archaeologists have pieced together much of the framework of this ancient attempt to conquer time, they have not ventured very deeply into the realm of symbolism and the possible meanings for human life that these calendars were said to possess. They admit, however, that the real purpose of the 260–day calendar, and its links with other cycles, was essentially astrological. The ancient Maya and Aztec skywatchers were both astronomers and astrologers, a situation similar to that in the West until the 17th century when a split between these two subjects occurred. In my opinion, the exploration of the meanings of the days and the possible "effects" of the rhythms of time is best suited to astrologers who are trained to think and work with a similar symbolic language. The astrological legacy of ancient Mesoamerica is too important to be left solely to the astronomers and archaeologists.

Chapter 2

The Restoration of the Sacred Calendar

My interest in the astrology of ancient Mesoamerica began in the mid 1970s, but it was greatly stimulated by several trips to Mexico in the early 1980s. For a long time I wasn't sure whether or not the 260–day calendar actually had an astrological effect. Having been influenced by the reports of the archaeoastronomers I was more or less of the opinion that the calendar was simply a most remarkable intellectual achievement for the cultures of Middle America. I didn't think that it actually worked in the way that the Western astrology I was familiar with did.

A few years later, I entertained the notion that the calendar might have actually been true for its users because they expected it to be so. I envisioned it acting as an elaborate structure of collective expectations that shaped the individual to a considerable degree. But the fact that so little was really known about the day–signs kept me from accepting any solution as final. I didn't want to make the same mistake the scientific establishment continues to make about Western astrology, that is, judging it without studying it. How could I honestly evaluate Mesoamerican astrology from just a few pitiful remnants?

In 1986 I teamed up with Angela Cordova, a Mexican–born psychic, in an effort to break into the symbolism of the 260–calendar via some rather unconventional methods. We devised a set of psychic experiments that over a six–month period generated a great quantity of information about the 20 day–signs. Using the psychic techniques of dream programing, channeling, dowsing and automatic writing, we came up with words, phrases and images for each of the days. The images, which became twenty tarot–like cards, were particularly helpful – the artwork was a way of bypassing the rational channels and allowing a more direct expression of the themes that were emerging from our subconscious minds. The results of this work, in the form of a book, cards, and chips, have been published by Llewellyn as *The Aztec Circle of Destiny*.

It was the psychic experiments that pushed my understanding of the day–signs to a new level. I began to understand some of the very contradictory reports that survived the Spanish conquest, and I began to see connections between these surviving manuscripts and our work. More and more, the internal structure of the day–signs, in terms of sequence and directional association, began to make sense. I was convinced that the 20 named days could be used as a divination device (that was obviously the case because it was still being used by some Maya communities) but I was still struggling with the idea that each day–sign had an influence on personality and character. There were several problems that had to be overcome before I felt I was on solid ground and could make that judgment.

The first obstacle in determining whether or not the day–signs "worked" astrologically for births has to do with the correlations between the Western and the 260–day calendar. After years of painstaking research, by the 1980s archaeologists and astronomers had generally settled on an approximate two or three day range called the Goodman–Martinez–Thompson (GMT) correlation. These researchers were concerned with not just linking the 260–day calendar with the Western calendar, but with linking the other calendars as well, including the katun counts. This correlation (stated as plus or minus a day or two) gives the Julian day number of the date that the Maya Long Count, a cycle of 5,125 years, began.

Using a computer program designed by Barry Orr, I did some date checking of my own. The program allowed me to input a base date of the 260–day calendar, then compute what day–sign would occur on any given date in our Western calendar. I checked out the few dates recorded shortly after the Spanish Conquest in both calendars. One of these was the date that Cortes took the Aztec city of Tenochtitlan. I also checked the ethnological reports on the present–day use of the 260–day calendar in remote Maya communities. My conclusion was that the GMT correlation was probably correct and that the first day of the present epoch, beginning with the day 5–Crocodile, was most probably August 12th, −3113, Julian day #584,284.

The next problem was to determine exactly when the influence of one day–sign began and the previous one ended. Archaeologists are not really sure when the day actually began for the Maya and Aztecs.

After a considerable amount of reading, I tentatively concluded that the day probably began at either midnight or sunrise, though arguments could be made for noon and sunset as well. One problem was a lack of information – this had never been clearly reported by the early friars who wrote about the customs of the Indians. It could be that this in itself makes a good case for the day beginning at midnight as did the Spaniards' day because if it didn't, the friars would have made a point of it. The Aztecs did begin their 52-year cycle at midnight, but other practices began at sunrise and some at sunset. It became apparent to me that I was on my own in this matter and would have to come to a final conclusion based on experience. One other related problem has to do with whether or not the day-signs were linked to the time zone of Mesoamerica. This is one problem that the archaeologists had probably never thought of, or if they did, had never taken seriously.

Finally, there is the problem of why should there be any astrological effect at all. In Western astrology, we have learned to advance ourselves in the field without the support of any physical explanations for why astrology works. However, as of the last thirty years or so, a few statistical studies have shown that astrology does in fact seem to work. For now, the critics of the subject will have to content themselves with this evidence, similar to what they will get if they make the same demands of psychology or particle physics. The problem, as I saw it, was to either come up with a physical explanation for a daily "astrological effect" shift, or devise an experiment in which I could separate personality traits and link them to specific day-signs. In both cases I was pushing the limits of my time and money. Without the benefits of a grant or the support of an institution, it soon became apparent to me that I would have to settle for a theory and a quasi-scientific methodology. The following is a report on how I tackled these two problems.

A Theory of Day Change

During the course of the day, the Sun appears to rise, culminate, set and then rise again. While we all know that the Sun doesn't actually do this motion itself (the rotating Earth does it), we have to accept it as our experience of the Sun. The day is divided into halves, daylight and night. Daylight is the time when solar energy is distributed to the Earth to be used by living things. Solar energy also warms the atmosphere, and also the land and water surfaces of the Earth. During the night, there is a lack of solar energy and living things sleep, essentially change operation modes, as the Earth's atmosphere and surface cools down. The day, therefore, is a combination of two phases, which meet at sunrise and sunset. There is, without question, a daily ebb and flow of solar energy. Since the origin of life, organisms have used this environmental binary "code" to orchestrate the diverse functions required to survive. These are called circadian rhythms. The sensing of light, or lack of it, is the basis of a kind of environmental entrainment and the switch from light to dark is a cue for changes in the organism.

During the daily cycle of light and dark, the amount of electromagnetic radiation reaching the Earth varies. Since the light and dark energies are balanced at sunrise and sunset, perhaps the places to look for a switch would be either the low point that occurs sometime at night, or the high point that occurs during mid–day. These are times when the solar signal strength is highest or lowest. If one were look at a cycle as starting low, peaking and then dropping down again, the way I am predisposed by my education to look at it, then the point during the night when solar energies are at their absolute lowest would be a logical starting point for the day. Studies have shown that rates of cell division are slowest before midnight, some pointing to about 10:30 local time. Also of interest is that ancient Chinese medicine teaches that the flow of Ch'i, the vital energy that surrounds us at all times, affects the body in a regular 24–hour cycle beginning at 3 AM local time.

It is known that many organisms, from the most primitive to the most sophisticated, respond to the regular fluctuations of solar energy and scientists have studied circadian cycles for many years now. Bodily factors like temperature, blood pressure, excretion of minerals and many other metabolic functions all operate on a 24 hour cycle. Biorhythms longer than the daily circadian cycle have also been studied by scientists. From the start of the 20th century the three popularly known biorhythms, the 23–day physical cycle, the 28–day emotional cycle and the 33–day mental cycle, were discovered. These are thought to begin at birth and run without adjustment for an entire life. While there have been many objections to this idea, there has also been some evidence in support of it. One study indicated that there were pronounced cycles of 14 to 17 days and also from 28 to 29 days. Some longer and shorter cycles were also noted. The main idea emerging from all this is that bodily rhythms are fairly regular and may be connected with either the counting of days or the cycle of the Moon, the latter being very apparent considering that lunar cycles range from 27 to 29 days.

Although nothing conclusive can be said about why a series of 13, 20 or 260 days should be of any consequence to humans, the existence of circadian cycles and biorhythms suggests that we are only just beginning to understand this aspect of biology. From another perspective, sunlight is electromagnetic energy. The body has been shown to have its own magnetic field. It may be the case that life–forms respond to a constantly fluctuating electromagnetic tide. From this perspective, life on Earth may be very much influenced by its cosmic environment.

It is possible that, since the time of its origins, life has structured itself around the constant rhythms of its environment. The cycles of day and night, and the cycle of the Moon were convenient pegs on which developing self–consciousness could establish a hold of some kind. Perhaps the ancient Mesoamericans discovered a powerful, though subtle, rhythm that imprints newborns creating variation in a population by means not understood at present. For now, we will have to proceed into an understanding of the day–signs without the benefit of a physical or biological explanation.

Determining the Influence of Day–Signs

The reader should keep in mind that I was in no way convinced that the day–sign astrology of the ancient Mesoamericans actually worked. I was, however, of the opinion that the 260–day astrological calendar formed an internally consistent set of symbols that could be used for divinatory purposes, much like the Tarot, Runes or I–Ching. My approach to this problem was to first ascertain whether or not I was looking for something as real as the astrology of the West that I was familiar with. Later, I would begin to piece together the meanings of the day–signs as they related to individuals.

The first thing I did was to gather together all the traditional and historical data on the day–sign meanings that I could find. There were ancient deities linked to the day–signs that, like the planetary rulers of the zodiac signs, I assumed would yield insights. Any myths or legends about these gods or the signs themselves were considered potentially relevant. As you will see in the descriptions of the day–signs, this data turned out to be both vague and contradictory in many cases.

Not having access to a large data bank of birthdays matched with specific psychological traits, nor having the time to put one together, I decided to start the research project modestly. I gathered together the birth data of many famous personalities who I knew something about. I also put together a long list of personal friends, relatives and acquaintances. When I had amassed about 400 names, I then sorted them out according to their day–signs using the above mentioned computer program and also an ephemeris that the program generated.

The next step was to look for patterns in the assembled data. What struck me immediately were the disproportionate totals among day–signs. For example, most of my close friends were born under five or six day–signs, and virtually none under five or six others. I also began to pick up on some patterns that linked all the names of one day–sign, one that brought in my knowledge of Western astrology. Although it was not clear at first, it appeared that certain zodiac signs and planetary placements occurred more frequently in the birth charts of those born under certain day–signs than others. This perception led me to making more complex astrological notations next to each day–sign, a technique that led to a major breakthrough.

What emerged from this additional information was a glimpse, in the symbolism of Western astrology, as to what each day–sign might really be about. For example, in my list of people born on the day–sign Dog, the prominence of the signs Leo and Scorpio, or the prominence of the Sun or the planet Pluto (which rule those two signs) was striking. Understanding what these symbols meant in combination was my opening to an understanding of the day–sign. While Dog was fairly simple, other day–signs were described by Western astrological symbolism in more complex ways, but there was always consistency. I realized that I was cracking a symbolic code by using another symbolic code. (I was also, and continue to be, aware that my personal selection of subjects would tend to bias an already subjective study, which is why I could not publish this exercise as a legitimate research paper.)

After the general astrological pattern of each day–sign emerged, I then followed up on these findings by computing the day–signs of clients whom I worked with regularly in my astrological consulting business. I was astonished how the patterns persisted in each chart read, and I soon found myself utilizing this newly found knowledge about the day–signs to add another perspective in the delineation of personality from a birth chart. The results of this practice have continued to be quite consistent, though I am still learning much about the day–signs. (The use of my results by others, and the fact that my delineations have been plagiarized several times, seems to confirm the general accuracy of the data I've assembled.)

As noted above, the problem of exactly when the day begins continues to be crucial to understanding the day–signs. We have seen that there may be significance to the regular ebb–and–flow of incoming solar energy. The low point, a possible starting point for the day, would then occur at night. What I have observed is that people born after midnight have the traits associated with the day–sign of that day. However, those born between sunset and midnight seemed to be more of a blending of day–sign influence, though more often than not it is the sign of the next day that will dominate.

Another observation suggests that time corrections for the longitude of birth may be a factor. In looking at some charts of clients born in Japan, I noticed that the day–sign of their birth did not correspond at all to my findings so I recomputed their birth as it would have occurred in Mexico. This changed their day–sign but it was far more descriptive of their personality and correlated better with their astrological charts. While I am not at all positive about it, it appears to me that Central Standard Time, the time–zone of Mexico, may be the key in calculating day–signs. Since nearly all the people on the list from which I derived meanings were born in the continental USA, most of their day–signs would be either correct or off by only an hour or two. People born in Europe or Asia, however, would need to calculate their birth time as if they had been born in Central Standard Time (six hours earlier than Greenwich Mean Time in England). Why this should be so is a mystery. Perhaps there is an ancient rhythm centered in that part of the world. Sixty–five million years ago a very large bolide (meteor, asteroid or fireball) hit the Yucatan peninsula and destroyed much of the life on

Earth. Perhaps there are still some reverberations from this event. One other thing I have noticed is that people born during daylight hours seem to display the qualities of their day–sign more obviously than those born during the night. Perhaps the amount of solar energy coming in at the time of birth has something to do with this variant, if it is indeed true.

The Four Directions

Once I felt I had a handle on the personality traits associated with each day–sign, I began to look for more subtle patterns in the sequence of days. One pattern that appears in the ancient writings and in the accounts of the friars shortly after the conquest is the linkage of day–signs with the four directions. In numerous pre–conquest diagrams, the day–signs are shown moving in their order around the four cardinal points in the sequence east, north, west and south. Because there are 20 days and each direction was linked to five days, there were five rotations of the named days. The pre–conquest books that focused on the structure of the 260–day period, called Tonalamatl, also displayed the signs in quarters. The assignments of days to directions appears below.

East: Crocodile, Serpent, Water, Reed, Earthquake
North: Wind, Death, Dog, Ocelot, Knife
West: House, Deer, Monkey, Eagle, Rain
South: Lizard, Rabbit, Grass, Vulture, Flower

Throughout the world, the four directions have served as the primary underpinning of cosmological, architectural, astrological and divinatory systems. The Chinese I–Ching, for example is based on eight trigrams that represent the four directions and the four points between them. The standard Western astrological chart has four angles that correspond literally to the four directions. The Tarot has four suits and Jesus has four evangelists. What is most striking to me is that the symbolism of the directions is fairly consistent throughout cultures and throughout history.

East is the place where the Sun rises. This is the direction of the new god, the god that is becoming symbolized by the light that is arising from the darkness. More commonly than not, ancient temples were built facing the west, so that the altar would be in the east. The pilgrim entering the main chamber would be gazing eastward at the image of the god, or at the figure of the priest. In the Middle Ages the Gothic cathedrals also were built this way. East is the direction of the "coming to power" or the "birth." It is the direction linked to Easter and to ideas of rebirth and the renewal of life. In Western astrology, the Ascendant, the point of the zodiac that rises in the east, is considered by many the prime significator of the personal identity.

West is the direction of the dying god, the place where the light enters darkness. To the ancient Chinese, the west was calm and peaceful, a place of repose. In Western astrology, west (the seventh house) is the direction in which we meet and merge with others, a place of joining and loss of ego. If east is the direction of the self, west is the direction of the not–self, the others.

North, in the northern hemisphere, is the direction of cold and ice. Perhaps for that reason it was associated with danger and difficulty. If one stands facing east, the north is to the left and left is called the sinister direction. The Chinese associated north with midnight and winter, and Western astrology has it linked to the fourth house, the house of cradle and grave. One could say that north symbolizes the turning inward of life, for protection against the elements.

South, again from the northern hemisphere, is the direction of the tropics, heat, and abundant vegetation. Here are forces that are life–giving and offer opportunity. Here also is where life triumphs over the rocks, unlike the situation in the north. In Western astrology, the south points to one's highest position in life as shown by the tenth house. The Chinese linked it to noon and summer. The south appears to be an outward direction that is connected to fruitfulness and mature power.

The day–sign data seemed to agree with this notion of the four directions. It appeared to me that those born under signs of the east have powerful self–motivated personalities, for the most part, while those born under signs of the west are more concerned with their relations with others. East people struggle with personal problems, west people with problems of cooperation. Those born under day–signs linked to the north appear to be involved in the development of the mind, yet they also seem to be emotional people who struggle with their feelings. Those born under day signs linked to the south appear to have emotions and feelings as primary issues in their lives. They are, by nature, emotional people, but struggle with the rational side of life.

In the sequence of the 20 day–signs, it appears that the signs of each direction build on each other, the first of the series being more concerned with basic issues associated with the theme of that direction, the last grappling with more complex issues. But this is by no means certain. I realize that the body of information I have put together in this book is founded on my own subjective experience and I hesitate to drift too far from what I consider reasonable limits. To better ground the material under exploration, we now need to look at these ideas from the perspectives of others.

The 13–day Periods

As we have already seen, the 260–day calendar is divided into units of 20 and 13. In much of the post–conquest literature on the day–signs, the potent influence of the 13–day periods, sometimes called the *trecena* or the "weeks", was stressed. Starting off each 13–day period was a day–sign labeled 1 (1–Crocodile, etc). This day–sign presumably had an influence that extended for 13 days, until the next number 1 occurred again – the 13–day period established a tone that affected all the days within it. In Western astrology this might be compared to one of the divisions within a sign. In a chart, for example, Mars may be in the sign Aries, but it is also in one of three decans or 10–degree segments that are said to modify the influence of the sign. The astrologer would then have to blend the qualities of the primary influence Aries with those of a sub–influence in order to accurately describe the effect of this planetary placement.

In order to test this idea, I took my list of names and day–signs and arranged them according to the 13–day period that they occurred in. It was clear to me almost immediately that those in each category were not nearly as similar as when I had arranged them according to day–sign only. However, I did feel that the 13–day period did exert a sub–influence on the day–sign. For example, it seemed that many people born in the week 1–Crocodile did have some of the qualities of that day–sign, but of a more subconscious quality. Apparently, a blending of influences was necessary to fill in important details about a person's Mesoamerican horoscope.

Another possible way to view the 13–day periods is to see them as what might be called "night–signs." It could be the case, and it seems to be so from experience, that the day–signs delineate the consciously projected personality while the 13–day periods describe the subjective, subconscious and reactive side of the personality. Since it takes the Sun thirteen days to cover the same sky distance that the Moon covers in just one day, perhaps there is a lunar (Moon sign) quality to these periods.

It also appears to be the case that there is a significant interaction between the direction of any day–sign and the direction of the day–sign that begins the 13–day period. For example, House is a sign of the west. The day–sign 3–House is the third day of a 13–day period that begins with 1–Crocodile, a sign of the east, the opposite direction. The issue I'm raising here has to do with the nature of any interaction between the eastern and western influences. It might be worth keeping in mind that day–signs preceded by 1, 5, 9 and 13 are consistent direction–wise while 3, 7, and 11 are cases of directional opposition.

The 260–day calendar then has twenty day–signs, four directions and twenty 13–day periods that each exert an influence on a birth. Like Western astrology, a reading of character would depend very much on the astrologer's ability to blend meanings, something that could never be conveyed adequately in print. Though there are further divisions of the 260–day period that warrant investigation, these will have to wait until the three primary qualities become better understood.

The Year–Bearers

In traditional Mesoamerican astrology, a birth was said to be influenced by the hour, the day, the 13–day period and also the year. Not much is known in regard to the hour, and although the day and night were probably divided into segments that had astrological meanings, we can't be sure about that either. A few things can be said about the year, however. An interesting feature of the 260–day calendar is that it meshes with the 365–day year in such a way that only four of the 20 day–signs can ever occupy the first of the year. These four day–signs were called the year–bearers and were said to give their influence to the entire year. The year–bearers, one for each direction, repeated in sequence and progressed in number. For the Aztecs these were the day–

signs Reed, Knife, House and Rabbit. After 52 years, each year–bearer would have occurred 13 times, once for each number. Also after 52 years, the calendar would have been 13 days out of step with the seasons because there was no leap year in the 365 day calendar of the Aztecs. At the 52–year point, a major calendar adjustment was made, the New Fire Ceremony occurred and a new era was said to begin. The New Fire Ceremony involved the extinguishing of all fires and lights in the city and the lighting of a new one at midnight (after a human sacrifice) from which the city's fires were relit.

Although it is not certain, the Aztecs probably began their year from the vernal equinox. The Maya (Classic period) used a different starting point, probably in July, and consequently had four different year–bearers. These were Ocelot, Deer, Grass and Earthquake. However, when the Spaniards arrived, they were using yet another set: Lizard, Water, Wind and Rain. The Maya of today are known to use the same year–bearers as the Classic Maya, and begin their year around March 6th or 7th. Because of these inconsistencies and the extreme generalism of assigning a particular quality to all born in a given year, I have not given much thought to the possible influence of the year–bearer on a birth.

In the next chapter some practical applications of Mesoamerican astrology will be presented. It is hoped that others will perceive patterns I have missed and add to the rehabilitation of what was once one of the world's great astrological traditions.

Chapter 3

Using Day–Sign Astrology

The reader must keep in mind that the recovery of ancient Maya and Aztec astrology is still very tentative. There are also many aspects of the ancient astrological tradition, such as the "Lords of the Night" and the "Thirteen Birds" that have not been discussed in this book because so little is known about them. Most likely some crucial elements have been lost forever. However, there are a few important concepts and techniques that could form the basis of an astrological reading, and there are some links with Western astrology that allow a reader trained in that tradition to utilize the day–signs in their work. I hope people find the material presented below to be useful.

The Polarity of Personality

Probably the single most important concept about the day–signs is that they form a personality matrix of 260 types, based on all possible combinations of the day–signs and the 13–day periods. The day–signs by themselves appear to indicate the more prominent personality characteristics. They seem to act like the Sun and the Ascendant as is understood in Western astrology – the parts of the personality that are more direct and outer oriented. The 13–day period appears to symbolize the subconscious instincts, urges, needs and responses – very much like the Moon does in the Western horoscope. In essence, we have here a classification scheme that is based on all possible combinations of twenty primary symbols that can assume both a solar, or yang, quality and a lunar, or yin, quality. In other words, the sign Crocodile can be both day–sign where it indicates personality traits that are directed outwards, and a ruler of a 13–day period where it indicates traits that are essentially responsive. The personality, therefore, is composed of two principle parts, the solar and lunar, male and female, yang and yin. A personality reading should begin with this basic distinction.

The Four Orientations

Beyond the day–sign and 13–day period distinctions are the four directions. Like the four elements, the four directions suggest something about the basic orientation of the personality. Signs of the east seem to be concerned with the establishment of the self, while those of the west get wrapped up in compromise and relationship. Signs of the north are defensive and appear to be distant in some ways while signs of the south express emotion. Quite possibly it is the signs of the north that struggle with emotions while those of the south struggle with mind.

In any delineation of personality using the day–signs, the directions must be taken into account. When there is a reinforcement of direction, which is the case when both the day–sign and the 13–day period are of the same direction, the effects are most obvious. Reinforcement of direction always occurs with the numbers 1, 5, 9, and 13. People born under these numbers may be more internally consistent, more forceful and have deeper convictions than those born with a mixture of directions.

It appears that a person born with the day–sign direction opposite the 13–day period direction may have a life of significant internal tension. The numbers that correlate with this condition are 3, 7, and 11. These people thrive on challenges and often achieve tremendous success in life through the overcoming of obstacles. It may be true also, that these people grow in life through the act of balancing and harmonizing the world around them, and also through the expansion of consciousness, a way of putting things into a larger perspective. In summary, for Western astrologers, it might be said that matched directions act like a conjunction and opposite directions act like an opposition. The other combinations present more complex problems for interpretation.

From another perspective, the directions of the 13–day periods divide the entire 260–day sequence into four sets of 65 days. The traditional book that contained the list of the 260 days, the Tonalamatl, was organized in such a way that all the day–signs belonging to a 13–day period of the east were located on one page. Those of the north had their own page, etc. In other words, the 260 days were divided by four and four lists of 65 days made up the book. Each set of 65 days was linked to one of the four directions, the direction of the leading day–sign or the 13–day period ruler. The point I'm trying to reinforce is that the influence of the directions on a day–sign is two–fold. First, there is the direction of the day–sign itself, second is the direction of the 13–day period. The ancient Mesoamericans thought enough of this second type of directional rulership to incorporate it into the standard form of their ritual compilations of the days.

Patterns of Relationship

The issue of compatibility of day–signs is an important one, but one not easily settled at the present time. Most likely, compatibility is affected by both the directions and the nature of the signs themselves. For example, east signs will tend to pair with west signs, and likewise, south and north. But there may also be certain sign preferences. For example, Wind types may generally prefer relationships with those born under Monkey or Earthquake because those are fairly cerebral signs and Wind types like to be mentally stimulated. Relationship compatibility is an area of day–sign astrology that will need years of study before some definite conclusions can be made. Practitioners of Western astrology should compare this problem with Sun–sign compatibilities where frequently the general rules simply don't work. In spite of this uncertainty a few things can be said that may serve to guide readers in the right direction. Experience seems to indicate the following:

1. Opposite day–signs direction–wise, for example Crocodile (east) and Eagle (west), seem to attract. There does, however, seem to be a tendency for this kind of combination to be one that contains many internal conflicts. Many relationships composed of opposite day–signs direction–wise are based on competition, conflict or constructive activity.

2. Like day–signs direction–wise, for example House and Monkey, are often based on agreements and cooperation. These are frequently strong relationships that do well in business and other practical matters.

3. East/east relationships tend to be stressful because both parties have strong personal needs that make cooperation difficult. West/west relationships may be too passive or accommodating.

4. Another type of opposition that can occur in the 260–day calendar is the opposition of day–signs themselves. When the 20 day–signs are strung around a circle, like the signs of the zodiac, ten pairs are formed. These are:

>   Crocodile – Monkey
>   Wind – Grass
>   House – Reed
>   Lizard – Ocelot
>   Serpent – Eagle
>   Death – Vulture
>   Deer – Earthquake
>   Rabbit – Knife
>   Water – Rain
>   Dog – Flower

I have noticed that a fairly large number of marriages or significant relationships involve this sort of pairing. It is true that each pair is an opposite direction–wise, thus reinforcing point 1 above.

Looking deeper into opposites one might consider that if all the 260 days were arranged into a circle, there would be 130 pairs of opposites. For example 1–Crocodile is opposite 1–Monkey and 2–Wind is opposite 2–Grass. It is possible that cross–relationships like these, or even ones spaced a specific number of days apart, could be significant. It is true that in the rituals of the Aztec merchants, days for departure were staggered in the 260–day calendar in such a way. Such arrangements can be read from the calendrical diagrams in the ancient codices that have survived the Spanish Conquest. There are also directional indications that can be read from these sacred books, but this is all beyond the scope of this book.

It is also possible that the Aztec deities that were linked with each day–sign (we don't have the complete Maya list) may offer some suggestions. For example, Wind was linked with Quetzalcoatl and Reed (and also Knife) with Tezcatlipoca. These two were symbols of the struggle between light and dark forces and suggest compatibility problems between these day–signs. Possibly Serpent and Rain, both ruled by water deities, have some basic compatibilities as do Monkey and Flower, ruled by deities who were in consort. Whether or not this proves to be a fruitful approach to discovering relationship patterns remains to be seen.

The Passage Through Life – Progressed Day–Signs

Since any astrological reading should include some forecasting, two simple techniques are presented here. The first involves simply following the course of the day–signs as they occur from day to day and comparing them with the day–sign of birth. One thing I have noticed is that the occurrence of the day–sign that is opposite one's day–sign of birth often coincides with a time of crisis and adjustment. This will occur at 130 days after the occurrence of the day–sign of birth. To find this day use Table II, find your 13-day sign column, and then go to the 13-day listing 10 columns away (begins with opposite). Count down to where your day-sign would be to find your opposite day-sign. Your final result is the number of the day that will bring on a crisis or period of adjustment. You can then turn to the ephemeris and determine past and future dates of this occurrence. Experience indicates that you should give a range of about a week before and a few days later from the "critical date" for the full trend to manifest.

There is a correlation with Western astrology that is relevant here. If you think of your birthday in the cycle as a conjunction, then the point 130 days from it is like an opposition. Experience seems to indicate that these two points in the cycle do coincide with personal events that fit the standard astrological description of these aspects. The conjunction (birthday) is hard to define in a general sense except that it usually strengthens the sense of self. The opposition (130 day point) tends to correlate with more objective events, public events, or decision making. A crisis at this point is more likely to involve encounters, relationships, or participation than the birthday point.

Quartering the cycle produces four sets of 65 days each. This was one of two ways (the other, and more common way, was in five sets of 52 days) that the 260–day cycle was depicted in the ancient Maya and Aztec books. At 65–day intervals in the cycle rituals were performed, and these points were called the burner ceremonies, though not much is known about them. My experiences suggest that the quarters of the 260–day cycle, aside from the above mentioned conjunction and opposition points, act as critical days and have the stress–producing qualities that Western astrologers would ascribe to the square or 90–degree aspect.

In the modern indigenous tradition the day–signs 65 days before and after the birthday, and the one 130 days away, are thought to constitute important components of the psyche and are actually seen as part of one's full personality. I have observed that when these points come up in the calendar, there will almost always be activity or discernable challenging trends in one's life. Major events will often fall within a day or two of one of these points and they are well worth noting ahead of time and studying.

There are other variations on relationships between day–signs that add to a description of the self and these are described in some detail by Carlos Barrios and Ken Johnson in their books. There is a pattern, called the Mayan Cross and based on the four directions, that is practiced by contemporary Mayan daykeepers. The day–sign of birth, taken as the center of the cross, is framed by four other signs with the east position, at the bottom of the grid, representing the future and west, at the top, the past. North (right) and south (left) signify feminine and masculine energy respectively. The day–signs that occupy these positions on the grid will relate to the day–sign in the center by a distance in the tzolkin of nine days ahead and behind for future and past, and seven days ahead and behind for masculine and feminine.

The Mayan Cross

	Past – Conception	
Masculine —	Day–sign —	Feminine
	Future – Destiny	

Example: Barack Obama

	Serpent	
Deer —	9 Reed —	Rain
	Crocodile	

The cross signs will form a pattern as follows: top and bottom will be a sign of the same direction as the center day–sign, left and right will be a sign of the opposite direction. In the example above, the day–sign, past and future are all signs of the east, the masculine and feminine positions are occupied by signs of the west. The usefulness in a delineation of personality by this method is something that readers should investigate for themselves.

I find that the quartering of the tzolkin from the day–sign provides similar information and also provides pivotal days to note on one's calendar that are often quite noticeable. Using the same example this arrangement uses the Classic Mayan and Aztec convention of placing east at the top of the cross, north to the left, west at the bottom and south at the right. Here the day–sign is placed in the east position signifying the emergence of self and the future. The west position 130 days from the day–sign (opposite in the tzolkin), signifies others, relationships and also the ancestral tradition. The north position (65 days ahead of the day–sign) signifies mind; the south position (65 days before the day–sign) emotion and feelings. A delineation would then take these positions and the day–signs located in them as indications of the various components of an emerging personality. Either of these schemes could be thought of as a means of locating areas of experience that need to be integrated into the self and readers are encouraged to test them out and see which works better for them.

9 Reed

9 Rabbit — Barack Obama — 9 Knife

9 House

Forty–day intervals from the birth day–sign also seem to coincide with changes, and 60–day intervals appear to be generally harmonious. Notice that these are simply multiples of 20. The idea of alternating waves of 20 days each, the first ten being up, the second ten down, comes to mind. If this approach turns out to be as productive as I suspect it is, then the ancient Mesoamerican astrologers will have to be given credit for discovering a master biorhythm.

A second kind of forecasting can be done using the Western astrological concept of secondary progressions. In this technique, a day is equated to a year. If you were 30 years old, 30 days after your birth would give symbolic information about that year of your life. Using the tables in this book, count ahead a day for each year of your life and arrive at the day–sign that rules your present year of life, or any other for that matter. Your actual day–sign would then rule your life from birth to your first birthday. The day after your birth would correspond to your life from age one to age two, two days after would correspond to age two to three, etc.

There are some fairly consistent patterns that emerge when using this technique. First, the day–sign that rules the year in question does seem to describe some of the more important trends of the year. For example, a year ruled by Grass may be a year of plodding and compromise, a year ruled by Serpent may be a year of upheaval and change and a year ruled by Flower may bring a relationship or partnership. Second, major life initiatives, such as career changes and relocations, seem to occur on years ruled by Crocodile (the first of the signs) or the beginning of a 13–day period (a sign led by the number one). Experience indicates that while this is generally true, sometimes the move or career change occurs a year before or a year afterwards. It is also possible that directional relationships between the sign ruling the current year and the birth day–sign may add further depth to the interpretation.

An example illustrating the above is the presidency of Barack Obama. He was born on the day–sign 9–Reed, in the 13 day trecena 1–Serpent. Counting a day for a year, the day–sign 4–Flower corresponds to the year 2008. He was elected to the presidency that year and began his term as president in 2009 with the day–sign 5–Crocodile. Here we see a major life change occurring as the last sign finishes and the first sign comes up. Another intriguing example is the life of John Lennon, born on the day–sign 10–Water. He teamed up with Paul McCartney, Ringo Starr and George Harrison as The Beatles in 1960 corresponding to the day–sign 4–Water and he died in 1980 corresponding to the day–sign 11–Water. As there are 20 day–signs, any given day–sign will come up every two decades, though the number prefix will differ.

Correlations with Western Astrology

One of the most remarkable things about the day–signs is their confirmation in the Western horoscope. In fact, it was this correlation that was responsible for a major breakthrough in my understanding of the day–signs. Exactly how this works is a mystery to me, but it does seem to work in a practical sense and I hope to eventually do some statistical testing to confirm my findings. The following list is the result of comparing hundreds of horoscopes, cast for the time and place of a birth, with the day–sign and 13–day period that was in effect on that day. I have found that astrological symbolism for the day–sign is usually most obvious, though that for the 13–day period is always present as well. The major pay–off here is that a reader of horoscopes, who understands the day–signs well, can cut through the myriad symbols of the horoscope quickly and locate the main themes.

The correlations between Western horoscope and Mesoamerican day–sign can take a number of forms. For example, prominence of the sign Cancer or prominence of the Moon in a Western horoscope means essentially the same things. They are two ways of symbolizing a kind of functioning, motivation and behavior. The several ways that a planet or sign in Western astrology can be considered prominent are by location relative to the horizon (usually rising, culminating, setting or at lower culmination), conjunction or aspect with key points in the horoscope (Ascendant, Sun and Moon) or by reinforcement (when a planet is in its own sign).

To illustrate how different horoscope patterns can point to the same thing, consider the following example. The day–sign Flower often correlates with a prominent Venus in the horoscope. One person born on this day–sign might simply have the planet Venus rising or Venus setting at the time and place of birth. Another might have an exact 45 degree separation (a semi–square) between the Sun and Venus, or the Moon conjoining Venus. A third person might have Libra (the sign of Venus) rising or the Sun or Moon in that sign. A fourth person might be born with a stellium in the 7th house, the house that corresponds with Venus.

Readers familiar with Western astrology will have to judge for themselves as to whether this pattern is as consistent as it appears in my experience. The idea that everyone born on a particular day will have such consistent symbolism in their horoscopes raises some major questions. For example, how could everyone born on the same day have the same kind of symbolism in their horoscopes? One explanation is that perhaps births everywhere tend to occur in spurts during any particular day, not at a consistent rate.

The Astrological Correspondences of the Day–Signs

Crocodile: The most common signs seem to be Cancer and Libra. The Moon is usually very prominent and so is Neptune. These two suggest the deep emotions and instincts of this day–sign. Saturn and Pluto, representing the strong defensive and territorial domination instincts, are present and prominent as well.

Wind: The most common signs found in the charts of this day–sign are Gemini and Pisces. Naturally, the rulers of these signs, Mercury and Neptune, may also be present. There is often a strong and somewhat stressed Saturn or Capricorn placement found also.

House: The signs Cancer, Leo, Scorpio and Capricorn appear to be the most common ones in charts of those born on this day–sign. To a lesser extent the planets Pluto and Saturn are prominent. There seems to be an important 12th house or Neptunian theme also in the chart.

Lizard: The signs Virgo, Sagittarius, and Scorpio are frequent, but I have also noticed a prominent Sun and Saturn, or Leo and Capricorn, in many cases.

Serpent: The signs Aries, Gemini, Leo and Scorpio are most commonly emphasized in the horoscope, or the planetary rulers of these signs Mars, Mercury, the Sun and Pluto. Also, the planet Uranus is frequently prominent in some way.

Death: Scorpio, Capricorn and Pisces are very commonly found with this day–sign. The Moon, Saturn and Neptune are also usually prominent.

Deer: The signs Taurus and Scorpio appear to be the most common in horoscopes of those born on this day–sign. Also prominent are the planetary rulers Venus and Pluto. Mercury and Jupiter may be important as well.

Rabbit: The signs Gemini, Aquarius and Pisces are frequently emphasized. Also the planets Mercury, Mars, Uranus and Neptune are linked or configured with other important parts of the horoscope.

Water: At least one of the three water signs, Cancer, Scorpio and Pisces, and the sign Aquarius, are usually prominent in the chart. Also Neptune, the Moon, Mars and Pluto seem to be strong.

Dog: Taurus, Leo and Scorpio are the main signs frequently found in charts of those born under this day–sign. Also, the Sun or Moon configured with Pluto, or its prominence, is common.

Monkey: The signs Gemini, Leo and Aquarius often appear prominently in the horoscope. The Sun and the planet Mercury are also quite powerful relative to the rest of the chart, or the 3rd house is strong.

Grass: Libra, Sagittarius, Capricorn and Pisces are the signs most often found emphasized in horoscopes of Grass births. Also, the planets Venus, Neptune and Pluto may be strongly placed.

Reed: Libra and Sagittarius are the typical signs found in the horoscopes of those born under this day–sign. Mars, Venus and Jupiter may also be strong and prominent.

Ocelot: Scorpio, Sagittarius and Aquarius are commonly prominent. In some cases, the relevant houses, the 8th, 9th and 11th are strongly emphasized instead.

Eagle: Most often the signs Virgo, Libra, Scorpio and Aquarius are emphasized. In some cases so is the Moon or the sign of Cancer.

Vulture: Taurus, Sagittarius and Capricorn are commonly emphasized in the horoscopes of those born under this day–sign. The planets Saturn and Pluto are often important as well. In one case, the natal Sun was located at the exact midpoint of Saturn and Pluto.

Earthquake: The signs Aries and Gemini and the planets Mars and Mercury are usually quite prominent. Also, Saturn and Uranus often stand out in some way, usually by house position (in an angular house) or by conjunction with an important planet in the chart.

Knife: Aries, Libra and Capricorn are commonly found signs in the charts of those born under this day–sign. Mars, Saturn and especially Neptune are also prominent.

Rain: The signs Gemini and Scorpio usually show up in some prominent way in horoscopes for this day–sign. There is also typically a prominent Mercury, Moon and Saturn.

Flower: The signs Libra and Pisces are most common, but Capricorn seems to be fairly frequent also. The planets Venus, Saturn and Neptune are usually emphasized in some way.

Part 2

The Delineations of the 20 Day–Signs

The Delineations of the 20 Day–Signs

In the sections that follow, the 20 day–signs are presented in terms of both traditional material and the modern interpretations discovered through my own subjective, but pragmatic, study of people known to me and notable people with public biographies. The first part of each section notes the traditional names and the symbolism and mythology associated with the day–sign. Also included are comments from two friars, Duran and Sahagun, who wrote about the Aztec calendar shortly after the Spanish conquest of Mexico. These friars were intent on eliminating the native traditions and their observations on the day–signs were done in the spirit of disgust. Their reports are superficial because of this bias, or possibly because their native informants were not experts in the subject. In many cases the traditional information appears to be contradictory and one is left with simply considering the more obvious properties of the symbol, something that is included in this section also.

The next section, titled "Experiential Observations", is a description of the day–sign as I have seen it operate in numerous cases. Since these day–signs appear to operate in some respects like the Sun–signs of Western astrology, the reader may want to consider the following. In some cases, usually with women from very traditional families or cultures, the description of the day–sign may fit the husband or other men in her life more than herself. This may be a case of the psychological phenomena of projection – that what is not comfortably held within, because of upbringing or societal restraints, is experienced externally through other people. I have found that women born after the middle of the past century, as a general rule, are less likely to project their day–sign on others than those born before this culturally transforming period.

After the description of the day–sign, the 13–day period that each numbered day falls within is listed. A few sentences add what might be relevant information about this sub–influence, though the interested reader should turn to the larger descriptions of the 13–day periods that follow the day–sign descriptions at the end of the book for more information. For example, a person born on 3–House, which falls within the 13–day period governed by 1–Crocodile, should study the latter day–sign as it will modify his nature to a noticeable degree and say something about subconscious and reactive qualities. At the very end of each day–sign delineation is a list of famous and notable people born under it. The listing is based on their birthdays as given in Wikipedia and calculated using computer software. These examples should be taken with a grain of salt as the birth times are generally not known and, given time zone differences, a few may actually fall into the previous or following day–signs. In addition, according to my observations, people born after sunset seem to be best described by the next day's day–sign, so readers are advised to think critically when considering these notable examples, though I would estimate that the vast majority are accurate.

Crocodile

Indigenous names
Maya: Imix or Imox
Aztec: Cipactli

Direction: East

The day–sign Crocodile began the sequence of the twenty named days during pre–Columbian times. Both Sahagun and Duran began their accounts of the sacred calendar with this sign. The several Tonalamatl (Books of Fate) that survive begin their listing of the 260 days with this day–sign. In Maya calendrics, the approximately twenty–year time periods called katuns were named for the day–sign they ended on. In all cases, this was the named–day Flower (Ahau in Maya), and it was preceded by a number from one to thirteen. For example, it was said that the Spanish arrived in Yucatan during katun 11–Flower, the katun that ended on that day. However, the next katun would always begin on the day 12–Crocodile. In fact, the entire 5,000–year creation epoch of the Maya that began in August –3113, the Long Count, began on the day 5–Crocodile.

The Maya name for this day–sign, Imix, probably refers to the Earth and its bounty and suggests the idea of protection and nourishment. The Maya glyph itself resembles a nipple. There are also connections between the word Imix and the Maya creation account. The Aztec word *Cipactli*, which means "prickly object" and also crocodile or caiman, had links to creation accounts as well. In Aztec myth, the Earth itself was the back of a Crocodile floating in a great pond. The Aztec symbol for the day–sign was that of the head of a crocodile with its lower jaw torn off. The explanation for this was that the god Tezcatlipoca ripped it off when he pulled the beast from the dark depths. Here is the notion of a violent creation where one of the most ancient gods pulls the Earth from deep water to its surface.

The Aztec deity linked to this day–sign was Tonacatecuhtli, the creator god itself. This god, who was actually a male–female duality, was the creator of all existence, living in the uppermost heaven called Omeyocan. The duality gave birth to the other gods, including

Quezalcoatl and Tezcatlipoca, who then took on a more direct role in the ongoing creation. Tonacatecuhtli was a remote god, and, as missionary activity forced belief changes on the native peoples, was often associated with the Christian god.

The characteristics of those born under this day–sign, according to Friar Duran's account, were quite positive. They were said to possess outstanding courage and strength and would be successful in farming, war and commerce. They were busy people who constantly worked to increase their wealth. Friar Sahagun also regarded the sign as positive except for 9–Crocodile, which was said to be perverse and prone to vice.

From a common sense perspective, one would think that those born on this day might have personality characteristics in common with the animal symbol. Crocodiles are relatively primitive animals, survivors from an earlier age. They dominate their environment due to brute strength, but are also extremely protective and nurturing of their offspring, guarding their eggs and then carrying or escorting their hatchlings to the water. Baby crocodiles ride on their mother's back for safety and protection from predators. Also, these animals tend to lie still for long periods of time, then burst into activity. In the previous edition of this book, and in many other books, this day–sign is called Alligator. Since alligators live only in the southern United States, and only crocodiles and caiman live in the Mesoamerican region, crocodile is probably the most appropriate translation of Cipactli.

Experiential Observations

Key Meaning: Primal creation and personal power

Those born on the day–sign Crocodile appear to have several key traits in common. They are energetic, practical, creative and initiating, but can also be dominating or parental towards others. They have strong nurturing instincts, are quite sensitive and require privacy. Many feel rejected by their families or parents, and in compensation, seek group friendships that make up for this loss. Some become founders of businesses, organizations or associations.

Crocodile types are often constantly at work, usually trying to maintain the integrity of their world. They relate to the world around them through their feelings and not their intellect. This causes them to be quite reactive to any changes taking place around them and they often rush in to keep the dam from breaking, so-to-speak. This reactiveness is probably behind a tendency to initiate activities. They are often found breaking ground or starting things up. It's because they have so much emotional concern for their world that they often achieve great success in life, not just because of sheer ambition. When motivated, the Crocodile type will work incessantly until emotional security has been restored and stabilized. However, when they do achieve emotional security, they may become extremely lazy and even lethargic.

Strong appetites, followed by rest periods, are a common characteristic of these people, although some may even develop an obsession with food or drink. Seafood is often a popular item on their menu. Eating and drinking are second-nature to these people and some even make careers out of it.

People born under the day-sign Crocodile have unusually strong instincts. While much of this is probably more like maternal instinct, some of it could be called genuinely psychic. They tend to be attracted to the psychic or futuristic sciences. When they follow their hunches, these people are nearly always successful in whatever they are attempting.

The Crocodile type is also extremely sensitive and touchy. They have a terrible time taking criticism and tend to react defensively. On the other hand, they can be among the most critical and fussy people known. In their dealings with the world, they often put on a tough exterior to protect themselves from what may be a harsh environment. Like the Crocodile they can be difficult to live with because of their hard, rough and even prickly, surface. They need privacy to recuperate from the stress of maintaining their defensive posture. In extreme cases they can become downright distant and reclusive. It is probably good for one born under this day-sign to have a private place that is all their own, a personal sanctuary of some kind. Crocodile types are attracted to and sometimes live in residences near the sea or a body of water.

Those who have close relationships with Crocodile types will notice their tendency to dominate others in a parental way. They have an unusually strong parenting instinct. If they don't have any children they will seek outlets by establishing nurturing relationships with people, pets, and plants. The maternal instincts of female Crocodile types can be awesome. Often they assume the role of parent, usually mother, towards others and either help them along their way, or clean–up for them. If the other person doesn't mind this, a dependency relationship will develop. If they do mind it, a power struggle may occur, one in which there is little hope of a rational solution. Because Crocodile types are so instinctive and emotional, they have problems reasoning things out and then acting on that reasoning.

Crocodile types will nearly always have a slightly unusual relationship with their own parents. In some cases this is due to the loss of a parent, in others due to their being dominated or rejected by their parents from birth onward. In all cases these relationships are characterized by emotional issues, and not necessarily those that have to do with property or money. Quite common among Crocodile types is a family rejection or critical parent complex. The feeling, real or imagined, that their parents expect too much of them, or don't want them, motivates them to create their own personal families. These may be small, but tight–knit, groups of friends that they put together, or they may actually join in with an existing family. The more enterprising Crocodile types will create a business or a professional "family", setting foundations for later, and larger, enterprises.

Creativity is a hallmark of those born under this day–sign. Although some Crocodile types are incredibly productive, others fail to realize some of their best and most creative ideas, in part due to maternal concerns of some sort, in part due to emotional inertia. The issue of having children is of intense concern to Crocodile types and they frequently botch this up by living an unconscious life, controlled by their feelings or emotions, or by avoiding the subject until emergency conditions arise. However, they can be excellent parents, very nurturing and sensitive to their offspring. Their weakness here lies in being overprotective and consequently dominating.

Crocodile types are best suited for occupations in which they can help others, nurture others or protect others. They like to be "at the steering wheel" and should probably not work for anyone else. In such positions they can be powerful leaders and bring to the world their own vision of security and harmony. On the other hand they need to become more objective and rational about their relationships with others. While this is difficult, it may spare them some emotionally draining power struggles.

The Influence of the 13–Day Periods

1–Crocodile
This is the first day of the 13–day period that begins with the day 1–Crocodile. It is the pure, unmodified form of this day–sign. Those born on it may exhibit the characteristics of the sign quite clearly. They are very powerful, have strong feelings about things and are not easily swayed by mere ideas.

2–Crocodile
This is actually the second day of the 13–day period that begins with the day–sign 1–Flower. Those born on this day may be quite creative, idealistic, and prone to fall in love easily. Relationships are important to them and contribute to their individual identity.

3–Crocodile
This is the third day of the 13–day period beginning with the day–sign 1–Rain. Those born on this day are ambitious, hard–working and easily stimulated on the intellectual level, but are also deeply emotive. They are often excellent communicators and many become teachers.

4–Crocodile
This is the fourth day of the 13–day period beginning with the day–sign 1–Knife. Those born on this day may find it necessary to sacrifice much of their personal life in order to realize their visions. They will need to develop their critical judgment as major life–altering and reputation–making choices will be presented to them during the course of their life.

5–Crocodile
This is the fifth day of the 13–day period beginning with the day–sign 1–Earthquake. While those born on this day might be extremely creative and full of ideas, they may also be somewhat unstable. They are dynamic, dominating, empire builders who thrive on constant change.

6–Crocodile
This is the sixth day of the 13–day period that begins with the day–sign 1–Vulture. Those born on this day may experience, or be unusually sensitive to, domination by others. The reverse is possible as well, where they are the dominators. Equality, balance and freedom from fears in life can be a challenge, but hard work and persistence will eventually pay off.

7–Crocodile

This is the seventh day of the 13–day period that begins with 1–Eagle. Independence and freedom from domination are important issues for those born on this day. They tend to be problem solvers, aloof and somewhat distant to those they don't know very well, but are good providers for their own family.

8–Crocodile

This is the eighth day of the 13–day period that begins with 1–Ocelot. These people are particularly well–informed and tend to become absorbed in making plans or effecting strategies. They experience great intensity in their relationships with the opposite sex.

9–Crocodile

This is the ninth day of the 13–day period that begins with the day–sign 1–Reed. These are often deep thinkers, somewhat opinionated, with strong psychic abilities. Sahagun reported that those born here would become sorcerers and astrologers.

10–Crocodile

This is the tenth day of the 13–day period beginning with the day–sign 1–Grass. Very much caught up in obligations and the affairs of others, those born under this combination have problems sustaining a strong personal center.

11–Crocodile

This is the eleventh day of the 13–day period beginning with 1–Monkey. Those born on this day are complicated people with strong artistic leanings. They have a compulsive need for attention and powerful creative drives.

12–Crocodile

This is the twelfth day of the 13–day period beginning with the day–sign 1–Dog. Loyalty and dedication to family is a characteristic of those born on this day. They are joiners and often founders of groups or associations.

13–Crocodile

This is the thirteenth day of the 13–day period that begins with the day–sign 1–Water. This might be the most emotionally intense of the thirteen forms that this day sign can take. These people dominate others without thinking, though their leadership is usually accepted by all.

Notables born under Crocodile

1 – Alan Watts, Billy Bob Thornton, Jenifer Aniston, Vanessa Redgrave, Boris Spassky

2 – Joe Biden, Lyle Lovett, Florence Griffith–Joyner

3 – Howard Hughes, Rita Hayworth, Frank Sinatra, Tom Hanks, Scott Hamilton

4 – Mao Tse Tung, Orson Wells, Robert Heinlein, Mark McGuire, Lucinda Williams, John F. Kennedy, Jr.

5 – Thomas Edison, Werner Heisenberg, Walt Disney, James Garner, John Goodman, Ben Vereen

6 – Wilma Rudolph, Louis Farrakhan, Peter Jackson

7 – W.C. Fields, Vincent Price, Hubert Humphrey, Berry Gordy, Marianne Faithful, Janis Ian

8 – Johnny Cash, Frederico Fellini, Richard Leakey, Sean Penn

9 – Ella Fitzgerald, Aretha Franklin, Glenn Close, Robert Plant

10 – Arnold Toynbee, Chuck Yeager, Janis Joplin, Phil Lesh, Kobe Bryant

11 – Linus Pauling, Sam Cooke, Joan Baez, Queen Latifah

12 – Zane Grey, Leonid Brezhnev, Bob Hope, A.A. Milne, John Fogerty, Olga Korbut

13 – John Cleese, Tony Blair, Patrick Stewart, Steve Winwood

Wind

Indigenous Names
Maya: Ik
Aztec: Ehecatl

Direction: North

Both the Maya and Aztec names for this day–sign suggest the idea of wind or breath, and also life itself. The Maya glyph for the sign includes a T–shaped design (possibly a symbol for the sacred tree of life) that has associations with the god of rain and wind. One could draw a connection between rain and the coming to life of seeds, the force that stimulates life and growth. The Aztecs symbolized this day by the mask of Ehecatl, a form of the god Quetzalcoatl. In this form, or manifestation, Quetzalcoatl was the wind god and his breath was funneled through the snout–like beak on the mask. Since Quetzalcoatl was a deity associated with intelligence, we might assume that the day–sign Wind had something to do with the workings of the mind. The Zapotec name for this day–sign means "fire."

Much has been written about Quetzalcoatl, though it is not completely clear as to whether he was a man, god or both. There appear to have been a number of Toltec priests who took on the name as a title which has added to the confusion. In the ancient mythologies, Quetzalcoatl, which literally means "feathered, or plumed, serpent", was one of the first creations of the creator duality. He, along with Tezcatlipoca, was said to have created the conscious universe. He was also associated with the creation of culture, the arts, the sciences, and also the astrological calendar and the planet Venus. Another side to the Quetzalcoatl myth is a story of his enlightened and god–like kingship which ended after he committed sexual sins with his sister. After he renounced his position and title he headed east, dying on a funeral pyre and merging with the rising Venus. There are several variants on this theme, some from Toltec sources, others gleaned from architectural inscriptions. The basic idea, though, is that he is both god and mortal. This reminds one in some ways of the Greek god Chiron, the centaur–educator who experienced death as a mortal.

Duran, in his recounting of the twenty named–days, describes Wind as producing fickle, inconsistent and negligent people who move from place to place. Sahagun regarded the sign as mixed in qualities, depending on the number attached to it. For example, 1–Wind people became astrologers if they are born into noble families, if not, they became demons. 9–Wind people were, according to him or his sources, "driven by the winds."

Wind, from the common sense perspective, is not seen except indirectly, yet it can be heard. It can be unpredictable, sudden and potentially destructive and it can have a cooling effect. Breath and fire are also linked to this day–sign. Breath is necessary for life – the dead do not breathe and a newborn's first breath brings it to life. People speak or communicate with each other with their breath. Fire also suggests life – it seems to be alive. It is there, or it is not. Fires also need air, or breath, or they go out.

Experiential Observations

Key Meaning: Adaptation, the mind and communication

People born under the day–sign Wind are generally mentally active and communicative, versatile and multi–faceted. They tend to be idealistic and romantic, fashion conscious or artistic, and somewhat non–committal or indecisive. They seem to have problems with issues of responsibility and obligation, these being their greatest challenges.

The Wind person is usually mentally wired. These types are thinking constantly and this intrudes upon their awareness of the intense emotional realities within and around them. To others, they seem very much alive and alert. To themselves, they feel confused and uncertain as to what information they should act on. Learning, speaking, reading, and other forms of mental communication appeal to them. Many have tried their hand at writing in one form or another. A conversation with one born on this day–sign is always interesting and stimulating. However, breadth, not depth, is their forte.

Most people born on this day–sign have more than one major interest or profession. Because their minds seem capable of grasping the similarities between seemingly different activities, they move from one to another with relative ease. Their biggest problem seems to be knowing both when and how to focus so as to not spread themselves out too much. Wind types are clever and very intelligent when it comes to learning. They enjoy playing many roles in life but do not seek out leadership positions, in fact, service seems to come easier to them.

Those born under Wind tend to be very sensitive to the way things around them appear visually. This is also true of their own appearance. They have strong aesthetic sensibilities and strive to create art, dress fashionably or decorate their homes. Also, music and the arts are of particular interest to them. Because they are so versatile, they often combine styles or mix fashions and are regarded by others as eclectic in their taste.

The imagination is a powerful factor for the Wind person and, when applied to human relationships, is a force behind strong romantic inclinations. Idealism, the obsession with a perfect future, is a typical problem for these people. Having a relationship with an image created in the mind, not the real person out there, usually leads to lovesickness and disillusionment. Often, those born under Wind experience disappointments in marriage or partnership because they overestimated the capabilities of their partner. Because of frequent romantic frustration, Wind people seek various kinds of escapes from life, some healthy and positive, others not so.

One of the great problems for those born under the day–sign Wind is the issue of commitment. Many have problems in marriage because they, or their partner, are not constant in their affections. Perhaps it is because they need variety to feel alive – or they project this quality onto the person they choose to mate with and then experience the problem outside of themselves. The worst thing a Wind person could do is to marry someone who is extremely traditional and limits their behaviors or stifles their interests. When they do find partners who allow them their needed freedom, they are more likely to settle down. Indecision is another issue for Wind people and is related to commitment problems. Because they are easily swayed by the strong opinions of others around them, they find it difficult to make a decision and stick with it. Their strong escapist urges and powerful imagination make it easy for them to avoid making decisions, though this often means unconsciously choosing a lifestyle that is complex internally, though inert externally.

Closely related to commitment is the issue of responsibility. Many

Wind types initially fear taking on challenges that involve responsibility, probably because they fear the conformity and obligations that arise from such situations. It is not unusual for those born under this day–sign to work for years under someone else before they finally accept an executive position or take the steps toward self–employment. Those that do usually succeed, but they need plenty of time before they can convince themselves of it.

There is no question that communications of all kinds are a source of potential success for those born under this day–sign. In many cases, talking is such a natural act that careers become based on it. Work that requires excellent communications, such as teaching, consulting, legal work and announcing, are areas where success may be found, especially so if there is room for the imagination to be exercised. Considering "wind" or the breath itself, I have noticed that there is often something very unique about a Wind person's voice or style of speech.

The Influence of the 13–Day Periods

1–Wind
This day begins the 13–day period called 1–Wind. Those born on this day have a strong need to communicate, explore and understand the world they live in. Their service instinct is strong and they are often teachers and counselors.

2–Wind
This is the second day of the 13–day period that begins with the day 1–Crocodile. Those born on this day are more independent, and also more domestically inclined than most Wind people. They have a strong intuitive sense and may even be psychic to some degree.

3–Wind
This is the third day of the 13–day period beginning with the day 1–Flower. Romance and love are major issues for these people yet they tend to have serious problems with commitment issues due to idealism and unrealistic expectations.

4–Wind
This is the fourth day of the 13–day period beginning with 1–Rain. Those born here are very complex, nervous, and are strongly attracted

to service related occupations. They are natural healers and teachers but sometimes lack the focus to achieve their full potential.

5–Wind
This is the fifth day of the 13–day period that begins with 1–Knife. Decision making can be a major problem for those born on this day and some have issues over responsibility. They are generally considerate people who usually have good mechanical and technical abilities and maintain high standards.

6–Wind
This is the sixth day of the 13–day period that begins with 1–Earthquake. Perhaps the most intense and unstable combination, these people need plenty of private time to rest and recuperate from the conflicting forces within and around them.

7–Wind
This is the seventh day of the 13–day period beginning with 1–Vulture. Those born on this day are somewhat aloof and hard to reach, a quality that may serve in leadership positions. They strive for success and status in more than one career.

8–Wind
This is the eighth day of the 13–day period beginning with 1–Eagle. Independence and personal freedom are primary concerns for those born on this day. These are people interested in minute details who can be unusually critical and mentally rigid.

9–Wind
This is the ninth day of the 13–day period that begins with 1–Ocelot. These are very complex people who are emotionally intense, often secretive and seductive. They are quite intelligent and are able to see the bigger picture in life.

10–Wind
This is the tenth day of the 13–day period beginning with the day 1–Reed. A respect for insight and intelligence, but also confusion, is characteristic of those born on this day. They have very strong opinions on philosophical or religious matters.

11–Wind
This is the eleventh day of the 13–day period beginning with 1–Grass. People born on this day are hard workers with much talent. They are very sensitive, which allows them to appreciate or even excel in the arts, but they can be hurt easily.

12–Wind
This is the twelfth day of the 13–day period that begins with 1–Monkey. An interest in the performing arts, music and dance is common to those born on this day. They also make excellent speakers, writers and teachers.

13–Wind
This is the thirteenth day of the week beginning with 1–Dog. Loyalty is an issue for these people, who tend to be joiners of groups. They are curious and discover personal power through identification with others in larger circumstances.

Notables born under Wind

1 – Charles Lindbergh, Roberta Flack, Arthur Penn

2 – Rod Serling, Fred Astaire, Todd Rundgren, Steve Wozniak

3 – John Updike, Judy Collins, Denzel Washington

4 – Clara Barton, John Wilkes Booth, Julian Huxley, Dave Brubeck, Rosie O'Donnell, Michael Jackson

5 – Booker T. Washington, Frank Zappa, Eric Clapton, Pat Buchanan, Will Smith

6 – Max Ernst, L. Frank Baum, Arnold Palmer, Dick Cheney, Lauren Bacall, Billy Crystal

7 – Joseph Stalin, Lou Gehrig, Wolfman Jack, Duane Allman, Sandra Bernhard

8 – Harry Truman, Alec Guinness, Patti Smith, "Weird Al" Yankovic, Ben Affleck

9 – Werner von Braun, Elizabeth Taylor, Cecil B. DeMille, Larry Flynt, Andy Warhol, Charles M. Schulz, Hillary Rodham Clinton, Richard Simmons

10 – Jimmy Durante, Otto Preminger, Richard Burton, Dinah Shore, George Lucas, Tom Selleck, Erica Jong

11 – Oswald Spengler, William Randolph Hearst, Billy Graham, Lawrence Welk, Richard Pryor, Whoopi Goldberg, Kristi Yamaguchi

12 – Al Pacino, Brian Boitano, Dennis Miller, Sarah Jessica Parker, Derek Jeter

13 – Laura Ingles Wilder, Richard Feynman, Spike Jones, Frankie Avalon, Martina Navratilova

House

Indigenous Names:
Maya: Akbal
Aztec: Calli

Direction: West

The Maya name for this day–sign means "darkness" or "night." The glyph may represent a jaguar or other animal associated with the darkness of the underworld. Jaguars, powerful nocturnal creatures of the jungle, were worshiped by many early Mesoamerican cultures. The Aztec symbol was that of a sectioned temple, with a stairway showing. The symbol thus reveals the interior of a temple, which were usually windowless, quite dark and not lit except indirectly. The Zapotec name for this day translates as "night."

The deity the Aztecs linked with this day–sign was Tepeyollotl, a jaguar–like god. He was called the "Heart of the Mountains" and was associated with caves, darkness, and the night. Earthquakes and volcanic activity were attributed to his influence. Tepeyollotl was an important god, one of the nine Lords of the Night, and was seen as an aspect of the Sun as it traveled beneath the earth at night.

In regard to this day–sign Duran reported that those born under it were private and inclined to seclusion. They were liked by their friends, they respected their parents but they didn't like to travel. They were to have peaceful deaths in bed. On the other hand, Sahagun reported that those born on 1–House were prone to vice and might die on the sacrificial block.

From a common sense perspective "darkness" and "night" suggest that House is a sign of privacy, aloneness, inaccessibility, mystery, and the unknown. "Interiors" and a temple suggest themes of containment, insulation, security and protection.

Experiential Observations

Key Meaning: Foundations of personal security

Those born on the day–sign House appear to have the following traits in common. They tend to be powerful, even physically dominating, people. They are organized, patient and show much endurance, and they work hard. They tend to be logical and systematic in their approach to problems but are also traditional and mentally rigid in some ways. Their concern for security in home and family is pronounced yet they treasure privacy and solitude and are inclined to be introspective. They are not the best team players.

One of the most obvious characteristics of people born under this day–sign is their tendency to dominate situations without really trying to. Some are simply physically large, some strikingly beautiful or handsome, while others may dress to enhance their personal power. Power may be exerted in subtle ways, but it is something others must contend with. In many cases, this power is completely legitimate, as when the person is a teacher, leader or healer. What seems to be true though, is that House people do not overtly seek power, they simply seem to feel it is their right.

Patience, endurance and hard work are natural strengths of those born under the day–sign House. They will work for years on a project with no sign of loss of interest or fatigue. Huge or extremely difficult projects appeal to them and they become dedicated to realizing their goals, no matter how long it may take. Science and math, or other systems of knowledge (including occultism, numerology, magic and astrology) often interest them because they aid in being organized about things. Traditions appeal to them and they have a great respect for history. Those born under House take a structural approach to life. The more things are organized, the more they are secure and under control. If it takes ten years or more to achieve this goal of organization, then they will do what is necessary.

Most people born under the day–sign House have powerful intellects and are capable of solving difficult problems. They tend to utilize the more conservative tried and true solutions, however, before they attempt something radical or unproven. The need to be organized and systematic is behind a tendency to be overly logical and possibly intellectually rigid, at least in some areas of life. While they have great strength of intellect, they also tend to be quite stubborn when it comes to changing their mind. This is probably due to the fact that they work so hard on seeing things a certain way, and they have built up so much mental inertia, that a change for them requires a near overhaul of the logical framework they have constructed. But it is true that those of strong, resilient mind, whether they be conservative or radical, eventually impress their views on the rest of the world. People born under House may leave a lasting legacy if they be writers, or thoughtful leaders.

Security, both mental and physical, is a major issue for those born under this day–sign. The physical security that a home, house, building or other structure represents may be a focus in life, or the emotional security that family ties offer may draw intense interest. Whatever the case, the House person usually places a very strong emphasis on these matters when it comes to the time to make crucial life decisions. Some may choose to work with or live near family, others may get involved in real estate. There is a strong territorial instinct in this day–sign and you can be sure that those born under it will know their exact boundaries – emotional and physical. If you are on their side, in their family or on their team, you will be well rewarded. Their personal territorial instinct translates to others and they can be extremely devoted to those they love or choose to protect.

As the symbol of the sectioned temple suggests, this is a day–sign that can be extremely private and a bit reclusive. On the surface this appears to be in contradiction with the fact that these people seem to know everyone, or at least all the people that are worthwhile for them to know. But this is just a manifestation of their deeply embedded political instincts. Ultimately, those born under this sign are not really team players and look forward to times alone, though these may be hard to come by in their busy, hard working lives. Often, they will be found living by themselves, or having a special area where they won't be disturbed. There is a part of them that cannot be accessed by others – and this may be a cause of serious problems in intimate relationships. However, this day–sign has a strong ego and usually doesn't cave in to outside pressures that try to take them away from their private space, whether this be psychological or physical.

The Influence of the 13–Day Periods

1–House
This day begins the 13–day period called 1–House. Those born under it may be extraordinarily territorial and concerned with maintaining their privacy. They have exceptional endurance and may become founders of organizations or businesses or work to preserve a tradition.

2–House
This is the second day of the 13–day period that begins with the day–sign 1–Wind. Those born here are communicators or teachers of traditions. They tend to be somewhat nervous but are mentally very clever. They struggle with personal complexities and responsibilities but are able to articulate the subtleties of life.

3–House
This is the third day of the 13–day period beginning with 1–Crocodile. These people are very domestic and usually have strong entanglements with family members. They are by nature busy and occupied and can also be quite dominating.

4–House
This is the fourth day of the 13–day period that begins with 1–Flower. Struggles in close relationships, or fear of them, are common with those born here. They may also be visionaries and exceptionally artistic or great appreciators of art.

5–House
This is the fifth day of the 13–day period beginning with 1–Rain. Concern for others is a major theme for those born on this day. This day–sign often confers high intelligence and deep insight. They may be attracted to the healing professions, often in unconventional traditions.

6–House
This is the sixth day of the 13–day period beginning with 1–Knife. Those born on this day find that personal sacrifices are necessary in relationships and family matters. This is a real struggle for them and often causes postponements of personal goals and complexity in social life.

7–House
This is the seventh day of the 13–day period beginning with the day 1–Earthquake. High intelligence along with extreme mental rigidity and lack of flexibility characterize these people. They need to learn to relax and flow with, rather than control, the events around them.

8–House
This is the eighth day of the 13–day period beginning with 1–Vulture. Those born on this day tend to be very successful in life, though often at the expense of others. These are politically conscious people who know their status, and those of others, at any given time. They struggle with security issues.

9–House
This is the ninth day of the 13–day period that begins with the day 1–Eagle. It is a day of independent leadership. Those born on it tend to become very successful when they follow their own path. They have critical minds and are capable of handling a lot of detail in their work.

10–House
This is the tenth day of the 13–day period beginning with 1–Ocelot. Those born on this day are competitive, but are also private and secretive. They have good insight and are very knowledgeable of things hidden or of psychologically–oriented subjects.

11–House
This is the eleventh day of the 13–day period beginning with 1–Reed. These are people who uphold principles, who are very faithful and consistent in many aspects of their lives. They often hold important and responsible positions in the world.

12–House
This is the twelfth day of the 13–day period beginning with 1–Grass. Those born on this day are courteous to all around them, though their private lives may be considered a bit strange to others. They can be very touchy, moody and sensitive and require privacy for healing.

13–House
This is the thirteenth day of the 13–day period beginning with the day 1–Monkey. People born on this day have a need for attention and

may excel as teachers or artists. They are very serious, however, and understand life in great depth.

Notables born under House

1– Susan B. Anthony, Walt Whitman, Maria Montessori, Marlene Dietrich, Wayne Gretsky, Buffy Sainte–Marie, Uma Thurman

2 – Joseph Campbell, Agatha Christie, Tommy Lasorda

3 – Isaac Asimov, Don Everly, Dennis Hopper, Garrett Morris, Katie Couric

4 – H.G. Wells, Frank Lloyd Wright, Rod Stewart, Donald Trump, Bill Murray, Levar Burton

5 – Konrad Lorenz, Dale Carnegie, Paul Anka, Jack Nicholson, Peter Gabriel, John Candy

6 – Paul Gauguin, Larry Hagman, Morgan Freeman, Alice Cooper, Billy Preston, Bruce Willis, Drew Barrymore

7 – Jim Thorpe, George Benson, Dan Rather, Joe Jackson, Richard Lewis

8– James Arness, Sid Caesar, Jeremy Steig, David Gilmour, K.D. Lang, Celine Dion

9 – T.E. Lawrence, Charlie Parker, Zsa Zsa Gabor, Dick Clark, Yuri Gagarin

10 – Joe Louis, Jack Kerouac, Eva Peron, James Randi, George Clooney, Jennifer Love Hewitt

11– Abraham Lincoln, Charles Darwin, Richard Wagner, Herbert Hoover, Jack London, Danny Kaye, Jonathan Winters, Tom Brokaw, Billy Joel, Kathie Lee Gifford, Jon Bon Jovi, Rufus Wainwright

12 – Gypsy Rose Lee, Aristotle Onassis, Rex Harrison, Alistair Cooke, Chevy Chase, George Carlin, Jeff Beck

13 – Roy Rodgers, Neil Simon, John Mayall, Michael Caine, Fred Rogers, Diane Keaton, Courtney Love

Lizard

Indigenous Names
Maya: Kan
Aztec: Cuetzpallin

Direction: South

The Maya called this day Kan, which means "ripe maize." The glyph for the day–sign is highly stylized but it suggests corn because it is frequently colored yellow and, in some of the codices, has young maize plants growing from it. The Aztec version of this day was symbolized by a blue lizard, probably referring to the edible common iguana of Mexico. Just what these two symbols have in common is not completely clear, and to further complicate things, the Zapotec word for this day–sign translates as frog, toad or roasted corn.

The Aztecs linked the old god Ueuecoyotl with this day. He was a god of dance and fertility and they consequently associated the sign with sexuality. Perhaps what was suggested by his rulership was the energy that is released through rhythmic dancing, a kind of primal energy that was related to sex and reproduction. The Maya name Kan, meaning "ripe maize", may be linked to this concept in the following way. Ripe corn is the mature product of the plant, its seed, and is not only edible and life sustaining, but it contains within it the potential of reproducing the plant from which it came. Perhaps what is suggested by this day–sign is the idea of sexual maturity and the mystery of procreation. Interestingly, frogs and toads are the sexually mature forms of animals that, considering the egg and tadpole phase, undergo a considerable evolution in their lives.

Duran reported that Lizard was a good and fortunate sign, the sign of those who become prosperous without great toil. He compared those born under it to lizards who wait for their food to come naturally toward them, rather than wasting energy in stalking prey. Sahagun describes 1–Lizard as a sign that produced people with strong bodies and much energy.

The idea of ripe maize, from a common sense perspective, suggest the sustenance of life and the reproductive abilities of the seed. Lizards, on the other hand, move quickly, yet they respond to opportunities. They (and also frogs and toads) tend to sit quietly on high perches and grab their food as it comes by. Lizards also hatch in clutches but soon disperse, each finding its own way in life. Quite possibly, the concepts of sexual maturity and independence, as well as passive–aggressive traits, are what the symbols imply.

Experiential Observations

Key Meaning: Individuality and sexual maturity

People born under the day–sign Lizard are usually interested in leadership, have a liking for performing and tend to be influential. They often have a reputation for being different or deviating from the status quo. They tend to become fanatically interested in one thing or another and hold to very high standards. Self–esteem is important to them. In relationships, they are strongly influenced by sexual matters, which often interferes with their efforts to maintain control and continuity in their lives.

People born under Lizard will often be found doing work that is creative or performance oriented. They have a strong desire to appear before the public in some way. It is a day–sign of leadership, or at least leadership where a personal performance is necessary. What is noteworthy is that these people thoroughly enjoy such situations and they are generally very competent, and sometimes outstanding, at what they do. Their standards are always high and this results in them becoming influential forces in the world around them.

Those born under the day–sign Lizard are usually quite individualistic. They compromise only under extreme pressure, and they harbor resentment if forced to comply. They often attract attention by being different, this action meeting their above–mentioned need to perform for the public in some way. More often, they are simply too involved in their own interests to be seriously concerned about what other people think of them, eventually becoming extremely individualized and highly specialized people. In some cases this leads to great fame, in others, a controversial reputation.

Superficiality is not tolerated by Lizard types. They take their interests very seriously and are often interested in heavy subjects like science, philosophy, religion and metaphysics. They are powerful thinkers, though they tend to lack flexibility of mind. Once they have thought out something, they will not be easily swayed by argument. It is this mental determination that allows them to accomplish as much as they do. Down deep, these people are very serious about their lives.

In relationship matters, sexuality is a major issue for those born under this day-sign. Lizard types are highly sexed individuals who have to do something with all that primal energy roaring within them. For many, this energy is channeled into work, music, ritual or other rhythmic and artistic projects. These people lead creative and productive lives and maintain stable, though usually somewhat unconventional, relationships with those of the opposite sex. However, others are confused about sex or have problems with it and let sexual matters interfere with the rhythm of their lives. In some cases overt sexual aggressiveness leads to unstable and controversial relationship patterns. In other cases sexuality is kept hidden, where it does just as much damage.

The term "lounge-lizard" may have relevance in understanding the nature of this day-sign. Like lizards, which perch on rocks or branches waiting for their meals to come to them, some Lizard types often appear on the surface to be lazy. But in reality, they are passive stalkers who work in full public view. It is their passive-aggressive nature that allows them to move upward socially without directly offending or displacing too many people.

The Influence of the 13-Day Periods

1-Lizard
This is the first day of the 13-day period beginning with Lizard. These people are usually physically strong, youthful and full of creative energies, sometimes to such an extent that they are perceived as unstable. They excel as musicians and can be good leaders if they can harness their strong emotional drives.

2-Lizard
This is the second day of the 13-day period that begins with the day-sign 1-House. Those born on this day are rather serious, responsible and dedicated. They are deep thinkers and usually very knowledgeable or well educated. They are traditional in their thinking but persistent in achieving their goals.

3–Lizard
This is the third day of the 13–day period beginning with 1–Wind. Far less structured than 2–Lizard, these people have complex minds and tend to be easily influenced by their environments. They are not always comfortable when in leadership positions and lean towards formalities for support.

4–Lizard
This is the fourth day of the 13–day period beginning with 1–Crocodile. A strong need for family security affects these people. They are often competitive and sometimes aggressive, often creative in real estate matters, attracted to or dependent on family or communal living conditions, and they make good group leaders.

5–Lizard
This is the fifth day of the 13–day period that begins with 1–Flower. Those born on this day tend to be strong–willed, sometimes outspoken, and this leads to challenges in relationships that make traditional marriages difficult. But they are also artistic and tasteful, some becoming performers and entertainers.

6–Lizard
This is the sixth day of the 13–day period beginning with 1–Rain. These are thoughtful but restless and complicated people, very caring of others, who are not sure exactly where they belong. They can be very romantic and enjoy traveling immensely.

7–Lizard
This is the seventh day of the 13–day period beginning with 1–Knife. Relationship patterns are usually highly unconventional with those born on this day. These are ambitious people who sometimes find it difficult to make decisions and find a balance between self–interest and self–sacrifice.

8–Lizard
This is the eighth day of the 13–day period beginning with 1–Earthquake. Success comes easily to these exceedingly busy people who never give up on their goals. They make excellent leaders and seem to be particularly fond of the arts but also require privacy.

9–Lizard

This is the ninth day of the 13–day period beginning with 1–Vulture. Those born on this day are serious and very politically conscious. They always know where they stand relative to others and will assume leading positions when appropriate. They are pragmatic and creative in political, social and economic matters.

10–Lizard

This is the tenth day of the 13–day period beginning with 1–Eagle. Creative freedom and independence are major issues for these people. They resist working for others and often become involved in self-employment that is creative or artistic and tend to be fussy or technically-minded.

11–Lizard

This is the eleventh day of the 13–day period beginning with 1–Ocelot. Those born on this day express their creativity through ideas. They are teachers, writers or communicators of some kind. They are warrior reformers and carriers of unusual or radical ideas.

12–Lizard

This is the twelfth day of the 13–day period beginning with 1–Reed. Determination and mental inflexibility characterize those born on this day. They are capable of great achievements through hard work and personal sacrifice. They stick to their guns and trust their own thinking, though it may be somewhat opinionated.

13–Lizard

This is the thirteenth day of the 13–day period beginning with 1–Grass. A need for calm, peace and understanding is common with those born on this day. They are internally complex, sometimes capable of self-undoing, but also often very successful in solving complex relationship issues and being good counselors.

Notables born under Lizard

1 – Phyllis Diller, Chuck Berry, Syd Barrett

2 – Grover Cleveland, Harry Houdini, Martin Luther King, Jr., Kirk Douglas, Carlos Santana, Vanessa Williams

3 – Arthur Conan Doyle, Elizabeth II, Grace Slick, Marilyn Manson

4 – Horace Greeley, Tommy Smothers, John Sebastian, Michael Phelps

5 – Isadora Duncan, Johnny Carson, Gene Hackman, Little Richard, Jessica Lang, Charlie Sheen

6 – F. Scott Fitzgerald, John Grisham, Mike Tyson

7 – William James, Otis Redding, Robert Duvall, Alvin Ailey, David Byrne, Martin Short, Sheryl Crow

8 – Buckminster Fuller, Bill Cosby, Gene Siskel, Jim Morrison, John Mellencamp, Joan Sutherland

9 – Henry Kissinger, Man Ray, Leonard Nimoy, George Foreman

10 – Greta Garbo, Red Skelton, Danny Elfman, Drew Carey

11– T.S. Eliot, Gore Vidal, Floyd Patterson, Billy Gibbons

12 – Pierre Auguste Renoir, James Doohan, Monica Lewinsky

13 – Fidel Castro, Spiro Agnew, Dean Martin, Gilbert Gottfried

Serpent

Indigenous Names
Maya: Chicchan
Aztec: Coatl

Direction: East

Both Maya and Aztec names for this day mean snake or serpent. The Maya glyph may be a representation of the head or scales of a snake. In Maya cosmology there were four celestial serpents, one at each of the four primary directions. These serpents, associated with rainfall, may have been linked with this day–sign. Among the Aztecs, this sign was symbolized by the head of a snake, one of the symbols of their goddess Chalchihuitlicue.

Chalchihuitlicue, goddess of ground water, sudden storms, whirlpools and other wild natural forces, was the Aztec deity linked to the day–sign Serpent. There is another side to this goddess though, that she represented the temporary beauty and fragility of nature. What seems to be suggested here is perfection at the edge of chaos.

Friar Duran wrote that those born under this sign were likely to be poor beggars with no home of their own. He compared them to the snake that lives naked, moving from one hole to another. Friar Sahagun reported that those born on the day 1–Serpent could be very successful if they did their penances. This delineation suggests that the good friar did not understand the day–sign very well and so resorted to a simplistic explanation of this personality type – and how it might benefit if Christianity was adopted. In several sources it was noted that the day 1–Serpent was a good day for merchants to begin long trading journeys. Also worth noting is that the Aztecs surrendered to Cortes on this day in 1521. It is one of the very few days recorded in both the Aztec and Christian calendars at the time of the conquest.

The symbol of the snake has been used in many cultures to signify a number of themes including sex, desire and the fusion of the male and female principles. Snakes also evoke fear and awe. Looked at without this bias, however, snakes are animals that have devolved, in a sense, to a more primitive (totally spinal) form. At one time they did have legs.

Snakes are carnivorous, live in the ground, and shed their skin in order to grow. They are mostly solitary animals, though some den together. Possibly those born on this day–sign reflect some of these qualities in their personality such as the ability to simplify, conquer territory and change when needed.

Experiential Observations

Key Meaning: The challenge of transformation

Those born under the day–sign Serpent are often strong–willed and charismatic people who project a mysterious or charismatic facade. They can be quite dramatic and are usually regarded by others as having sex appeal. Serpent types are emotionally–driven and have such strong reactions that they sometimes explode with anger causing great upheavals in relationships. They may not be easy to reason with, but are quite intelligent and usually well–informed. They tend to become fanatical about one subject or another. Death and sex fascinate them and they can become obsessive about these matters.

Serpent types are always noticed, yet often not much is known about them. Few get to know them really well and, as a result, they are often hard to describe accurately. Typically, they project an aura of mystery, or they are just simply charismatic in some way and manage to attract a number of followers. They are often found prancing around one stage or another – or attracting attention by lurking in the shadows. Leadership comes naturally to them in part due to their ability to grab the attention of others. They are quite strong, physically and mentally, and are capable of living under very stressful conditions. On the other hand, failure to nurture themselves adequately is a common weakness of these types.

The emotional power of those born under this sign is remarkable. For some, a needed emotional release comes when they are under the effects of alcohol. Other people will not want to be in their way when they are angry or upset. They are very affected by their feelings and occasionally overcome by them – in a sense, they "wrestle with the serpent." In this regard, they are capable of doing violence to themselves and to others, though not necessarily consciously. One of the effects of this character trait is illustrated by the periodic upheavals in relationships and family matters that they tend to experience. When these powerful emotional energies are harnessed, Serpent types can be quite constructive and creative, pouring out products or performances without any apparent rest. There are some Serpent types who appear calm and steady, but they experience upheaval and crisis in life through others. They are projecting this dynamic character trait, not internalizing it.

Some Serpent types have a noticeable sex–appeal, but others are sexually frustrated. The key factor here has to do with personal centering. It would appear that once their lives are in balance, their deep reservoir of primal emotional energies becomes enticing to others who respond to such things. Serpent types excel in the dramatic arts and have a tendency to keep the act going long after the curtain has come down.

Those born under Serpent are usually of high intelligence and very well–informed. They tend to be interested in subjects that involve strategy and transformation, particularly psychology. Many Serpent types spend years in therapy, or become therapists themselves. It may be that this sign is so in touch with the issues of survival, change and transformation that they try to learn as much about it as they can. One subject that both scares and attracts them is death. Often those born on this day–sign have had strong death experiences, such as the deaths of those close to them. Others may have simply been through some powerful emotional upheavals connected with death in some way. Obsessions with death are common with this sign and it is important that this part of life–experience be acknowledged and well–understood.

The Influence of the 13–Day Periods

1–Serpent
This day is the beginning of the 13–day period called 1–Serpent. It was regarded as a good day, particularly for merchants and for receiving favors. Those born under it are likely to be sexually provocative, powerful and have good leadership abilities, although their lives will be filled with changes and transformations.

2–Serpent
This is the second day of the 13–day period that begins with 1–Lizard. Sexuality is a particularly important issue to those born on this day. They are powerful people who like the limelight and are intent on realizing their goals.

3–Serpent
This is the third day of the 13–day period beginning with 1–House. These are serious and deeply emotional people who enjoy the night and living in seclusion. They are also capable of extreme intellectual feats.

4–Serpent
This is the fourth day of the 13–day period beginning with 1–Wind. Teaching and other forms of communication come easy to those born on this day. They are energetic and idealistic, full of ideas, but often have problems dealing with their feelings. They should probably avoid alcohol or drugs.

5–Serpent
This is the fifth day of the 13–day period beginning with 1–Crocodile. There is much emotional and sexual power in this combination and those born under it are often charismatic achievers. Some may have problems handling power but most turn this emotional energy toward blazing trails and establishing traditions.

6–Serpent
This is the sixth day of the 13–day period beginning with 1–Flower. Those born here are creative artists and romantic lovers that tend to become fanatical about their relationships. They are fond of dance and music, and have a good sense of rhythm.

7–Serpent
This is the seventh day of the 13–day period beginning with 1–Rain. This is also a more intellectual form of the day–sign Serpent. Those born here may be good speakers, communicators, teachers, psychologists, healers or group leaders who have strong concerns for the well–being of others.

8–Serpent
This is the eighth day of the 13–day period beginning with the day 1–Knife. These people have a strong sex drive, tend to run risks, experience strong feelings about relationships and often feel compelled to make personal sacrifices for a relationship. They often have problems making important decisions, but once made are committed to them.

9–Serpent
This is the ninth day of the 13–day period beginning with 1–Earthquake. This is a particularly volatile day and those born on it tend to lead rather extreme lives. They tend to be intellectual, spontaneous, and competitive, but also somewhat dominating.

10–Serpent
This is the tenth day of the 13–day period beginning with 1–Vulture. These people are usually attracted to positions of leadership and responsibility that confer status. They have strong feelings that drive them toward what they perceive as their rightful destiny or place in the world, a place that usually is of high visibility.

11–Serpent
This is the eleventh day of the 13–day period beginning with 1–Eagle. Those born here have a strong sense of freedom and often refuse to compromise their principles. They have powerful minds capable of grasping profound concepts and organizing vast amounts of information.

12–Serpent
This is the twelfth day of the 13–day period beginning with 1–Ocelot. These people are very secretive and discreet, though quite knowledgeable of human nature and how it can be changed. They make good psychologists or healers.

13–Serpent
This is the thirteenth day of the 13–day period beginning with 1–Reed. Leadership and instruction come naturally to those born on this day, though they tend to be somewhat authoritarian. They are strong–willed and enjoy intellectual sparring or debate, though they often lack the flexibility to see other points of view.

Notables born under Serpent

1 – Oscar Wilde, Bob Guccione, Lionel Richie, Pat Benatar

2 – Yasser Arafat, Noam Chomsky

3 – Robert Baden–Powell, Wilford Brimley, Carrie Fisher

4 – Andrew Carnegie, Phil Silvers, Grace Kelly, Angelina Jolie

5 – Upton Sinclair, Mircea Eliade, J. Paul Getty, Andy Griffith, Marilyn Monroe, Gary Larson, Michelle Kwan

6 – John Huston, Ridley Scott, Luciano Pavarotti, Vanna White, Eminem

7 – Mario Andretti, Tom Clancy, David Letterman, Matt Damon

8 – Stephen Wright, Carmen Electra

9 – Ben Hogan, Clint Eastwood, Lily Tomlin

10 – Ulysses S. Grant, Ray Kroc, Gene Autry, Jack Palance, David Janssen, Jose Arguelles

11 – Herman Melville, Willy Mays, Dick Smothers, Stephen Hawking, Matt Groening, Nancy Kerrigan, Venus Williams

12 – W.K. Kellogg, Arthur Miller, Charlie Watts, Jeff Goldblum

13 – Ruth Benedict, Katharine Hepburn, Joan Crawford, George W. Bush, Jodie Foster

Death

Indigenous Names
Maya: Cimi
Aztec: Miquiztli

Direction: North

Both the Maya and Aztec names for this day refer to similar ideas. Cimi is the Maya root word for death and the glyph for the day is that of a skull. The death god itself was symbolized by a skull. The day–sign was also associated with the owl, a bird of the darkness and one regarded as an omen of death. The Aztecs symbolized this day–sign with the figure of a skull and linked it with the Moon god. The idea of white things that shine in the night appears to be suggested by both the skull and the Moon.

The Aztec god Tecciztecatl was linked to this day–sign. He was one of the more ancient gods, a male form of the Moon, and was depicted as an old man who carried a seashell on his back. In the Toltec/Aztec story of creation, Tecciztecatl played an important role in Aztec mythology. When the gods gathered at Teotihuacan to create the present age, they decided that some of them should throw themselves into a fire as a sacrifice so that the world could begin. Tecciztecatl was one of these sacrifices, but it took him several tries before he could go through with it. After four attempts, he finally succeeded in his self–destruction and his sacrifice changed him into the Moon.

Duran described this day–sign as one producing weak, sickly and faint people. They tended to be forgetful, timid and of poor appetite. On the other hand, Sahagun described those born on the day 1–Death as people who became rich and experienced upward mobility. According to him, 2 and 8–Death were unfavorable days on which to be born.

Skulls, death, the Moon and owls suggest the dark, the night, the underworld and the unknown, and also physical death and transformation. This suggests that Death may be a sign of secrecy, privacy and personal crisis.

Experiential Observations

Key Meaning: Sacrifice for community

The day–sign Death seems to be a sign of politics, obligations, sacrifice and faith. Those born under it tend to be involved in civic affairs, or they are at least very interested. They are not confident leaders and will often comfortably accept a secondary role or position. Tradition appeals to them, and since they have a strong faith, so does religion. Often those born under this sign are unsure of where their life is headed, and faith or instinct are all they can go on. They are materialistic, very concerned with domestic security and have an interest in real estate, or perhaps work with homes or houses. Close experiences with death, either their own, or those close to them, affect them in a profound way, shaping their destiny.

Those born on the day–sign Death tend to be very politically conscious. They are concerned with what is happening in the world, or their neighborhood, and they like to feel that they can do something about it. They co–operate well with others and rarely allow their egos to get in the way of progress toward the collective goals they believe in. Those that make politics a career will often align themselves with powerful allies, even those more powerful than themselves.

Death types take all kinds of responsibilities very seriously. They can be depended on to do the best job they can, but because their notions about responsibilities are often extreme, one way or the other, they are often caught off–guard when crises occur. Obligations to others, and a sense of duty also tend to dominate these people. In many cases, their lives become so bound up with the lives of others that it may be difficult to say where self–interest begins and obligation ends. Because Death types are usually polite and hesitant to speak their true feelings, they tend to give in to others more often than may be necessary or even reasonable.

There is a tendency for Death types to form partnerships with rather strong individuals. The actual power dynamics of the relationship may not be clear on the surface, but underneath there is usually a good deal of psychological manipulation by one or the other; probably both. In many cases, the person born under the day–sign Death plays a passive, victim–

like role and allows the partner to appear to be the leader. However, the victim, or martyr, holds on to a good deal of the power and can influence events from behind the scenes, or indirectly.

Life, its meaning and mysteries, fascinates these types. For some, the unknown is overwhelming and they learn early on in life that it is only faith that can carry them well beyond the limits of their understanding. In many respects, they live deeply subjective lives, searching for emotionally satisfying answers to life's great questions. In some cases they simply do not want to know, and avoid learning too much. This may be in part due to their associations with powerful others whose confident decisions and choices affect them profoundly. Religion, spirituality and metaphysics appeal to them, especially traditional religions and philosophies. Here they find powerful forces that can guide them through life and give it meaning. Often life is experienced as a personal sacrifice of some sort by those born on this day, and religion or spirituality gives this sacrifice meaning. Religion also plays into their sense of obligation toward others and the community.

Intellectually, Death types are usually conservative, or at least they lean in that direction. Once they become attached to a set of ideas and beliefs, usually traditional or structural, they stay with them for life, which gives them a certain kind of wisdom. They are not enthusiastic about new ideas, though they may politely listen to whoever challenges what they believe to be the truth. There is also a noticeably materialistic streak to those born under this day–sign. They want to make money and they know what to do with it once they get it.

People born under this day–sign are very sensitive to causes. These may be those of the poor and needy, the oppressed, and the sick, and also those of the environment and quality of life. At the bottom of this trait are strong instincts and a strong sense of responsibility and duty. Although they may be sympathetic to such things, real "down and dirty" activism is not usually their style. They often prefer to support a cause, but let others handle the action.

Death is a day–sign that seems to be quite security conscious. Many of those born on this day invest their money carefully, often in real estate, and use it wisely. This may be due in part to experiences with financial limitations or actual poverty early in life, or possibly a strict upbringing. They are not comfortable taking risks, except maybe on political issues, and prefer a life of domestic security to that of adventure. While they aspire to be wealthy, they don't pretend to be, and if they have wealth, you'd never know it. This day–sign prefers to cut a low profile and can be very attached to home and family.

The actual experience of death, personal, in the family or with a close friend, often leaves a strong mark on these people and they never forget it. Talking about such an experience is difficult for them and they prefer to avoid the subject. Because of this tendency to keep strong emotional experiences to themselves, Death types are often regarded by others as somewhat distant and even remote. They are hard to know well, and to complicate things further, they tend to manifest two distinctly different personalities depending on the environment they are in, or on how much they've had to drink. Often the real problem here is one of inhibitions. This is a repressive sign that needs to lighten up now and then for the sake of their own mental health. But some born on this day have both a public and a private personality and this is sometimes reflected in having two or more residences.

The Influence of the 13–Day Periods

1–Death
This is the first day of the 13–day period beginning with the day 1–Death. Those born on this day tend to be very strong and successful people who rise in life and achieve great honors. They are moderately inclined toward leadership roles, but prefer to work cooperatively with others who are often very powerful.

2–Death
This is the second day of the 13–day period that begins with 1–Serpent. These people are extremely emotional, even volatile, though usually this part of them is not seen. They are private people, sometimes very secretive, who can also be intensely religious.

3–Death
This is the third day of the 13–day period that begins with 1–Lizard. Those born on this day can be very creative, but also very opportunistic. They have high standards, like being in the spotlight, and are usually quite influential, though often relying strongly on others for inspiration.

4–Death
This is the fourth day of the 13–day period beginning with 1–House. This combination produces people who are somewhat compulsive and often emotionally repressed, yet are very productive in practical matters. They prefer to keep much to themselves and are not particularly communicative except when it comes to serious topics.

5–Death
This is the fifth day of the 13–day period beginning with 1–Wind. Those born on this day are full of ideas but often nervous and anxious, this being reflected in the difficulties they have in making firm decisions. They sometimes fear the weight of responsibilities and obligations.

6–Death
This is the sixth day of the 13–day period that begins with 1–Crocodile. Real estate and other matters connected with housing and domesticity interest those born here. They have some leadership qualities and are sensitive to and concerned about the physical and material environment they live in.

7–Death
This is the seventh day of the 13–day period beginning with 1–Flower. Dedication to others, and personal sacrifice to the needs of others, is characteristic of those born on this day. These are hard–working and very idealistic people who prefer to work closely with others.

8–Death
This is the eighth day of the 13–day period that begins with 1–Rain. Those born here are creative people, often concerned with the health and well–being of others who will make personal sacrifices for such things. They can be somewhat fearful and anxious, however, and tend to hold on to what they have.

9–Death
This is the ninth day of the 13–day period beginning with 1–Knife. Consideration for the lives of others is prominent with those born on this day, and they will be quick to make concessions or sacrifices even if this involves some risk. There is a marked practical streak in these people who often display talent for design or construction.

10–Death
This is the tenth day of the 13–day period beginning with 1–Earthquake. Those born here are quite intellectual, but they may also be fearful and anxious, feeling that their security may be threatened at any moment and so they become defensive and often take risks. They may also tend to become over–involved in social issues and political matters.

11–Death
This is the eleventh day of the 13–day period beginning with 1–Vulture. This is a materialistic combination that is sometimes quite ambitious, but commitments to professional growth will cause stress in personal matters. These are skeptical people who will see the negative in things before the positive, a trait they work hard to overcome.

12–Death
This is the twelfth day of the 13–day period that begins with 1–Eagle. Freedom is attractive to those born on this day, but this conflicts with their sense of responsibility and duty. They tend to achieve this desired freedom later in life. They are often good with details and getting things organized.

13–Death
This is the thirteenth day of the 13–day period beginning with 1–Ocelot. Those born on this day are often distant and remote people who when approached are actually quite knowledgeable and willing to share their wisdom. They are often spiritual or religious, though this is a private matter with them.

Notables born under Death

1 – George H. W. Bush, Colin Powell, Jane Fonda

2 – Anthony Quinn, Madeleine Albright, Evel Knievel, Doug Henning, Joan Jett

3 – Kurt Waldheim, Barry Goldwater, Paul McCartney, Roger Ebert

4 – William Burroughs, Carol Burnett, Brigitte Bardot, Don Henley, Tom Cruise

5 – Charlie Chaplin, John Madden

6 – Eric Heiden, Paul Shaffer
7 – John Glenn, Melissa Etheridge
8 – Ted Danson, Bill Gates, Robin Williams
9 – Paul Robeson, Freddy Mercury, Sid Vicious
10 – L. Ron Hubbard, Ozzy Osborne
11– Paul Volcker, Eriq La Salle
12 – Ingmar Bergman, Bonnie Raitt
13 – Thomas Merton, Jose Feliciano, Peter Jennings

Deer

Indigenous Names
Maya: Manik
Aztec: Mazatl

Direction: West

The Maya glyph for this day, which is probably a grasping hand, does not seem to refer to anything specific. It is possible, according to some archaeologists, that there is a link with this day–sign and the Maya god of hunting. The Aztecs symbolized this day by the head of a deer and regarded it as a sign of timidity. It seems probable that both Aztec and Maya versions of this day had a connection with hunting and game.

For the Aztecs, the ruling deity of the day–sign Deer was Tlaloc. He was a major god and shared top honors with the war–god Huitzilopotchli on the major pyramid in the Aztec capital city. Tlaloc was the old agricultural god, the god of rains and of the Earth. He was said to live on top of a mountain in a place called Tlalocan, a paradise of water and life. Tlaloc corresponded to the Mayan god Chac, also a god of rain.

Duran wrote that those born on this day were woodsmen, fond of the outdoors and liked hunting. They had a wanderlust and often left their homeland to live in foreign and distant lands. It was easy for them to leave their parents and their homes. Sahagun noted that these people were extremely timid and shy.

From the common sense perspective, Deer are herd animals that have no fixed residence and roam about, within certain limits. The males tend to be independent and strive to dominate a herd of females. While the young learn survival skills from their mothers, the males fight with one another for sexual rights.

Experiential Observations

Key Meaning: Fellowship and family vs.
freedom and independence

The characteristics of those born under the day–sign Deer are not exactly as the ancient symbols would seem to suggest. While they are generally peaceful people, they can also be very bold in speaking up for what they feel to be right. While they can be inspiring and generous towards others, and even dominating at times, they do not have particularly strong desires for leadership. They do have strong feelings about family and tradition and these matters often control their lives. This may be due to their hard to suppress need for companionship. Their aesthetic sense is usually highly developed and they often dabble in one or other of the arts. Those born on this day–sign are very sensual and sexually inclined, yet are also quite intuitive and very sensitive to the concerns of other beings.

The day–sign Deer seems to imprint on those born under it a tendency to unquestionably follow their own instincts and feelings. This usually translates into doing what they want to do, whenever they want to. They have no hesitation about speaking their mind on controversial subjects and are usually quite knowledgeable about such matters. Mentally, they combine a powerful intuition with good reasoning abilities. They can be strong–minded and, as one would expect, are not easily convinced or swayed from their intellectual positions. To others, they can appear dominating, and they often are, indirectly. But they don't really want to dominate or lead, they merely know what they know well and as a result can be quite inflexible at times.

Deer is a sign of participation in the community. Those born under this day–sign are often deeply involved with family, community and tradition, and in some cases, socio–political traditions. Family or community may be such a strong issue that crucial life decisions are often based completely on these concerns. The need for the security of close relationships with others is at the base of this tendency. Partnership appeals to them, and yet they have a difficult time of it because their need for freedom creates conflicts. What usually happens is that Deer people experiment until they find a way to have both companionship and personal space, and this often means unconventional and even experimental relationships. The more conservative Deer types will struggle with this conflict and some tolerate turbulent or frustrating relationships while others escape from stable relationships only to seek another. The more radical Deer–types make their own rules when it comes to partnering. It seems that those born under this day–sign are happiest when they feel free enough to be themselves, no matter how unconventional this is.

Deer is a sensual sign. On one level, food and eating are important to them. The aesthetic sensibilities are usually strong with these people and not a few of them are artists, musicians, poets or writers. Most of the time their taste in these matters is quite sophisticated. They have a strong sense of rhythm and enjoy dancing and other sensual body movements, including sex. In fact, their strong sex drive may be part of the problem they have in maintaining stable relationships. In this area, experimentation seems to be the rule, while in other aspects of relationships they tend to be more traditional. This tendency frequently pushes them into wrestling with moral and ethical considerations.

Those born on this day–sign are really very complex people with both traditional and unconventional qualities. They are concerned with family and social integrity, yet they will take risks in intimate matters that have the potential to destabilize their social life. They tend to be generous people, quick to offer food, drink or help when appropriate. They will display strong feelings for animals and plants, but will not hesitate to blast someone who they feel is stepping into their territory. They belong to a group or family, but they love to "go stag." In the final analysis, however, these are trustworthy people who, for all their weirdness, are usually pillars of society.

The Influence of the 13–Day Periods

1–Deer
This is the first day of the 13–day period beginning with the day 1–Deer. Those born on this day are quietly adventurous though powerful people with strong sex drives. They subtly dominate others yet maintain a stable home life.

2–Deer
This is the second day of the 13–day period beginning with 1–Death. Those born on this day often find themselves in predicaments where they must sacrifice something in order to move forward. They are very peaceful people who are motivated by ideals, have a strong sense of group consciousness and have plenty of family obligations.

3–Deer
This is the third day of the 13–day period beginning with 1–Serpent. There is explosive potential in those born on this day that could lead

them to high positions of power and fame. Their feelings are so strong about some things that only personal, hands–on experiences can change their minds. They are often somewhat reckless and sexuality is also an important issue for these people.

4–Deer
This is the fourth day of the 13–day period beginning with 1–Lizard. These people are usually genuinely strange, often inventors or simply harmless eccentrics who march to their own beat. They are well ahead of their time in many matters and this makes it difficult for them to have normal relationships with others.

5–Deer
This is the fifth day of the 13–day period that begins with 1–House. Those born on this day are serious about life, can be quite intellectual, and tend to be caught up in family matters. Their sincerity is noteworthy. They live out their fantasies about freedom more through their imagination than in reality.

6–Deer
This is the sixth day of the 13–day period beginning with 1–Wind. Those born here are extremely mentally active, great with conversation, articulate but sometimes too clever for their own good. They struggle with the need for freedom versus the responsibilities of family and community.

7–Deer
This is the seventh day of the 13–day period beginning with 1–Crocodile. This combination produces energetic, strong, charismatic, emotionally intense people who are original and creative. They are little concerned with what others think about them and blaze their own trails.

8–Deer
This is the eighth day of the 13–day period beginning with 1–Flower. Close relationships are a major concern for those born on this day. They are deeply emotional and have a hard time being alone, so they strive to join with others quickly and easily.

9–Deer
This is the ninth day of the 13–day period beginning with 1–Rain. Those born on this day can be very intellectual and quite possibly artistic as

well. They have a deep concern for the welfare, and even the healing, of their community or family often setting high standards.

10–Deer
This is the tenth day of the 13–day period beginning with 1–Knife. Relationship matters can become extremely complicated for those born on this day. Decision–making is something that weighs heavily on them. Practical solutions to problems often involve some personal sacrifice.

11–Deer
This is the eleventh day of the 13–day period beginning with 1–Earthquake. Those born on this day can be quirky or highly original. They are also very powerful and influential, though they are regarded by others as having questionable ideas.

12–Deer
This is the twelfth day of the 13–day period beginning with 1–Vulture. Dominating or maintaining a superior position toward others comes naturally to those born on this day. As leaders they are popular though often somewhat off–beat. They are often obsessed with their social position.

13–Deer
This is the thirteenth day of the 13–day period beginning with 1–Eagle. A strong need for freedom and also for clarity drives those born on this day. Relationships are generally unstable factors in their lives, though they tend to thrive in those that are open or unconventional.

Notables born under Deer

1 – Immanuel Kant, Leon Spinks, Steve Forbert

2 – Joseph Haydn, John Kenneth Galbraith, Tiny Tim, Stephen Gaskin, Sonny Bono, Merle Haggard, Elton John, Caroline Kennedy, Colin Farrell

3 – Carlos Castaneda, John McCain, Meryl Streep

4 – Alan Leo, Malcolm X, Rona Barret, Captain Beefheart, Prince Charles

5 – Ian Fleming, Mother Teresa, Jackie Robinson, John Denver, Elizabeth Stanton

6 – James Michener, Jackson Pollock, Alice Walker, Jimmy Fallon

7 – Kurt Vonnegut Jr., B.B. King, Allen Ginsberg, Johnny Depp

8 – James Coburn, Jack Nicklaus, Kenny G.

9 – Raymond Burr, Martha Stewart

10 – Lewis Carroll, Amelia Earhart, Malcolm Forbes, Ellen DeGeneres

11 – Franz Boas, Ozzie Nelson, Julia Child, Burt Reynolds, Jamie Lee Curtis

12 – Steve Allen, Rosemary Clooney, 14th Dalai Lama, Alicia Keys

13 – William McKinley, Stephen King

Rabbit

Indigenous Names
Maya: Lamat
Aztec: Tochtli

Direction: South

The Maya name for this day, Lamat, was a name for the planet Venus, and its glyph was also that planet's glyph. Venus, next to the Sun, was the most carefully watched celestial object of the Maya astronomers. It was associated with drunkenness because of its association with Quetzalcoatl/Kukulkan, the man–god who sinned while intoxicated. The Aztecs symbolized this day by the head of a rabbit. The connection between the two is not obvious, though they do have the idea of drunkenness in common.

The Aztec ruling deity for this day–sign was Mayauel, an earth/fertility goddess and also the goddess of the intoxicating beverage pulque. Pulque was a liquor made from the agave plant, though this plant was used for many other things as well. Here, in the idea of intoxication, could be the connection with Venus.

Most of the Aztec sources regarded this as a tricky day, one on which anything could happen. Duran doesn't say much about the sign except that those born under it fell into the same category of destiny as Deer. Friar Sahagun, probably fascinated by vice, carried on for several pages about how those born on the day 2–Deer were extremely prone to intoxication. From the common sense perspective, rabbits are alert, quick and move rapidly when startled, often in erratic patterns. They reproduce rapidly and eat vegetation. There are also traditions that link humor with rabbits. The planet Venus doesn't tell us much except that perhaps there are two sides to those born on this day. The Morning Star phase of Venus was considered powerful and even dangerous, while the Evening Star phase was linked to a monstrous deity.

Experiential Observations

Key Meaning: Opposition, risk and daring

The day-sign Rabbit appears to be a sign of intense energy that, at times, lacks a focus. Those born under it are nervous and always busy at something. Debating and arguing appeals to them. They have a great need for physical activity and are noted for their flexibility or rhythm. They can be extremely intelligent, but they are also somewhat paranoid and even a little crazy. They like to perform, play games, and take risks. They appreciate music and have a good sense of humor, but they also have a self-destructive side to them.

Those born on the day-sign Rabbit have minds that never quit. They need constant stimulation and are fond of talking, debating, reading, writing or other forms of communication. This nervous energy also translates into bodily tension and the need for physical outlets as well. They can be quite competitive and enjoy sparring with others. Some find the military much to their liking. Many will purposely adopt an opposing or unpopular point of view just to keep some tension in the atmosphere. Some like to exercise, others dance, but all need to keep moving about. These are people who can do enormous amounts of work in very little time, and not seem to be tired from it.

Rabbit types have a strong need for attention. Many born on this day are performers or entertainers. They are quite ego-centric, but they are not as confident of their abilities as one would think. Because of this, they tend to avoid taking on large responsibilities, or if they do, handle them best from behind the scenes. Ultimately, they are not naturally good at sustaining a self-managed business project and would often rather serve than lead, or at least share the limelight.

The minds of those born on this day are complex. They can be of high intelligence but they can also be quite paranoid about certain things. Their capacity for subtlety of mind causes them to be interested in details, mysteries, intelligence gathering work, psychology and the occult. They tend to be suspicious of every new person they meet, though once they know you they can be very loyal friends. Such complex minds appreciate a good joke, perhaps as an escape or just an appreciation of subtlety. These are people who love games, languages, codes, and taking risks. Some become addicted to gambling. Ultimately, the mental complexity of Rabbit types is so intense that some, including themselves, might label them crazy.

There is a self–destructive side to the day–sign Rabbit that may be what the Maya and Aztecs were alluding to. Some born under this sign become addicted to drugs or alcohol, perhaps as a way of stimulating their already complex minds. Once this becomes a habit, and Rabbit types can be obsessive–compulsive, a cycle of self–destruction sets in. It is probably true that these people should avoid substances that only serve to stimulate their sensitive minds. Other kinds of addictions are also possible with this type. Those born on this day who have good self–control will often be found working around people in weakened conditions, as in hospitals or in a psychiatric capacity.

The Influence of the 13–Day Periods

1–Rabbit
This is the first day of the 13–day period beginning with the day 1–Rabbit. Those born on this day display the characteristics of the day–sign clearly. They are energetic and capable of doing many things at once. They are more inclined to take on leadership roles than some of the later days of the period.

2–Rabbit
This is the second day of the 13–day period beginning with 1–Deer. This day was regarded in ancient times as a day of drunkenness and it's possible that those born here are very sensitive and should avoid alcohol or drugs, though it is not certain. In general though, those born on this day tend to be unique individuals with brilliant, though somewhat unstable, minds.

3–Rabbit
This is the third day of the 13–day period beginning with 1–Death. Those born here tend to be politically conscious and quite active in community affairs. They tend to be easily influenced by others, however, and may also develop addictions.

4–Rabbit
This is the fourth day of the 13–day period beginning with 1–Serpent. A very high powered combination, those born here may be literally

exploding with nervous and sexual energy and need acceptable outlets. Their drive to be creative is strong and interactions with them are always stimulating. Others may perceive them as both outrageous and brilliant.

5–Rabbit
This is the fifth day of the 13–day period beginning with 1–Lizard. Those born on this day are highly independent and very detail oriented. They are not particularly inclined towards leadership, though their competency and knowledge often forces them into it. They like the limelight and sometimes push the limits of what they can handle.

6–Rabbit
This is the sixth day of the 13–day period beginning with 1–House. This is a more stable combination, in terms of life style, and those born here are more focused and are able to stay with one thing for long periods of time. However, they tend to have very complex and weird minds which makes them hard to understand.

7–Rabbit
This is the seventh day of the 13–day period beginning with 1–Wind. Those born on this day tend to be highly nervous people, always busy and very communicative. They tend to be idealistic, and can be quite outspoken at times, though do well as communicators.

8–Rabbit
This is the eighth day of the 13–day period beginning with 1–Crocodile. Those born on this day can be very competitive and intellectually dominating. They make good leaders and administrators and are fond of traditions, which they will nurture. Sometimes they are founders of traditions.

9–Rabbit
This is the ninth day of the 13–day period beginning with 1–Flower. These people can be very sociable and are often artistic. Because they think so idealistically, they tend to have problems with relationships or with "fitting in" in general. Consequently, they often become depressed and find it difficult to change or move forward.

10–Rabbit
This is the tenth day of the 13–day period beginning with 1–Rain. This is a very mental combination and those born here tend to be highly–

strung and nervous. They do well in occupations such as teaching or consulting and like to think of themselves as healers.

11–Rabbit
This is the eleventh day of 13–day period beginning with 1–Knife. Those born on this day often give up a good deal in life in order to achieve harmony which seems to be an intangible goal. They are good with tools and with eye–hand coordination but sometimes have questionable judgment.

12–Rabbit
This is the twelfth day of the 13–day period beginning with 1–Earthquake. Those born on this day often lead lives of constant change requiring careful scheduling. They will take risks and are often first in their field. They can be brilliant and original in the arts and sciences, and they enjoy a good debate.

13–Rabbit
This is the last day of the 13–day period beginning with 1–Vulture. A strong ego and a tendency to dominate others with ideas is often found in those born on this day. These are high–caliber competitive people who love to win in games of one–up–manship.

Notables born under Rabbit

1 – Beatrix Potter, Roger Daltrey, Dale Earnhardt Jr., Tobey Maguire

2 – Evangeline Adams, Elvis Presley, Leonard Bernstein, Sugar Ray Leonard

3 – Tony Bennett, Walter Mondale, Joe Cocker, Whitney Houston

4 – Jorge Luis Borges, Dick Button, Gary Busey, Bette Midler

5 – Brian Wilson, Billy Jean King, Liam Neeson

6 – Jerry Lewis, Sally Field, Wynton Marsalis, Tara Lipinski

7 – Georgia O'Keefe, Nelson Rockefeller, Ed Asner, Carl Sagan

8 – Babe Ruth, Jane Goodall, Robbie Robertson, Cyndi Lauper

9 – John Hurt, Jimi Hendrix, Rob Reiner, Bjorn Borg, Scott Weiland

10 – Robert E. Lee, Norman Mailer, G. Gordon Liddy, Cybill Shepherd
11 – Lizzy Borden, Joseph P. Kennedy, Paul Ford
12 – Bo Diddley, Ike Turner, Roger Maris, James Cameron
13 – George Orwell, David Carradine, Paul Kantner

Water

Indigenous Names
Maya: Muluc
Aztec: Atl

Direction: East

The Maya glyph for this day appears to be that of a fish head, most probably a reference to water. It is possible that the glyph may also suggest jade, another symbol for water. The Aztec symbol for this day was a sectioned view of a valley or canal filled with water. This image was said to symbolize the human passage through life.

The Aztec deity linked to this day–sign was Xiuhtecuhtli, the god of central fire, time and life. He is the central deity of the nine Lords of the Night portrayed on the famous cosmogram from the Codex Fejervary–Mayer. In this diagram, he is seen as the source of life for the entire manifestation around him, and he is also being nourished by the blood of the manifestation. It appears that the concepts of centering, life–giving and self–feeding might be connected with this day–sign.

Duran reported that this sign was evil. Those born under it suffered throughout the course of their short lives. They were sick, frustrated and angry people. Sahagun reported that those born on 1–Water would be both fortunate and unfortunate in life. However, 3–Water was decidedly favorable, though subject to sudden loses, and 4–Water and 5–Water were unfortunate and perverted. These reports are typical of the friars who were hostile to the indigenous astrology.

It makes sense to consider the obvious. Water is necessary for life – it brings plants to life. It is plastic and changeable and it conforms to the container it is placed in, yet it can cause damage if not contained. Perhaps this is relevant information for those born under this day–sign.

Experiential Observations

Key Meaning: The power of the emotions

The day–sign Water appears to be a sign of strong feelings and emotions. Those born under it have powerful imaginations and often live in a fantasy world. The strange and bizarre fascinate them. Many are psychic. Many create illusions as successful performers or artists, while others associate themselves with show business or romantic life–styles. There seems to be a concern with public recognition of some sort or another. Water types can be dominating and their strong feelings often arouse sexual or violent energies in them or around them. They are risk–takers who act independently. One of their greatest challenges is in regard to taking responsibility for their own lives. If they can do this, there are no limits to their reach.

Water types have strong emotions and feelings that are easily aroused. In some cases these are so deep and so intense that violent or sexual feelings take over the personality. These primitive, very territorial drives then operate openly with little conscious resistance. On a less dramatic level, this condition translates negatively into compulsive and addictive behaviors, including abuse of power, sexual obsessions, drinking, and use of drugs. On the positive level these emotional drives lead Water types into deep commitments and help them persist in achieving goals. Which way the emotions lead probably has much to do with early childhood experiences.

Many of those born under this day–sign display psychic abilities, or they have an interest in psychic phenomena. Undoubtedly this is something that stems from having unusually strong feelings and reactions to things. In some cases a talent for psychism is noticeable and a few actually make a career of it. For most, this conscious linkage with the subconscious depths manifests as creative artistic ability or vision. These people are artists who produce sounds and colors from their souls, not superficial illustrators or imitators. Leaders born under Water have a vision that they attempt to realize during the course of their lives. Whether psychic, artist or visionary, Water types are driven by forces that most of us have no idea even exist.

Those born on this day also have a natural show–business flair that is both a blessing and a curse. If circumstances allow them to exercise this legitimately, as performers or artists, then they are generally very successful. If circumstances work against them, they tend to drift into unrealistic and even dangerous life–styles. They seem to be concerned with recognition, which may be due to a deep–seated inferiority complex. Their "performances" are usually quite powerful and arouse strong feelings in others. Many find them charismatic and sexual.

There is an uncompromising quality to this sign that often leads to great success in career matters. Nothing is done halfway, it is everything or nothing – and this is what it takes to be at the top of a profession. Those born under this day–sign have strong, independent minds and are capable, and very willing, to solve their problems by themselves. They tend to have a problem with taking responsibilities though, possibly because they anticipate getting in over their heads, which they do all the time anyway. This problem is one that is probably affected by early childhood experiences. In particular, it is usually their mother that makes the deepest imprints. When they have good role models, leadership and responsibility are not problems. Once Water types get control over their strong feelings, they make excellent leaders and handle responsibilities well. This is a day–sign that, by nature, takes responsibilities very seriously, hence the problem with this issue.

Ultimately, Water types do get recognition for their accomplishments, whether these be positive or destructive. These people are not moderate, they tend to go to extremes. They are constantly attempting to control, or at least monitor, a host of nearly uncontrollable urges. Their intense behaviors and bizarre interests take them well beyond the worlds of ordinary people and there they find opportunities to exercise their personal power. By most people's standards, they take plenty of risks along the way.

The Influence of the 13–Day Periods

1–Water
This is the first day of the 13–day period beginning with the day 1–Water. Those born on this day have and project great personal power and are usually very well known. Their artistic or creative abilities are considerable.

2–Water
This is the second day of the 13–day period beginning with 1–Rabbit. These people are clever and forceful and make controversial leaders. Some have serious emotional weaknesses that they must overcome before they achieve the success they seek in life.

3–Water
This is the third day of the 13–day period beginning with 1–Deer. Those born here are roamers and strong individualists, often with a vision. They are motivated by strong emotions which they may later rationalize. Their interests lean toward the rhythmic, spiritual or psychic.

4–Water
This is the fourth day of the 13–day period beginning with 1–Death. A more practical and materialistic bent is found in those born on this day. These people have an emotional depth that is rarely seen. Many were, or are, dominated by their mothers.

5–Water
This is the fifth day of the 13–day period beginning with 1–Serpent. Those born on this day are creative and artistic, but tend to experience great emotional disruptions in their lives from time to time. They project sexual and emotional power and make good leaders.

6–Water
This is the sixth day of the 13–day period beginning with 1–Lizard. These are very serious and committed people who seek the limelight or leadership positions. They tend to dominate others without much effort and attract loyal followers.

7–Water
This is the seventh day of the 13–day period beginning with 1–House. Repression of feelings and emotions can cause many problems for those born on this day. These people need a stable home life and good relationships with their parents.

8–Water
This is the eighth day of the 13–day period beginning with 1–Wind. Those born here may be driven to learn as much as they can about what ever they may be interested in. They can be nomadic, roaming from

place to place or interest to interest, or they focus on communication in which they naturally excel.

9–Water
This is the ninth day of the 13–day period beginning with 1–Crocodile. This is a very powerful combination and those born on this day usually become recognized as leaders. Since their feelings are so strong, and they are not particularly rational, their actions are often controversial.

10–Water
This is the tenth day of 13–day period week beginning with 1–Flower. A weakness, and yet a strength, for love and romance affects those born on this day. They tend to be visionary and artistic or champions of a cause.

11–Water
This is the eleventh day of the 13–day period beginning with 1–Rain. Nurturing and caring for others is a major theme in the lives of those born on this day. They tend to assume parental roles and often have strong mothers, both themes sometimes encouraging a dominating attitude toward the people around them.

12–Water
This is the twelfth day of the 13–day period beginning with 1–Knife. Personal sacrifices may be necessary for those born on this day to have successful relationships. Their conflicts between self–interest and cooperation are severe at times.

13–Water
This is the last day of the 13–day period beginning with 1–Earthquake. Those born on this day are particularly emotional people who struggle with issues of self–control. They are risk–takers, tend to be nomadic and often stray in relationships.

Notables born under Water

1 – Joseph Conrad, Carly Simon, Liza Minnelli, Brooke Shields

2 – George C. Scott, Lorne Michaels, Mickey Rourke, John Travolta

3 – George Washington, Margaret Mitchell, Shirley MacLaine, Mick Jagger

4 – Jefferson Davis, Edvard Munch, Rock Hudson, Madonna

5 – Benjamin Disraeli, Bill Clinton, Bobby McFerrin

6 – Al Capone, Walter Cronkite, Norman Schwarzkopf

7 – Wolfgang Amadeus Mozart, Mel Blanc, Rupert Murdoch, Dick Cavett

8 – Thelonius Monk, Joan Rivers, Mary Tyler Moore, Paul Reubens, Oprah Winfrey

9 – George Eastman, Salvador Dali, Indira Gandhi, Sidney Poitier, Sammy Hagar

10 – Kenny Rogers, John Lennon, Julia Roberts

11 – Simon Bolivar, Muddy Waters, Saddam Hussein, Neil Young

12 – Woodrow Wilson, Lon Chaney Jr., Herbie Hancock, Diane Sawyer, Daryl Hannah

13 – Thor Heyerdahl, Christina Aguilera

Dog

Indigenous Names
Maya: Oc
Aztec: Itzcuintli

Direction: North

Both Maya and Aztec glyphs depict this day–sign with the head of a dog. Maya sources often show a dog holding a torch, possibly alluding to the myth in which a dog brings fire to humans. The Aztecs believed that the dog was the companion of the human soul after death in the underworld. A crucial point in entering the afterlife was the crossing of a river, and it was a dog that did the guiding.

The Aztecs linked this day with the god Mictlantecuhtli, the god of souls in the underworld and ruler of Mictlan, the land of the dead. The connections between dogs, this day–sign and the underworld are obvious. What seems to be suggested though is the idea of loyalty.

Duran described this day–sign in positive terms. It was considered fortunate and happy, and those born under it were courageous, generous, successful and likely to have many children. They were good friends and always willing to help out those who asked for favors. Sahagun reported that those born on the day 1–Dog would become rich.

Since both the Maya and Aztec symbol was that of a dog, it is logical that people born on this day might have similar personality characteristics to that animal. For example, dogs are social animals that live in packs. Together they establish a social order, the alpha male and female being the leaders. Dogs are carnivorous, somewhat nomadic, yet also very territorial. Within the pack, and as pets, they are very loyal.

Experiential Observations

Key Meaning: Loyalty and participation

As logic and the ancient sources suggest, the day–sign Dog has much to do with loyalty. Those born under it have a strong team or group instinct and they will stick by their allies in times of trouble. They enjoy being the leader, but will wait until it is their turn for the position. Transportation seems to hold a special appeal, though they are not fanatical travelers. Creativity, political and artistic, seems to be a common feature of those born here. The father, often the most important parent, is a source of guidance or conflict. Emotional maturity is also an issue for those born on this day.

Those born under the day–sign Dog are usually good team players. Loyalty is definitely one of their best traits. They instinctively know who has what rank and this understanding allows them to be patient and wait their turn for leadership. Their experience as followers and good team members is excellent preparation for the leadership positions they may seek. Many born under this day–sign come to run their own business and they make good employers. They know how to inspire loyalty in others because they have such a good understanding of it themselves.

One characteristic of those born under Dog is a liking for short–distance travel. Owning a car, boat or even plane is an important issue for them. They like patrolling their "territory" but are not so keenly interested in really distant places. They have a strong neighborhood interest and will usually know everyone on their block or in their town.

Dog types are frequently very creative. The arts, particularly music and drawing or painting seem to appeal to them. While they are, in most cases, not particularly daring or experimental in these areas, they have a good sense of harmony and rhythm and often achieve a respectable level of popularity. They approach their art–form as a craft to be learned and mastered and are technique conscious. Other Dog types reveal their creativity in the social and political arenas. Some aspire to public positions while others attempt to provide social leadership through teaching, education or social service work. Politics is important to them and they are usually well–informed regarding current events.

For those born under the day–sign Dog the father is usually the most influential parent. In some cases the father provides a legacy, financial or career–wise. This creates a situation where the son or daughter has no choice but to follow the pattern set by the parent. For some, this situation is not so favorable. The father may be distant, or there may be rivalry between child and parent and much time may be spent in rebellion. Ultimately, the Dog type must make peace with their parent, and accept what they were, or were not, given. The idea of father or parent has even deeper connotations when looked at from a larger cultural perspective.

Those born under Dog will often have a strong loyalty to community, city or country and will become involved in the political process. Some may even become nationalistic leaders who help guide their community, large or small, into the future.

One of the problems that Dog types have in close relationships has to do with emotional maturity. These people have strong feelings about territory and can be quite jealous when it comes to sharing and trusting in relationships. They need to know clearly just what the pecking order is and where the boundary lines are drawn. If these are not clear, an insecurity crisis occurs and the response is usually not friendly. A double standard is sometimes held by Dog types. There will be one set of rules for the mate, and one for them. It is in these instances that some real work on emotional maturity is needed. Ultimately, the territorial instinct of this day–sign is deep and not easily accessible.

The Influence of the 13–Day Periods

1–Dog
This is the first day of the 13–day period beginning with the day 1–Dog. Those born on this day are natural leaders and strong community supporters. They have a sharp wit and may often be perceived as antagonistic.

2–Dog
This is the second day of the 13–day period beginning with 1–Water. Strong individuality, enthusiasm, and powerful drives are characteristic of those born on this day. Artistic creativity is also usually prominent.

3–Dog
This is the third day of the 13–day period beginning with 1–Rabbit. Born on this day are competitive people with clever minds and much nervous energy. They are often artistically creative or work with art or decoration.

4–Dog
This is the fourth day of the 13–day period beginning with 1–Deer. Those born on this day have very strong team instincts and yet are very original or even eccentric individuals. Family matters shape their lives significantly, yet they love to roam.

5–Dog
This is the fifth day of the 13–day period beginning with 1–Death. Politics, community and social causes have special appeal for those born today. They are very consistent in their political and philosophical positions.

6–Dog
This is the sixth day of the 13–day period beginning with 1–Serpent. Powerful and influential are the people born on this day. They are charismatic and have strong and persistent drives, as well as talent, for leadership and performance.

7–Dog
This is the seventh day of the 13–day period beginning with 1–Lizard. Those born on this day are highly individualistic people, very influential, who enjoy the limelight. They have strong sex drives and erratic relationship patterns.

8–Dog
This is the eighth day of the 13–day period beginning with 1–House. These people are emotionally deep and hard to reach, but they are also strong leaders. The consistency in many aspects of their lives is remarkable.

9–Dog
This is the ninth day of the 13–day period beginning with 1–Wind. Those born on this day tend to be concerned or infatuated with ideas and ideologies. They are often teachers or powerful speakers who influence others with their words.

10–Dog
This is the tenth day of the 13–day period beginning with 1–Crocodile. People born on this day have strong emotional attachments to others, especially family members. Parents and parenting are major issues for them.

11–Dog
This is the eleventh day of the 13–day period beginning with 1–Flower. These people become deeply involved in relationships, but often suffer due to loyalty problems, theirs or another's. They are idealistic and quite resistant to acknowledging what is really happening.

12–Dog
This is the twelfth day of the 13–day period beginning with 1–Rain. Those born on this day make good teachers and educators. They are very loyal and dedicated to those they love.

13–Dog
This is the last day of the 13–day period beginning with 1–Knife. Personal sacrifice for community, group, family or partner characterizes those born on this day.

Notables born under Dog

1 – Andy Rooney, Hunter S. Thompson, Bill Maher, Julia Louis–Dreyfus, Lance Armstrong

2 – Al Jolson, Lindsey Buckingham, Robin Quivers

3 – Thomas Cole, Mae West, J. Robert Oppenheimer, Nelson Mandela, Barry Manilow, Newt Gingrich, Eddie Murphy

4 – Olympia Dukakis, Kevin Bacon, Branford Marsalis, Bonnie Blair

5 – Franz Anton Mesmer, Louis Prima, Alex Haley, Bob Marley, Rob Zombie

6 – Brigham Young, Mohandas Gandhi, Emmett Kelly, Herb Alpert, Connie Chung

7 – Golda Meir, Anwar El–Sadat, Mariah Carey

8 – Edgar Rice Burroughs, Dylan Thomas, Willy Nelson, Jerry Garcia, Pamela Anderson

9 – Mark Twain, Howard Carter, Adolph Hitler, Cole Porter, Alex Trebek, Steven Spielberg

10 – Florence Nightingale, Veronica Lake, Graham Nash, Vladimir Putin, J.K. Rowling

11 – Frederick Remington, Russell Crowe, Eddie Vedder, Justin Beiber

12 – Stephen Crane, Max Planck, Jimmy Hoffa, Sammy Davis Jr., Allen Toussaint, Shannon Miller

13 – William H. Taft, Diane Arbus, Phyllis Schlafly, Tim Robbins

Monkey

Indigenous Names
Maya: Chuen
Aztec: Ozomatli

Direction: West

The Maya glyph for this day–sign appears to be a stylized head of a monkey. The name "Chuen", however, translates as "craftsman" or "artisan." The Aztecs also symbolized this day with the head of monkey, and it too was considered a day for artists and craftsmen of all kinds.

Xochipilli, the Aztec god of flowers, art, dance, and singing, was the patron deity of this day–sign. He was called the "Flower Prince" and, along with his artistic side, was considered an inspirer of drinking and irresponsible sexual activities.

Duran wrote that this was the day–sign of clever actors who had many friends and were found among kings and nobles. If female, she was a good singer, very pleasant and easily persuaded in any matter. Sahagun reported that 1–Monkey was a popular entertainer, singer, dancer or scribe.

Common sense suggests that those born under this day–sign are in many ways like the animal it was named after. Monkeys are intelligent, clever, and they imitate what they see. They live in groups of extended families, are curious and communicative, and are also very sexual animals.

Experiential Observations

Key Meaning: Performance and artistry

Both traditional and common sense descriptions of this day–sign seem to match the personalities of those born under it. These are multifaceted people, with considerable talent for performance or artistry. They seek attention from others and are drawn to positions of leadership. Although they are somewhat distant from others emotionally, they have strong personal desires that drive them to accomplish their goals. Monkey types are very communicative, interested in everything around them and are quick learners.

On the most basic level, those born under this day–sign are the clowns and entertainers of the twenty named–days. They need attention and learn very early how to get it by putting on a performance. Actors, artists, musicians, designers and writers make up an unusually large percentage of people born on this day. Many are multi–talented and seem to switch from one art form to another with little effort. Those that do not practice an art form will seek other ways to get attention, in some cases in less socially acceptable ways.

Perhaps it is the cultivation and development of personality that is the core issue for Monkey types. The mask of the self, the social personality, appears to be the strong point, or the object of obsession, for those born on this day. Life is experienced as theater and the mask becomes all important. In careers where personal presentation is crucial to success, as in performing or sales, a developed personality is a real asset — and it is this type of career that attracts Monkey types.

Many Monkey types assume positions of leadership. By nature they are not followers and therefore the choice is either independence or leadership — but leaders get attention. There is a tendency to constantly promote themselves which is often perceived by others as attractiveness or even charisma. Much of this is done unconsciously. It may be the case that Monkey types have egos that are really very insecure and require compensation by getting the world to acknowledge their worth. However, some compensate a little too much and can be overbearing and dominating.

Emotionally, those born under Monkey are somewhat distant and aloof when in close relationships. They may fear losing their center to another and so they keep up a good defense. Another possibility is that they really don't want a close relationship and enjoy playing the field — which is just another way of getting attention from the world. This emotional distancing is attractive to others as it lends an air of mystery to their already dramatic character. On the other hand, Monkey types have powerful drives and a strong desire nature. Their sexual desires are usually strong and often motivate them to accomplish things they wouldn't ordinarily do. The desire for leadership and attention is also behind many accomplishments. Perhaps these drives are one and the same.

Monkey types are usually very communicative and curious. They are interested in everything that passes in front of them and will go out of their way to learn how something works. They make excellent teachers and are equally good students. Mentally, they are capable of working with details, but they excel at generalities. This quality helps them immensely when it comes to handling a leadership position. Many less flamboyant natives of this day–sign turn out to be reporters, writers, lawyers or other communicators.

The Influence of the 13–Day Periods

1–Monkey
This is the first day of the 13–day period beginning with 1–Monkey. Strong leaders and dominant personalities are born on this day. They rise in life because of their way with words and their dramatic stance.

2–Monkey
This is the second day of the 13–day period beginning with 1–Dog. Those born on this day are dedicated to their work, friends and lovers. They also have natural leadership qualities.

3–Monkey
This is the third day of the 13–day period beginning with 1–Water. These are very intense individuals who can be most uncompromising, which may lead to great success in some cases. They are attracted to the limelight but have a complex emotional life and sometimes problems with responsibilities.

4–Monkey
This is the fourth day of the 13–day period beginning with 1–Rabbit. These are exceptionally clever people who can play any role they wish to. They may be perceived by others as a little crazy or self–destructive.

5–Monkey
This is the fifth day of the 13–day period beginning with 1–Deer. Unconventional and artistic are words that describe these people. They have problems in close relationships due to a conflict between traditional and freedom–loving needs.

6–Monkey
This is the sixth day of the 13–day period beginning with 1–Death. Those born on this day are very political in nature and are concerned with social relations. They enjoy the spotlight, or are at least concerned with what others think about them. Self–worth issues may be a challenge when they are in leadership positions.

7–Monkey
This is the seventh day of the 13–day period beginning with 1–Serpent. These people can be real powerhouses. They are driven by strong desires toward leadership positions where they then tend to dominate as well as lead.

8–Monkey
This is the eighth day of the 13–day period beginning with 1–Lizard. These people are very competent artistically, quite aggressive and they usually have a strong sex–drive. They enjoy leadership as long as it doesn't deny them their freedom.

9–Monkey
This is the ninth day of the 13–day period beginning with the day 1–House. These people excel at activities that require precise calculations. They can be manipulative and dominating, but also very consistent.

10–Monkey
This is the tenth day of the 13–day period beginning with 1–Wind. The mental activity or mental power of these types is remarkable and they make good teachers and communicators. They can be controversial in speech and are restless and sometimes emotionally distant, leading to problems in relationships.

11–Monkey
This is the eleventh day of the 13–day period beginning with 1–Crocodile. Those born on this day can be very dominating of others. They seek to nurture and protect those they love, but may do so to extremes.

12–Monkey
This is the twelfth day of the 13–day period beginning with 1–Flower. Concern for love and relationships dominate those born on this day. These are addictive romantics who also excel in the arts and theater.

13–Monkey

This is the thirteenth day of the 13–day period beginning with 1–Rain. Those born on this day make good teachers and healers. They are mentally very alert, well–informed and are involved in their communities.

Notables born under Monkey

1 – Helen Keller, Joan Miro, Ronald Reagan, Mario Cuomo

2 – Jack Benny, Morley Safer, Harrison Ford, Gene Simmons

3 – John James Audubon, Hank Aaron, Andy Kaufman, Winona Ryder

4 – Duke Ellington, Sean Connery, Tina Turner, David Bowie, Patty Hearst

5 – Johnny Weismuller, Carl Reiner, Bill Bradley, Richard Wright, Cat Stevens, Garry Trudeau

6 – Buffalo Bill Cody, Igor Stravinsky, Ricardo Montalban, Bill Moyers, Bob Hayes, Bob Costas

7 – Count Basie, Claude Levi–Strauss, Anita Bryant, Jackson Browne, Lindsay Lohan

8 – Douglas Fairbanks, Jacques Cousteau, Boris Yeltsin, Peter Frampton

9 – Samuel Beckett, Fay Wray, Dustin Hoffman, Serena Williams

10 – Aleister Crowley, Nikita Khrushchev, Humphrey Bogart, Maureen O'Hara, Arlene Dahl, Neil Armstrong, Charles Manson, Don Imus, F. Lee Baily, Pierce Brosnan,

11 – Stanley Kubrick, Tom Arnold, David Duchovny

12 – P.T. Barnum, Robert De Niro, Laraine Newman, Val Kilmer

13 – Burt Lancaster, James Woods, Barbara Streisand, Ray Romano

Grass

Indigenous Names
Maya: Eb
Aztec: Malinalli

Direction: South

This is one of the more confusing day–signs. The Maya name Eb does not have a clear translation. The glyph has elements that suggest both death and water, which it has been suggested implies harmful rains. In the Quiche Maya language the name for this day–sign means "tooth." The Aztec name Malinalli translates as "twisted" but is also the name for a type of grass that was used to make household tools such as brooms, brushes, sacks and cords. This grass was also used to draw blood for offerings from a hole made in the tongue. The Aztec glyph for the day–sign contains a jawbone, or bottom half of a skull, with plants growing out of it.

The Aztec deity Patecatl, the god of medicine and surgery, was the patron god of this day–sign. The use of herbs for healing, and also for transforming consciousness, were among the skills attributed to Patecatl. It is possible that the plants shown in the Aztec glyph represent herbs, but this is not certain. The meaning of the skull is not clear either. Perhaps the grass growing out of the skull is a symbol of life coming from death.

Duran's description of this day–sign emphasized the chronic ill–health this sign was supposedly prone to. People born on this day, he reported, would experience a regularly occurring cycle of health and sickness which did not lead to death. Sahagun regarded 1–Grass as a dreadful day where people found what they wanted only to lose it. 2–Grass and 6–Grass were also considered unfavorable, though 7–Grass, and possibly 8–Grass, were favorable.

Since the Mayan and Aztec names for this day–sign are not in agreement, there is some uncertainty as to what this day–sign is about. The Aztec symbol of grass, from a common sense perspective, suggests practical usefulness, in its use as a tool or a herb. It also suggests the idea of regeneration as grass is a perennial – it dries up and then comes to life again.

Experiential Observations

Key Meaning: Cooperative usefulness

People born under Grass appear to be relaxed, pleasant, somewhat casual and easy going. Sometimes they are plodding. They are slow to anger, often repressing it, and are generally courteous and kind. Very sensitive and even touchy, these people can be easily hurt on the emotional level. Grass types are hard workers and quite ambitious, but they compete politely with others and prefer peace to conflict. They are generous, popular and very practical people.

They enjoy the pleasures of good company, have excellent manners and anticipate the needs of others. They are generous and giving people who usually expect nothing in return. Relationships are extremely important to them, particularly those of a romantic nature. They need relationships or at least some kind of social life, and are not happy without them. This strong need for relationships suggests their tendency to make personal sacrifices for others. Grass types are usually very popular people, and if they work in the entertainment field they usually experience much success.

Most people born on this day–sign are very sensitive; they can be emotionally fragile, psychic or simply very aware of the emotional and psychic dynamics that go on around them. This awareness is at the core of their politeness and personal refinement. Grass types can be easily hurt through rejection or by criticism, but they don't usually let on to others that something has upset them, this is kept to themselves. These types are soft on the surface but hard underneath.

There is a deeper side to Grass types that is not always so pleasant. They tend to hide their anger and resentment which, over time, can become poisonous to them and to others around them. In some cases, they repress powerful urges for power and sexuality. It appears that this day–sign is concerned with the refinement process on the emotional level, but this also implies the need for some constructive ventilation of raw feelings and urges.

People born under Grass often have strong, almost driving, ambitions and they work very hard to achieve their goals. They don't over–stress themselves, however, it is their persistence that counts most. At times they can be plodders, doing the same things over and over again as if they find security in always keeping up the same pace. But they are also competitive, though they prefer to avoid direct competition. Working alone is often a good solution to their dilemma of self–interest versus self–sacrifice. Ultimately, Grass types want peace, almost at all costs, and will work very hard to avoid a fight or even bad feelings.

There seems to be a very practical bent in the Grass mentality. Many born under it are problem solvers, designers or engineers. They can handle details well and, after an appropriate amount of deliberation, make their decisions and execute commands. Some have a strong investigative streak and are attracted to careers that search, dig or uncover things. The idea of recycling, or reusing things appeals to them.

Popularity and public success is often seen in the lives of those born under this day–sign. In general, Grass types are conservative and practical and present to others a message that does not upset or challenge the status quo. In some cases the message is somewhat old–fashioned or outdated. In more positive situations they come across as peaceful and relaxing and therefore generate fewer negative responses. If they are performers, and many are musical performers, they play the hits that the crowd loves. Their sense of what is going to be well–received qualifies them as advertisers, promoters or spokespeople.

The Influence of the 13–Day Periods

1–Grass
This is the first day of the 13–day period that begins with the day 1–Grass. Those born on this day take on the characteristics of the day–sign in its purest form.

2–Grass
This is the second day of the 13–day period beginning with 1–Monkey. Those born here enjoy entertaining and hosting and have a good sense of humor. They are often quite creative and make good teachers.

3–Grass
This is the third day of the week 13–day period beginning with 1–Dog. These people are quick to dedicate their lives to a cause, or are particularly serious and committed to their work. They enjoy working with groups or with a team.

4–Grass

This is the fourth day of the 13–day period beginning with 1–Water. Those born on this day are emotionally intense, romantic and have a very strong desire nature. They are often leaders, but they lead in a casual and polite way.

5–Grass

This is the fifth day of the 13–day period beginning with 1–Rabbit. A friendly kind of competition plays a prominent role in the lives of those born on this day. These are clever and intelligent people who make their moves deliberately but decisively.

6–Grass

This is the sixth day of the 13–day period beginning with 1–Deer. Those born on this day are individuals not easily influenced by the opinions of others. They are generous and strongly attached to family, but strive to be free–agents. They may be leaders, but do so indirectly.

7–Grass

This is the seventh day of the 13–day period beginning with 1–Death. These are conservative people who have strong feelings, which they usually suppress, about community and political matters. They are often involved with homes and real estate matters.

8–Grass

This is the eighth day of the 13–day period beginning with 1–Serpent. Those born on this day are very sensitive yet determined individuals. They seek power, either personally or through association.

9–Grass

This is the ninth day of the 13–day period beginning with 1–Lizard. These are intelligent people, deep thinkers who take life seriously. They often must sacrifice a good deal of personal freedom in life for one reason or another. They tend to be somewhat lazy, however.

10–Grass

This is the tenth day of the 13–day period beginning with 1–House. Deep, private and emotional are those born on this day. They are hard workers and good problem solvers.

11–Grass
This is the eleventh day of the 13–day period beginning with 1–Wind. Those born on this day are excitable and often concerned with communication and transportation matters. They have much nervous energy and need to be constantly busy.

12–Grass
This is the twelfth day of the 13–day period beginning with 1–Crocodile. These are strong characters, emotionally intense, who work well alone or in a shared leadership position. They are creative and dedicated people who nurture and protect those close to them.

13–Grass
This is the thirteenth day of the 13–day period beginning with 1–Flower. Those born on this day are romantically inclined and very much influenced by ideals, which may produce unrealistic expectations in relationships. They are often conceptually artistic or skilled in crafts.

Notables born under Grass

1 – Friedrich Nietzche, Moe Howard, Billie Holiday, Jim Croce

2 – J. Eric S. Thompson, Reba McEntire, Michael Keaton, Ben Stiller

3 – Margaret Mead, Albert King, Pete Townshend, Stevie Wonder, Dan Aykroyd, Paula Abdul

4 – Lee Marvin, Hugh Hefner, Lee Harvey Oswald, Howard Stern

5 – Dwight D. Eisenhower, Reverend Jim Jones, Mike Myers, Nicole Bass

6 – Cab Calloway, Liberace, Sun Ra, Mel Brooks, Jerry Lee Lewis, Joe Lieberman

7 – Spencer Tracy, Robert F. Kennedy, Anne Frank, Tom Petty

8 – Claude Debussy, Rod Steiger, Nancy Pelosi

9 – Hugh Downs, George McGovern, Mickey Mantle, Angelica Houston

10 – Franz Kafka, Thurgood Marshall, Ayatollah Khomeini, H. Ross Perot, Duane Eddy

11 – Robert Louis Stevenson, J. Edgar Hoover, Nat King Cole, Carl Bernstein, Gene Wilder

12 – Yitzhak Rabin, Bob Weir, Jeff Bridges, Sharon Osbourne

13 – Karl Marx, Vladimir Lenin, Arthur M. Schlesinger, Lucille Ball, Martin Mull

Reed

Indigenous Names
Maya: Ben
Aztec: Acatl

Direction: East

The Maya connected this day–sign with ideas of growth and development in both the corn plant and in human life. The various versions of the glyph are stylized, but may suggest some kind of vegetation. The Aztecs symbolized the day with a depiction of either some type of reed–like standing plant, or arrow shafts with feathering. It is probably the case that the day–sign name Acatl refers to the type of reed that was used to make arrows and darts.

The Aztec god Tezcatlipoca, a powerful Toltec deity, was the ruler of this day–sign. He was, along with Quetzalcoatl, one of the offspring of the creator duality and one of the primary forces behind the existence of the world. Tezcatlipoca was a god of the dark side, a powerful magician and warrior, believed to have a special control over the rhythm of the twenty named–days.

In Duran's account of the day–signs, Reed was considered a somewhat neutral sign. Those born under it were supposedly hollow, like the reed. This made them heartless, complaining, empty and insignificant, though they could very well be wealthy. He reported that they were inclined to spend their days lying naked in the sun. Sahagun was a bit more optimistic about this sign and indicated that those born under 2–Reed could become rich.

Taking the symbol literally, one notes that reeds are tall, strong and rigid. They were used to make arrows and other projectiles which were designed to fly straight and then hit a target. Possibly, people born under this day–sign would reflect these characteristics.

Experiential Observations

Key Meaning: The integrity of belief

People born on the day–sign Reed are usually well–respected by their friends and peers. They are popular and accomplished, and are usually quite competent at whatever they try. Often they are risk–takers or pioneers who stick by their principles when facing opposition. In some cases this amounts to being opinionated, and many do tend to be intellectually rigid and prone to argue when confronted. Although they love to relax and enjoy life, they are capable of intense work and can be extremely disciplined if necessary. Status seems to be an important issue. Many are intellectuals or well educated, usually in fields concerned with human nature.

Those born under the day–sign Reed are frequently highly regarded by others for one accomplishment or another. In some cases they are simply way ahead of their competitors, or have made their mark on the field they work in. In other cases, it is simply just a matter of general competency; the ability to excel at whatever they set their mind to or put their hands on. Another characteristic common to Reed types is their popularity and status with others. For some this is simply a well–deserved fame, for others, respect and recognition from their peers. Although Reed types have enemies, even they respect their successful ways.

What is probably the source of the competency described above is the integrity and personal confidence that Reed types exude. These people will stick to their guns when under fire, keep a stiff upper lip when in trouble and, like the reed, remain firm when pressed. There is a militant side to them, and although they don't deliberately seek conflict, they seem to thrive in it. They can be politely aggressive, or crusaders for a cause, as for them life is something to be won through strength and conviction.

Reed types are ambitious and clear about their goals and intentions. These people also have principles, often of a moral or ethical nature, that govern their behavior toward others. Some Reed types are attracted to religious or philosophical studies, others are simply concerned with justice. If a person born under Reed does not receive a good liberal education, this broad–minded orientation may become distorted resulting in a mind that tends toward being opinionated and judgmental.

People born under Reed work very hard and they are far–sighted. They know the value of consistency and are capable of disciplining themselves to accomplish a task, regardless of the time it takes to reach the goal. Frequently, they take risks or pioneer the way in their work, their inner confidence allowing them to do things that others would shy away from. They can take criticism because they know themselves so well. One important attribute of most of those born under this day–sign is that they want to learn. This openness to new ideas keeps them in the forefront of their field. Most people born on this day are well–educated or knowledgeable, while those that fear education become eccentrics.

Closely related to the love of knowledge is the love of open spaces. Reed types won't tolerate restraint – they must be free to do as they choose. For this reason, many Reed types enjoy travel, as well as hiking, riding, skiing, etc., because of the freedom of movement such activities provide.

Teaching, politics, and the social sciences seem to appeal to those born under Reed. They have good instincts for reading the character of others and a talent for diplomacy. Reed types communicate well because they understand other people – they know where others really stand on important matters. Like psychologists, they learn to judge and form expectations of others that are realistic. They are insightful and deep thinkers. Although Reed types may have personal philosophies that range from conservative to liberal, their common ground lies in the breadth of their minds.

One of the more problematic traits of Reed types is extremism. For some, this is compensated by their accomplishments in the world, for others this could be a real problem. Reed is not a moderate day–sign. Those born under it are high–powered achievers who are capable of burning themselves and their friends out when they get carried away. Once interested in something, these people will not stop until they've learned everything about it or have accomplished what they set out to do. Sometimes others have to slow them down or even stop them from what may be destructive obsessions. Fortunately, Reed is usually a very balanced day–sign and those born under it often catch themselves in time.

The Influence of the 13–Day Periods

1–Reed
This is the first day of the 13–day period beginning with the day 1–Reed. People born on this day are usually extremely ambitious and tend to be very conscious of their social position in life. They have important ideas to express and do this with great power or skill.

2–Reed
This is the second day of the 13–day period beginning with 1–Grass. Those born on this day are more laid–back than ruthlessly ambitious and some are even a bit reserved. They have a strong need for relationship and have plenty of patience.

3–Reed
This is the third day of the 13–day period beginning with 1–Monkey. Performance is an issue for these people, whether in politics, teaching, entertainment or salesmanship. They can be forceful and charismatic, sometimes projecting sexual power into whatever they do.

4–Reed
This is the fourth day of the 13–day period beginning with 1–Dog. Those born here are usually very dependable and constant people. They are deep thinkers who are challenged to live a moral and ethical life and establish high standards of conduct.

5–Reed
This is the fifth day of the 13–day period beginning with 1–Water. This is a powerful combination. Those born under it are hard driving individuals, ambitious and very capable in their chosen field. Control of their emotions can be a real challenge, however.

6–Reed
This is the sixth day of the 13–day period beginning with 1–Rabbit. Intellectual debate on general principles are enjoyed by those born on this day. There is also a militant streak in these people.

7–Reed
This is the seventh day of the 13–day period beginning with 1–Deer. This is a highly independent combination and those born under it tend to do their own thing. They are adventurous and enjoy traveling.

8–Reed
This is the eighth day of the 13–day period beginning with 1–Death. These are people who are motivated by feelings of political and social obligation. They see personal sacrifice as meaningful action.

9–Reed
This is the ninth day of the 13–day period beginning with 1–Serpent. Here is another powerful combination and those born under it tend to be driven by their emotions to attain positions of power. They are often well–educated and articulate, but tend to preach.

10–Reed
This is the tenth day of the 13–day period beginning with 1–Lizard. Those born on this day are natural leaders and performers – though also respected for their intellect. They have extremely high standards and usually make a strong impact in their field, sometimes emphasizing a point of view that is radical in some ways.

11–Reed
This is the eleventh day of the 13–day period beginning with 1–House. People born on this day are hard workers with phenomenal endurance and commitment to what they do. They tend to be very cerebral, perhaps too much so, and often become teachers or advocates of a concept.

12–Reed
This is the twelfth day of the 13–day period beginning with 1–Wind. People born on this day are quite restless and love variety. They make excellent teachers as they are usually multi–faceted individuals who excel at communication.

13–Reed
This is the last day of the 13–day period beginning with 1–Crocodile. Those born on this day can be dominating people, but in a parental kind of way. They can be good teachers but are often complex individuals with strong, often inflexible, ideas about life.

Notables born under Reed

1 – Ralph Waldo Emerson, Michael Moore, Randy Quaid

2 – Pearl S. Buck, Ed Sullivan, Forest Whitaker

3 – Annie Besant, George Wallace, Larry King, Jim Henson, Joni Mitchell

4 – Rodney Dangerfield, Jerry Brown, Deepak Chopra, O.J. Simpson,

5 – Angela Davis, Nadia Comaneci, Justin Timberlake

6 – Percival Lowell, Harold Ramis, John McEnroe

7 – Ted Williams, Audrey Hepburn, Jerry Fallwell, Sissy Spacek

8 – Andres Segovia, Aldous Huxley, Frank Oz, Mia Farrow

9 – United States, Judy Garland, Dione Warwick, Freddie Prinze, Barack Obama

10 – Sigmund Freud, Carl Jung, Alan Alda, Jesse Jackson, Salmon Rushdie, Mel Gibson

11 – Franklin D. Roosevelt, Adelle Davis, David Brinkley, James Brown, Quentin Tarantino

12 – Ralph Nadar, Bela Karolyi, Joe Namath

13 – Louis Henri Sullivan, Menachem Begin, Marvin Gaye, Michael Crichton, Diana Ross

Ocelot

Indigenous Names
Maya: Ix
Aztec: Ocelotl

Direction: North

The Maya name for this day-sign probably refers to an earth god, but the glyph does show spots, possibly the spots of a jaguar. In Maya myths, the jaguar is associated with the earth, or the interior of the earth, hence the connection. The Aztec name Ocelotl means ocelot or jaguar. The symbol for the day is the head of this animal, which is associated with darkness and the night.

The Aztec goddess Tlazolteotl was the ruling deity of this day-sign. She was a witch goddess, known as the Lady of Filth, who was invoked when sins were confessed. The Aztec military had two basic branches, the ocelot and the eagle warriors. The ocelot branch were the scouts, spies and advance guard — the warriors of the dark and the night.

Duran gave a rather long description of this day-sign beginning with a comparison to the jaguar itself. Those born under it were supposedly daring, proud, conceited and desirous of powerful positions. They were mercenary, but enjoyed going to war. Women born under the day-sign were likely to be snobs. Sahagun said virtually nothing about this day-sign.

Since both Maya and Aztec symbols agree, we might assume that the nature of the jaguar will be reflected in the character of those born on this day. Jaguars or ocelots are solitary, nocturnal, secretive, stealthy and powerful animals. They are also carnivorous.

Experiential Observations

Key Meaning: Investigation and healing

In many ways, those born under the day-sign Ocelot are indeed like the animal after which the sign is named. They are secretive and private and yet are also very sensitive and often psychic. They have a pronounced aggressive streak yet seem to be able to avoid direct confrontations with others. In relationships, Ocelot types tend to become deeply involved, often to the point where one person is feeding on another. They make good counselors and therapists. Many of those born under Ocelot are religious or spiritual people, or have been affected strongly by such matters.

Privacy is something that those born under Ocelot need, yet their tendency to become involved in entangled relationships often makes this difficult. By nature, these are secretive people who find that controlling information helps them maintain power. They have an inborn sense of strategy and make good planners and investigators.

Ocelot types are also quite aggressive and competitive. These are people who will fight to make a point, though they usually do so in somewhat indirect ways. In conversation they can be cutting and sarcastic, but they do use subtlety and rarely come right out with what they think. Ultimately, this could be a problem for them when others catch on to what they are really saying. This passive–aggressive approach can go on for years before a real crisis is reached. The experience of breaking off long–standing ties and friendships is something common to this day–sign.

Those born under this day–sign tend to have rather complex relationships with spouses, relatives and friends. They tend to become deeply involved with others on many levels and they also base some of their security needs on these relationships. When things turn sour, they find themselves caught up in a network of ties and obligations that are difficult to throw off easily and quickly. Frequently, their relationships become based on dependency, where one person needs the other for survival. In some cases whole networks of people are needed to keep their lives afloat and circumstances become quite complex. Ocelot types, at worst, can be socially maladjusted and dependent. At their best, these are people who can heal sick human relationships, or simply explore them to their fullest.

Ocelot types often display various kinds of psychic abilities. They are very sensitive in general and can read people intuitively. Some develop other psychic senses or master divination techniques. On another level, medical and healing arts often appeal to them and they find their way to a diagnosis using their powerful instincts. When this psychic ability is combined with their tendency to become deeply involved in human relationships, what emerges is the doctor or counselor. At their very best Ocelot types are healer/confessors and provide a necessary service to humanity. Like the Aztec goddess Tlazolteotl, they consume the negative by-products of human relationships.

The expansion of the mind and the alterations of consciousness are the foundation for the psychic ability and intuitiveness described above. In some cases, Ocelot types experience this in a negative way. Drugs, alcohol, bodily abuse or extreme beliefs can turn this sensitivity into confusion. Some become mentally unstable, others become spaced-out. Those born under Ocelot should realize this potential weakness and not place themselves in mentally detrimental situations.

Most people born under this day-sign are intelligent and well-educated. They display a facility for communication and are often powerful and persuasive speakers or writers. Negatively, they can dominate conversations or attempt to impose their views on others. They have powerful imaginations and are capable of visualizing all sorts of things, from the sublime to the paranoid. Possibly the best type of education for Ocelot types is one in which psychology and social sciences are emphasized.

The Influence of the 13-Day Periods

1-Ocelot
This is the first day of the 13-day period beginning with the day 1-Ocelot. Those born on this day have complex personalities but sometimes become influential and powerful when they find ways to express their deep feelings. They have a strong need for privacy, however, and more often fly below the radar.

2-Ocelot
This is the second day of the 13-day period beginning with 1-Reed. People born on this day are usually quite visible and strive for leadership positions. They can be very clever and manipulative and use their intellect as a tool.

3-Ocelot
This is the third day of the 13-day period beginning with 1-Grass. These are compassionate people who keep their anger to themselves. They are committed in relationships, though they usually hold most of the power.

4–Ocelot
This is the fourth day of the 13–day period beginning with 1–Monkey. Born on this day are people who are sexual and seek attention, but reveal very little of themselves. They tend to be possessive and jealous in love.

5–Ocelot
This is the fifth day of the 13–day period beginning with 1–Dog. Loyalty and constancy in close relationships are important to those born on this day, though there are often problems with long–term commitments. They are creative and have good strategic instincts which help them to overcome difficulties.

6–Ocelot
This is the sixth day of the 13–day period beginning with 1–Water. Those born on this day have strong emotions that often get the best of them. They are compulsive about many things and tend to have complex private lives.

7–Ocelot
This is the seventh day of the 13–day period beginning with 1–Rabbit. These people are clever with words and tend to thrive on both contradiction and competition. In social matters they are masters of one–upmanship and always ready to face challenges head on.

8–Ocelot
This is the eighth day of the 13–day period beginning with 1–Deer. People born on this day are individualistic and uncompromising, and often attain powerful, though independent, positions in life.

9–Ocelot
This is the ninth day of the 13–day period beginning with 1–Death. Privacy is important to these people. They are basically conservative and self–sacrificing and take an active interest in their family or community.

10–Ocelot
This is the tenth day of the 13–day period beginning with 1–Serpent. This is a most powerful combination and those born on this day need to understand the proper use of power, otherwise they tend to be manipulative and dominating.

11–Ocelot
This is the eleventh day of the 13–day period beginning with 1–Lizard. These popular people are determined and not easily swayed. As a result they have no fears about going against the current or becoming associated with radical causes.

12–Ocelot
This is the twelfth day of the 13–day period beginning with 1–House. Those born on this day are strong characters, but can be very private and aloof as individuals, even if in the spotlight. They tend to stay near their homes and families, but have powerful minds that enjoy a challenge.

13–Ocelot
This is the thirteenth day of the 13–day period beginning with 1–Wind. Active minds and a tendency to communicate excessively characterize those born on this day. They always have something to say which makes them good teachers or counselors.

Notables born under Ocelot

1 – Khalil Gibran, George Patton, Nolan Ryan, Laura Nyro, Antonio Banderas

2 – Richard Nixon, Ethel Merman, Stan Lee, Twyla Tharp, Shakira

3 – Joseph Stalin, Enrico Fermi, Lech Walesa, Iggy Pop

4 – Charles Ives, Bette Davis, Cass Elliot, Chelsea Clinton

5 – Stephen Foster, Kofi Annan, Keith Richards, Arlo Guthrie, Steven Tyler, Tiger Woods

6 – J.P. Morgan, Jack Kemp, Cindy Crawford

7 – Israel Regardie, Muhammad Ali, John Landis, Sarah Palin

8 – Nancy Reagan, Paul Newman, Margaret Thatcher, Lenny Bruce, Marlee Matlin

9 – Ernest Hemmingway, Charleton Heston, Linda Ronstadt, Jon Stewart

10 – Alan Turing, Jim McKay

11 – Benjamin Spock, Edward R. Murrow, Charles Bronson, Randy Newman

12 – Henry Ford, Yul Brynner, Arnold Schwarzenegger, Donna Summer, Alec Baldwin

13 – Emily Dickinson, George Bernard Shaw, Edgar Cayce, Sarah Ferguson

Eagle

Indigenous Names
Maya: Men
Aztec: Cuauhtli

Direction: West

There is not any obvious agreement between Maya and Aztec versions of this day–sign. The Maya word Men is actually part of the verb "to do" and the glyph is that of a head with a line of dots behind the eye. It has been suggested that this refers to the old Moon deity. The Zapotec word for this day–sign means "mother" or "female animal." It may be that the great mother goddess, whose symbol was that of an eagle's claw, was being evoked in this day.

The Aztec version of this day–sign, Cuauhtli, clearly translates as "eagle." The symbol was that of a flayed human face, or a torn–out eye, apparently symbolizing the pain and suffering of human sacrifice. The associated deity was Xipe Totec, a corn god, for whom such sacrifices were made. The idea here was one of renewal; the skin of a dead victim was made to come "alive" again when it was worn by a priest of Xipe Totec.

Friar Duran's account of this sign doesn't make things any clearer. He simply said that it has the same nature as the day–sign Ocelot except for a few differences. These were addiction to theft, miserliness and a tendency to hide things. Sahagun reported that 1–Eagle produced people who were brave, daring and presumptuous.

Disregarding the Maya idea of "mother" and the human sacrifice theme surrounding the Aztec glyph and the god Xipe Totec, eagles have the following characteristics. They are high–flying, powerful birds that make high nests. Unlike vultures, they are mostly solo flyers. They are hunters, birds of prey. The Aztecs associated the eagle with the Sun, possibly because of its high–flying abilities. It was believed that eagles were the carriers of sacrificed human hearts to the Sun, the carriers of "food" to the Sun. In this view, the eagle plays a nourishing role. Perhaps this is one link to the Maya notion of this sign as "mother." Still, it isn't clear from this information just what kind of character one born on this day–sign should have.

Experiential Observations

Key Meaning: Vision and perspective

Those born under the day-sign Eagle tend to be easy-going yet independent. They can be loners who have their own unique ideas about life. Eagle types have powerful minds, in some cases scientific and technical, in others, critical and exacting. They are perfectionists who can be quite rigid intellectually, yet they are usually open to new ideas. Eagle types are both ambitious and escapist, though they usually work hard to perfect one aspect of their lives or another. Most Eagle types are popular with others, and most are genuinely friendly people, though they prefer unconventional relationships.

Eagle types tend to be almost free spirits. They would probably just take-off for parts unknown but they usually have complex relationship entanglements to handle, so they don't. But they treasure their time alone and tend to keep a good distance from most people. Eagle people have their own set of rules in life which develop from their unique perspective on things. Others often regard them as simply deviant from the norm. They are usually a bit ahead of their time in their thinking, and they tend to be experimental in many areas of their life. At worst, Eagle types become too self-involved, at best, they pioneer changes and further new developments in the social world.

Many people born under this day-sign are noted for their intellect. Frequently Eagle types have an interest or background in philosophy or science, or the more technical aspects of their chosen field. They are perfectionists with exacting, critical minds that require challenges. Making plans and layouts seems to be particularly appealing to them. Most have high standards and are ambitious about one thing or another, though mostly it is the intellectual challenges that keep them hard at work. Negatively, they tend to think in rigid patterns and are not easily influenced by other's ideas, unless they are genuinely interested in them. Eagle types can be intellectually stubborn, out of habit more often than not.

Oddly enough, there is an escapist side to this day-sign. For some this is simply a lazy streak, for others drug or alcohol use or abuse. On a more positive level, many Eagle types are concerned with making the world a better place and they only appear to be escapist to others. The creation of a fantasy, an escape from society or a personal journey within – these are things that appeal to this sign on a deep level. Perhaps this is a way to simulate the high, soaring flights of an eagle.

Those born under Eagle are usually popular and well–liked, which is interesting since they are the ones who tend to frequently bend the rules. Most have relatively dramatic personalities and thrive on attention – but they are also shy. Although they seem to fascinate others who only see them from afar, they are also immensely popular with those who know them up–close. One thing Eagle types find uncomfortable is competition. They will compete when necessary, and can be very serious about such things, but they usually try to avoid it. Competition with themselves is more their style and is perhaps the basis of their personal ambitions.

Eagle types are very interested in relationships and will make life choices that compromise their free–wheeling instincts in order to explore them. Most of the time this innate conflict forces their relationships into unconventional patterns. Since they are great believers in freedom, their relationships stress this not only for themselves, but also for their partners or friends. These people struggle with jealousy, which they strive to eliminate from their lives.

The Influence of the 13–Day Periods

1–Eagle
This is the first day of the 13–day period beginning with the day 1–Eagle. Those born on this day intensely pursue personal interests, even if this creates instability in relationships. They are extremely independent and original people capable of improving any situation they happen to be a part of.

2–Eagle
This is the second day of the 13–day period beginning with 1–Ocelot. Those born on this day are strong characters who will fight hard to realize their goals and follow their ideals and interests. They are generally private people, often loners in life, who hold to high standards in whatever they do.

3–Eagle

This is the third day of the 13–day period beginning with 1–Reed. People born on this day are often notably intelligent and are often found in the teaching or communication professions. They have strong philosophical interests but can also handle details well.

4–Eagle

This is the fourth day of the 13–day period beginning with 1–Grass. These are compromising people who are deeply involved with social life. While they are independent and original in many ways, they want very much to participate in life and have long–lived careers.

5–Eagle

This is the fifth day of the 13–day period beginning with 1–Monkey. Those born on this day are natural performers, entertainers and also teachers. Conventional relationships present problems for them as they have strong sexual drives and a need for variety.

6–Eagle

This is the sixth day of the 13–day period beginning with 1–Dog. Loyalty and faithfulness are major issues for people born on this day, and these conflict with the need for freedom. Being a team–player is a real test for them.

7–Eagle

This is the seventh day of the 13–day period beginning with 1–Water. People born on this day are highly independent and always follow their own instincts, not those of the crowd. They have strong feelings and a keen appreciation for the arts, particularly music, and can project their emotions powerfully to an audience.

8–Eagle

This is the eighth day of the 13–day period beginning with 1–Rabbit. Aloof and hard to pin down are ways to describe those born on this day. They love their freedom and as a result form relationships only with those that allow them free–rein. Others are kept at a distance.

9–Eagle

This is the ninth day of the 13–day period beginning with 1–Deer. People born on this day are highly independent and original. They are usually ahead of their time in one way or another but tend to be unusually rigid in their thinking. Relationships present problems for them and they tend to be somewhat nomadic.

10–Eagle
This is the tenth day of the 13–day period beginning with 1–Death. This is one of the more conservative versions of Eagle, but there is still a good deal of independence. They straddle the fence on many issues and try to compromise, but will fight if necessary.

11–Eagle
This is the eleventh day of the 13–day period beginning with 1–Serpent. This is a very powerful combination and those born under it have a gift of personal power. The intelligent use of this energy can be a benefit to humanity.

12–Eagle
This is the twelfth day of the 13–day period beginning with 1–Lizard. These are popular and charismatic people. They are detailed thinkers who have good judgment and good taste.

13–Eagle
This is the last day of the 13–day period beginning with 1–House. Those born on this day are private, yet popular. They are distant and hard to reach, but are very much involved in public life. Their concern for security is strong and many of them devote their lives to making money or buying property.

Notables born under Eagle

1 – Peter Hurkos, William Westmoreland, Stevie Nicks, Jimmy Connors, Fred Norris

2 – Henry David Thoreau, Arthur Godfrey, Pat Nixon, Raquel Welch

3 – Errol Flynn, Peter Lorre, Robert Wagner, Michael Stipe

4 – John F. Kennedy, Dick Van Dyke, Woody Allen, Dick Dale, Maria Shriver

5 – Gertrude Stein, Woodie Guthrie, Howard Cosell, Angus Young

6 – Winston Churchill, Gene Kelly, Roy Clark

7 – Richard Alpert, Ringo Starr, Sigourney Weaver, Conan O'Brien

8 – Tex Ritter, Tony Danza, Bryan Adams

9 – Aaron Copland, Red Foxx, Chick Corea, Chris Evert

10 – John Adams, Laurence Olivier, Spike Lee, Gillian Anderson

11 – John Dewey, Phil Donahue, Daniel Day–Lewis

12 – Bing Crosby, Cary Grant, Ricky Nelson, Susan Sarandon, Michael Jordan

13 – Marie Curie, Bill Haley, Merv Griffin

Vulture

Indigenous Names
Maya: Cib
Aztec: Cozcacuauhtli

Direction: South

Cib, the Maya word for this day–sign appears to refer to an insect, possibly the bee. The glyph itself seems to depict a shell, and there are some jaguar features in a few of its several versions. The bee and the shell may refer to the Bacabs or four directions, the jaguar to the night and the dead. However, this is not clear and probably should be left to Maya scholars. The Aztec word Cozcacuauhtli means eagle with a collar, their way of describing the vulture. The Aztec glyph is clearly the head of this large bird which they regarded as a sign of riches.

The Aztec goddess Itzpapalotl was the ruling deity of this day–sign. She was a beautiful black goddess, called the Obsidian Butterfly, who represented ultimate evil and was the bringer of nightmares. Itzpapalotl was one of the Tzitzimime who were strange insect–like creatures that swooped down to earth from the four quarters during eclipses to consume humans. This may be the link with the Maya symbol that seems to combine insect, four quarters and the darkness.

Duran reported that this day–sign indicated a long life and good health. Those born under it were said to be tall, muscular and inclined to go bald. They were prudent, wise, discreet and made good teachers and givers of advice. Sahagun noted that this was a sign of the aged.

The Aztec version of this day–sign provides some help in determining what it might be about. Vultures are large soaring birds that clean up what others have killed. They are dominating animals, pushing other scavengers out of the way. Vultures are also quite social in that they soar in groups. Possibly people born under this day–sign have some of these characteristics.

Experiential Observations

Key Meaning: Authority and status

Serious, deep, realistic and pragmatic are words that describe those born under the day–sign of Vulture. These people are hardened to life and sometimes a bit callous in their handling of relationships. Vulture types are status–conscious. They can be authoritative and dominating – though many find themselves in the reverse position, dominated by others. They are also competent, critical and rejecting when something hasn't met the usually high standards that they have adopted.

This is a particularly heavy day–sign in that those born under it face life very seriously. Some are philosophical about such matters, others sing the blues. There is a sense of limits and fatality in these people that makes them seem ultra–realistic and pragmatic. They know nonsense when they see it and will give credit where it is due. There is a private side to them, perhaps simply the response to a consciousness filled with judgments and evaluations. Whatever the reason, they need time to be alone and are often somewhat of a mystery to others.

Many Vulture types can seem hard and insensitive. They have a tendency to downplay the feelings of others. Perhaps their own experiences, ones that have led them to their realistic positions, are behind this trait. They had to work hard, or were deprived, and yet they made progress. Why shouldn't anyone else? Most have an excellent sense of judgment, are extremely competent at what they do, and critical of how others do the same thing. They want the best for themselves, and for those close to them, and will reject what is not up to their standards.

Vulture is a day–sign concerned with authority and position. Those born under it are acutely conscious of their social or political status at any given moment. For most Vulture types, this means that they are self–conscious when around people who can judge them in some way, and this often becomes a rejection–complex. Many have had problems getting along with their parents, in particular the father. For many females this can be somewhat oedipal and they tend to have relationships with father figures. Yet, for all the problems they may have with bosses and higher–ups, they are strongly inclined to take on authoritative roles themselves. Most Vulture types make excellent managers or business people, though some would rather have others do the managing for them while they simply exert control from the top. The worst thing that could ever happen to one born under this day–sign is to experience a fall from power, disgrace or ruin. But in reality, this happens to very few members of this generally pragmatic group.

Although most Vulture types maintain their authority and high position relative to others, not a few are victims. They face the authority issue that is central to this day–sign from the other side. Some are simply taken advantage of by others, some are even beaten and abused. In some cases, this is more a social issue, where the majority reject what the Vulture type believes in. Many female Vulture types are so insecure that they live their lives through a man; their father or husband. Often, they choose a husband that outwardly displays the normal Vulture characteristics, or has a career that carries with it authority and prestige. In such a situation, projection of their day–sign qualities onto another is their mode of operation. They have set up a life with rigid standards and a pecking order – but they are also the victims within it.

It is in the giving of advice that many Vulture types excel. Their challenges in life, plus their acute awareness of what works and what doesn't in society, give them the ability to make good judgments for others. In many cases, their high status alone accounts for the value of their advice. The critical faculties of this day–sign are usually very good and they can be exacting in judgment or in business matters.

Although it seems that Vulture is a serious, fatalistic sign, and this is true, don't underestimate the ability of these people to enjoy a laugh. What better way is there to lighten the load? Many have an excellent sense of humor and some are great comics – though usually sarcastic and cynical.

The Influence of the 13–Day Periods

1–Vulture
This is the first day of the 13–day period beginning with the day 1–Vulture. Those born on this day can be somewhat elitist, and often at the top of whatever field they play in. They often demonstrate leadership or will do things that are advanced or ahead of their peer group.

2–Vulture
This is the second day of the 13–day period beginning with the day 1–Eagle. People born on this day are loners, yet they may be quite popular with others. They are perfectionists and very devoted to rules and regulations.

3–Vulture
This is the third day of the 13–day period beginning with the day 1–Ocelot. These are private people that are hard to reach which makes them all the more elevated in the minds of others. They tend to become deeply involved in their own thinking, or in some form of strategic planning.

4–Vulture
This is the fourth day of the 13–day period beginning with the day 1–Reed. People born on this day are great and respected teachers, but usually somewhat above the level of others. They make excellent philosophers and religious theorists, though they tend to be somewhat opinionated.

5–Vulture
This is the fifth day of the 13–day period beginning with the day 1–Grass. This is a less harsh version of this day–sign and is usually well–respected. Those born under it tend to become deeply involved in relationships and matters of love and affection. Often they experience rejection or deep loss.

6–Vulture
This is the sixth day of the 13–day period beginning with the day 1–Monkey. People born on this day are creative, artistic and often work in the entertainment fields. They have good leadership qualities.

7–Vulture
This is the seventh day of the 13–day period beginning with the day 1–Dog. Constancy and persistence characterize people born on this day. Once they have chosen a goal, they never give up on it and they take it to the limits. They don't strive for leadership but can handle it if necessary.

8–Vulture

This is the eighth day of the 13–day period beginning with the day 1–Water. Those born on this day are sensitive, highly imaginative and sometimes even fragile. They are deeply emotional people who fear rejection but have the power to compensate for this kind of wounding in constructive ways.

9–Vulture

This is the ninth day of the 13–day period beginning with the day 1–Rabbit. These are particularly complex people who play games of one–upmanship with others. They are masters of their world and know when to make strategic moves.

10–Vulture

This is the tenth day of the 13–day period beginning with the day 1–Deer. There is usually a noticeably deviant streak to those born on this day. Some are loners. They have their own particular view of things and may completely disregard any opposition to it.

11–Vulture

This is the eleventh day of the 13–day period beginning with the day 1–Death. Perhaps one of the most politically conscious days in the entire 260–day cycle, this one produces people who are totally involved in status, reputation and "the score."

12–Vulture

This is the twelfth day of the 13–day period beginning with the day 1–Serpent. People born on this day have compulsive urges to power and prominence. They are tireless and fanatical in the accomplishment of goals, have very high standards, and are often great achievers in life.

13–Vulture

This is the last day of the 13–day period beginning with the day 1–Lizard. Those born on this day are fiercely independent, popular and extraordinarily competent at what they do. They can be very self–conscious and excessively concerned with what others think about them.

Notables born under Vulture

1 – James Joyce, Alan Freed, Burt Bacharach, Garrison Keillor, Jimmy Page, Michael Douglas, Twiggy

2 – Boris Karloff, Ingrid Bergman, Ray Bradbury, Eppie Lederer (Ann Landers), Pete Rose, Prince Harry

3 – Ayn Rand, Bob Dylan, Van Morrison, Reggie Jackson

4 – Winslow Homer, W.C. Handy, Debbie Reynolds

5 – Pablo Picasso, George Burns, Albert Camus, Regis Philbin, Robert Redford, Chuck Norris

6 – George Armstrong Custer, James Earl Jones, Oliver Stone

7 – William Tecumseh Sherman, Truman Capote, Ted Nugent, Hillary Swank

8 – Joseph Smith, Guglielmo Marconi, Patsy Cline, Al Sharpton, Stevie Ray Vaughan

9 – Mary Cassat, Doris Day, Marlon Brando, Warren Buffet, Tori Spelling

10 – Marshall McLuhan, Arthur C. Clarke, Colin Wilson, Brian Jones, Stephen Stills

11 – Calvin Coolidge, Buster Crabbe, William F. Buckley Jr., Elizabeth Dole, Anthony Hopkins, Smokey Robinson, Rudy Giuliani

12 – George Martin, Buddy Holly

13 – Neil Diamond, Aaron Neville, Rush Limbaugh, Tatum O'Neal

Earthquake

Indigenous Names
Maya: Caban
Aztec: Ollin

Direction: East

The Maya name for this day–sign is Caban, which translates as "earth." The glyph's curving line may be a representation of a young earth goddess. The traditional lore about this day was that it favored commerce, matchmaking and medicine. The Aztec name Ollin translates as either "earthquake", "movement" or "rocking motion." This day–sign's glyph, which looks like a bow but may represent the Sun on the horizon, appears in the center of the Aztec Calendar Stone. It is the day–sign that rules, and gives its name to, the present creation. The god in the middle, with tongue sticking out, is the Sun god, Tonatiuh. Legend has it that the present age will end with earthquakes.

The Aztec deity linked to this day–sign was Xolotl, the dark side of the planet Venus, its evening star phase. This god was described as a monstrous, troubled animal whose function was to bring the Sun down into the night.

Duran had a lot to say about this day–sign. First, he identified it with the Sun, because the Sun moves or rolls through the sky. Males born under it were said to shine like the Sun, although females would be foolish, stupid and stubborn. However, both were likely to be rich and powerful. The sign was said to be very positive and well–omened and promised elevation in rank. Sahagun reported that 1–Earthquake was a favorable sign, but those born under it had to do their penances in order to have it operate positively. 4–Earthquake was the day the Sun was worshiped and fed sacrificial victims.

If this day is correctly interpreted to mean earthquake, then it would follow that people born on that day might be unstable, and prone to sudden and destructive events. If it is rocking motion or movement that was implied, then the ideas of swinging from one point to another, or constantly shifting focal points or balance might be more accurate. Another key concept might be that of progress and continuity.

Experiential Observations

Key Meaning: Pushing the limits

The minds of those born under the day–sign Earthquake are unusually active. They are cerebral, rationalizing, and clever. Their ideas are usually quite liberal or progressive and, for some, a little too far out. Many people regard those born under this day–sign as slightly crazy, or at least extremist. Their sense of humor is usually excellent. They often seek leadership positions but tend to be controversial. Their power comes from the strength and conviction of their ideas.

Earthquake types are thinking all the time. They tend to believe that the world can be made logical and that rational solutions are the only solutions. They can be brilliant engineers or strategists who pioneer new solutions to stubborn problems. For some, however, this capacity to rationalize everything they perceive leads to misjudgements and poor choices. It is probably due to the sheer intensity of their rational minds that these people often fail to take into account the human dimension of emotions and feelings.

So much mental activity leads to views that can be based on abstractions or unrealized ideals. In fact, most Earthquake types are progressive, liberal or even radical in their thinking when compared with the norm. This tendency to be a bit ahead of their time can lead to a feeling of elitism, on the one hand, or to being labeled extremist on the other. Many of those born under this day–sign do have problems adjusting to the stress and strain of conflicting viewpoints and, sooner or later, they reach points where privacy and rest become vital to their mental health. Some constantly straddle the boundary between what their society labels sanity and insanity. Some experience nervous breakdowns.

Earthquake personalities usually have a great sense of humor. Possibly this is due to the sharpness of their minds and their ability to make practical use of close observations of human nature. Many have made comedy a career, although most simply appreciate a good joke and love to laugh. Clowning comes naturally to them. Humor is a way of steadying or stabilizing one's hold on reality. When a comedian falls down, we laugh because that shouldn't happen. Much humor is based on the re–creation of uncomfortable and embarrassing situations. Could it be that Earthquake types thrive on laughter because they sense the boundary between comfort and embarrassment more than most? And does this mean that those born under this day–sign live their lives on shaky ground?

In social matters Earthquake types tend to be strongly influenced by intellect and communication. This can be a problem if a partner is very emotional and needs attention in this department. Although those born under this day–sign are very interested in others, close relationships usually suffer somewhat because of their tendency to become too involved with their own interests. In other words, this is not always the most cooperative and compromising of the day–signs. In some cases a compliant and compromising mate could make things easier for them.

Earthquake types tend to seek out leadership positions or solo positions, possibly because they know how hard it is for them to follow the path of another. These are fiercely independent and stubborn people who can't stand being told what to do and they, as one would imagine, pay the price for this tendency in their close relationships. As leaders, they are usually regarded as progressive and possibly a little threatening to followers of the status quo. If leadership is something that is not open to them, they will seek work that allows them a great deal of freedom. Night work, constantly changing schedules and long hours are preferable to being forced into conformity.

The Influence of the 13–Day Periods

1–Earthquake
This is the first day of the 13–day period that begins with the day 1–Earthquake. Those born on this day tend to be very driven. Sometimes living in extreme conditions, they struggle to maintain equilibrium in life, and in the process, many come to develop a good sense of humor.

2–Earthquake
This is the second day of the 13–day period beginning with the day 1–Vulture. These are ambitious people who tend to assume an elitist mantle. They make excellent leaders, though possibly a little too extreme for some.

3–Earthquake
This is the third day of the 13–day period beginning with the day 1–Eagle. Born on this day are people who are popular and freedom–loving. They have a strong tendency to take risks or to do things that their peers would regard as unconventional or radical.

4–Earthquake
This is the fourth day of the 13–day period beginning with the day 1–Ocelot. These are complicated people who can be difficult to understand. They are extremely cerebral and tend to have serious problems balancing this quality with their emotions and feelings, which are also very strong.

5–Earthquake
This is the fifth day of the 13–day period beginning with the day 1–Reed. Those born on this day strive for leadership positions and often achieve great success in life. They are deep thinkers, good teachers, and usually very progressive.

6–Earthquake
This is the sixth day of the 13–day period beginning with the day 1–Grass. Relationships are important but challenging for those born on this day. They understand the importance of compromise as they strive to reach ideals, but their own self–centeredness creates more problems than they care to admit.

7–Earthquake
This is the seventh day of the 13–day period beginning with the day 1–Monkey. Leaders, entertainers and people with public image consciousness are born on this day. They make good teachers or salespeople.

8–Earthquake
This is the eighth day of the 13–day period beginning with the day 1–Dog. Although essentially loners, these people are also team players when necessary. They are dedicated, and with a strong interest in their community, they strive to serve.

9–Earthquake
This is the ninth day of the 13–day period beginning with the day 1–Water. Those born on this day tend to struggle with conflicts between

mind and feelings. They tend to lead somewhat unstable lives, not knowing quite where they fit it, but they can overcome these tendencies if they have creative outlets.

10–Earthquake
This is the tenth day of the 13–day period beginning with the day 1–Rabbit. Too clever for their own good may be a way to describe those born on this day. Their powerful minds rationalize their actions. Finding potential solutions to problems is where their talents lie.

11–Earthquake
This is the eleventh day of the 13–day period beginning with the day 1–Deer. These are very independent types who are often motivated to do whatever they feel like doing when they want to do it. They have a very strong sex drive and often stray in relationships.

12–Earthquake
This is the twelfth day of the 13–day period beginning with the day 1–Death. These people are pragmatic thinkers, status watchers and community upstarts. They know much, but there are many issues they avoid confronting.

13–Earthquake
This is the thirteenth day of the 13–day period beginning with the day 1–Serpent. A potentially explosive but also brilliant combination. These are powerful people, often very accomplished, known and respected for their ideas.

Notables born under Earthquake

1 – Dorothea Dix, Jackie Gleason, Dolly Parton, Jay Leno

2 – Thomas Jefferson, H.P. Lovecraft, Jimmy Dorsey, Johnny Unitas

3 – Washington Irving, Shirley Chisholm, Jimmy Buffett

4 – Theodore Roosevelt, Ted Kennedy, Carole King, Dave Davies

5 – Daniel Webster, Hank Williams, Gilda Radner, Michael J. Fox, Demi Moore

6 – Alfred Hitchcock, Joseph McCarthy, Edmund Hillary, Steve McQueen, Sidney Pollack

7 – Frank Borman, Waylon Jennings, Gordon Lightfoot, Mary Lou Retton

8 – William H. Rehnquist, Jimmy Carter, Shirley Temple, Barbara Walters, Richard Gere, Elvis Costello

9 – B.F. Skinner, Peter Falk, Melanie Griffith

10 – Nikola Tesla, Sinclair Lewis, Martha Graham, Cameron Diaz

11 – Timothy Leary, Jim Nabors, Peggy Fleming, Jackie Chan

12 – Horace Mann, Buddy Guy, Maria Muldaur

13 – Benjamin Franklin, Carroll O'Connor, Michael Dukakis, Alanis Morissette

Knife

Indigenous Names
Maya: Etz'nab
Aztec: Tecpatl

Direction: North

There is good consistency between Maya and Aztec names for this day–sign. The Maya name translates as "sharp implement" or "knife" and its glyph seems to show a blade of some sort. The Aztec name means "flint" or "flint knife" and the symbol for the day is clearly that of a flint sacrificial knife.

The Aztec deity associated with this day–sign was Tezcatlipoca, in his form as Chalchiuhtotolin, the Jeweled Turkey. It was said that Knife was neither good nor bad, as day–signs go, but if one seized the moment, much good fortune could result. This idea is in line with the nature of this manifestation of Tezcatlipoca.

According to Duran this was the worst of signs, harsh, hard and sterile. After emphasizing that the sterility part was the cause of great sorrow because this was a shameful thing, he goes on to say that otherwise they were fortunate. Sahagun reports that 1–Knife indicated good fortune and produced brave warriors and chieftains who gained honor and riches.

One would think that the symbol of a knife, consistent in both Mayan and Aztec traditions, would be suggestive. Knives are sharp, they cut or penetrate and they are tools. Knives made of stone are cold and, as sacrificial knives, they offer victims to the gods.

Experiential Observations

Key Meaning: Cooperation versus self–interest

People born under Knife tend to be practical and mechanically inclined, or at least have good coordination. They are extremely social people who spend much of their lives struggling in close relationships. They can be very polite, compromising and self–sacrificing, but when pushed they tend to have hot tempers. They are subtly dominating people, yet they usually work for others. Vanity and self-absorption is probably the source of many problems in their life.

Knife types have very practical minds. They are adept at solving mechanical problems, working with tools or even mastering finger coordination for a musical instrument. They are often extremely interested in the more technical aspects of what they do and they have a good head for detail. Many born on this day find satisfaction in engineering, photography, crafts, or the arts. Success or competency in these matters does not necessarily mean success in human relationships – a point that Knife types must learn eventually.

Social life, parties, group events, love affairs and partnerships, can become obsessive to those born under this day-sign. They simply can't help themselves from getting excited when around others. They can be model friends and lovers, until you get to really understand their inner conflicts. They try to be polite, courteous, and non-competitive. They will sacrifice part of themselves for another. This may help in a "sale" but ultimately, many of them are totally unrealistic about relationships. Their ideas about how relationships should be maintained may be in direct conflict with their own needs — which they have already sacrificed, and on some level, they are angry about having done so. This pattern results in relationships that are stressful, very much a struggle for both partners. Older Knife types may have learned this lesson, but many younger ones keep making the same mistakes about this basic self-interest versus cooperation issue.

Although those born under Knife appear to be calm and polite on the surface, underneath there is fire. While they will avoid a conflict by repressing their feelings for a long time, when finally pushed too far they will explode with pent-up rage, or at least say some things that you wouldn't expect them to. They can be intensely jealous. This aspect of them allows for a kind of domination of others – more through fear of those inner fires than anything else. In fact, most Knife types are very uncomfortable dominating others consciously and usually work for or with someone else.

A keen mind and an enthusiasm for new subjects is common to those born under this day-sign. Many are well-read, or at least read frequently. They are curious and open to learning, a process that helps them to develop good judgment in social matters. These are people that thoroughly enjoy sharing a discussion on some technical subject with others. While they are very interested in the romantic/physical aspects of relationships, they are equally interested in a good conversation.

The great weakness of those born under Knife is their vanity. They can be very self–absorbed people both in their work, or in regard to their appearance. This may be a sign of personal insecurities that they try to appease by receiving praise and compliments from others. In close relationships many are quite jealous, another indication of their deep personal insecurities.

The great strength of this day–sign is in regard to personal sacrifice. These are people who, for whatever psychological reason, will put their own interests aside in order to meet the needs of others. Some will do this for their country or for the needy, others in less dramatic ways.

The Influence of the 13–Day Periods

1–Knife
This is the first day of the 13–day period beginning with the day 1–Knife. Born on this day are strong people who bear well under pressure, sometimes experiencing a deep personal loss of some sort. They are not afraid of anything.

2–Knife
This is the second day of the 13–day period beginning with 1–Earthquake. These are very cerebral people, problem solvers, quite mechanical or dexterous, who tend to be intense and dominating and sometimes take calculated risks.

3–Knife
This is the third day of the 13–day period beginning with 1–Vulture. This is perhaps the vainest of the combinations. Those born here may be very competent and adept at gaining status in what interests them.

4–Knife
This is the fourth day of the 13–day period beginning with 1–Eagle. These are independent people who struggle with authority issues. They are often creative in business and assume leadership positions based

on their knowledge of technical details. In relationships they tend to compromise too often.

5–Knife
This is the fifth day of the 13–day period beginning with 1–Ocelot. These are people who are very active mentally, but tend to experience powerful transforming events in their lives that challenge them to their emotional limits.

6–Knife
This is the sixth day of the 13–day period beginning with 1–Reed. Concern with morals and ethics in matters of relationships tend to dominate those born on this day-sign. They usually find themselves in complex situations where they must assume the role of leader or teacher – yet they really don't want to.

7–Knife
This is the seventh day of the 13–day period beginning with 1–Grass. Those born on this day are very social, compromising and polite. They make personal sacrifices readily, without even thinking about it.

8–Knife
This is the eighth day of the 13–day period beginning with 1–Monkey. These are busy and creative people, very much concerned with performances and productivity, often found in careers where there is interaction with the public.

9–Knife
This is the ninth day of the 13–day period beginning with 1–Dog. Loyalty in relationships characterizes those born on this day. They will stay with a relationship long after it ceases to nourish their needs.

10–Knife
This is the tenth day of the 13–day period beginning with 1–Water. Perhaps the most emotional form of Knife, those born on this day tend to be easily upset and angered, and are also possessive in close relationships. They need to manage their self–destructive tendencies.

11–Knife
This is the eleventh day of the 13–day period beginning with 1–Rabbit. Clever, cerebral and technically complex would describe those born on

this day. They enjoy controversy, but need others to realize their plans or dreams.

12–Knife
This is the twelfth day of the 13–day period beginning with 1–Deer. People born on this day are social, but tend to be somewhat nomadic at the same time. They can be generous and sharing, but also a little strange and deviant.

13–Knife
This is the last day of the 13–day period beginning with 1–Death. A strong sense of community and political issues dominates those born here. They are very willing to sacrifice their time on behalf of a greater cause, but they expect something in return.

Notables born under Knife

1 – Jackie Onassis, Howie Mandel

2 – Leon Trotsky, James Dean, Paul Simon, David Lynch, Mick Fleetwood, Charles Barkley

3 – Glenn Miller, Che Guevara, Gary Hart, Maury Povich, George Stephanopoulos, Dana Carvey, Jon Lovitz

4 – Jules Verne, Alfred Adler, Douglas McArthur, Ansel Adams, R.D. Laing, Richard Branson

5 – Lyndon Johnson, Harry Belafonte, Francis Ford Coppola, Cher, Dan Quayle

6 – Tony Randall, Harry Chapin, Hulk Hogan

7 – Bruce Lee, David Crosby, Goldie Hawn, Dorothy Hamill

8 – Eleanor Roosevelt, Art Linkletter, Jesse Helms, George Harrison

9 – J.R.R. Tolkien, Norman Vincent Peale, Alan Greenspan, John Malkovich

10 – Benito Mussolini, John Belushi

11 – Geraldine Ferraro, Christopher Reeve, Chris Farley, Britney Spears

12 – Rudyard Kipling, Jean Piaget, Louis Armstrong, Lou Reed, Martin Scorsese

13 – Perry Como, Gene Roddenberry, Fidel Castro, Hussein of Jordan, Gary U.S. Bonds

Rain

Indigenous Names
Maya: Cauac
Aztec: Quiahuitl

Direction: West

Both the Maya and Aztec names for this day-sign refer to "rain" or things related to rain such as storms or thunder. The Maya glyph has cloud symbols in it, the same ones that appear on drawings of the Celestial Dragons, the bringers of storms and rain. The Aztec glyph is the head of the rain-god Tlaloc.

Tlaloc, the ruler of the day-sign Deer, was the principle nature deity for the Aztecs and also for earlier cultures in Mexico. He was ruler of water, rains and fertility, hence his appearance as the glyph for this day-sign seems to be right. However, he probably wasn't the ruling deity of the day. In the codices, rulership seems to point to the Sun god Tonatiuh, the deity that occupies the center of the Aztec calendar stone. Other sources link this day to the goddess Chantico, the goddess of hearth and home. Chantico was actually a fire goddess, but a very domestic one – and water is an element needed in the home.

Duran wrote that all those born on this day were to have bad luck in life. They were to be blind and have many physical deformities and handicaps. Sahagun agreed, in a sense. According to him, 1–Rain began a string of very bad days. Those born on the first day were likely to be sorcerers and soothsayers. 8–Rain was also bad, but 7 and 13 Rain were favorable.

As rain seems to be the common theme in both Maya and Aztec sources, common sense suggests that issues of fertility and nourishment, and the idea of the sustaining of life, might be relevant to those born on this day. The concept of "rain" also suggests the need for shelter. Since rain falls on everything, it might also imply universalism.

Experiential Observations

Key Meaning: The healing of mind and body

Rain appears to be a sign of youth and curiosity, at least on the surface. Those born under it are restless, mentally active, talkative and friendly. They are a little insecure and tend to imitate others rather than pursue a unique direction in life. They are multifaceted and often accomplished in several areas. There is a deeper side to this day–sign though. Many are drawn to the study or practice of religion, spirituality or philosophy. They seem to have good intuition and can improvise when in a tight spot. A concern for the welfare of others, especially the public, is noticeable. They are often found working in occupations that cleanse, purify or heal.

One of the most obvious characteristics of this friendly day–sign is their youthfulness. You will see them involved with children as a career, or perhaps simply just acting like one. This is a day–sign that does not grow old, it just keeps moving. Curiosity and an openness to new ideas characterizes these people, though they sometimes fail to capitalize on what they discover. As a rule, they are nervous and restless and need to constantly exercise their minds in some way. Many talk for a living. All this nervous energy and driving curiosity leads them to develop along several lines, making them multifaceted, interesting, and consequently popular people.

Rain types are more inclined to imitate than to innovate. They respect tradition and the forms created by those that came before them, whether this be in art, science or business. It is from imitation that they learn, but it is also imitation that leads them to conform with the times. Perhaps they imitate because they are so receptive and easily influenced by others. Although some real characters are born under this day–sign, most follow a beaten path and few are pioneers. It is precisely due to this imitative and non–deviant streak that Rain types make excellent teachers and instructors. They are believable and understandable to others, not intimidating or incredible.

Those born under Rain have an interest in the deeper meanings of life. Many become religious, or at least have a deep respect for religious institutions. Others approach spirituality in a more personal way. Meditation and other consciousness raising techniques may appeal to them. Some find philosophy of great interest and use this knowledge to put their life experiences into perspective. Rain types want to know what is really going on in this life and they seek answers to their questions. Perhaps it is the powerful intuition that they all seem to have that causes them to look beyond the mundane world we live in.

Rain types are usually compassionate and will devote time to helping those in need. Many become activists for one cause or another. They have a deep concern for the welfare of others and can be very nurturing in times of crisis. Some find an outlet for their strong protective and nurturing needs in public or volunteer work of some sort. They are loyal friends and devoted parents. In close love relationships, Rain types tend to become over–involved, sometimes to their detriment, though this seems to be more the case with women than men. They value sex as a shared ritual, not just as entertainment.

The cleansing and healing process has a special importance for those born under this day–sign. Many become doctors or healers of some sort. Their natural instincts to protect and nurture, combined with excellent intuition, technical aptitude, and a mind capable of grasping details, makes them well suited for such work. For some, cleaning in and of itself is a sacred ritual, whether it be themselves, their home, an object or another person. It is not simply a matter of controlling their environment, it is more a case of taking proper care of it. On the other hand, Rain types can be excessively neat and make the rest of the world anxious about disturbing the perfection around them.

The Influence of the 13–Day Periods

1–Rain
This is the first day of the 13–day period beginning with the day 1–Rain. Those born on this day are caring and sensitive people with a strong concern for the public. They are excellent role models, communicators and teachers.

2–Rain
This is the second day of the 13–day period beginning with the day 1–Knife. Relationships are extremely important to these people, who are generally practical and self–sacrificing. They are dedicated to their work and often excel in technical skills.

3–Rain
This is the third day of the 13–day period beginning with 1–Earthquake. Born on this day are strong, individualistic people who strive to be independent. They tend to be very nervous and unsettled in life but often achieve much over time.

4–Rain
This is the fourth day of the 13–day period beginning with 1–Vulture. Born on this day are people who know their place and would like the rest of the world to do the same. They can be obsessive about cleanliness and order.

5–Rain
This is the fifth day of the 13–day period beginning with 1–Eagle. These are freedom loving people who have a hard time working for others. They tend to enter into very unusual relationship situations.

6–Rain
This is the sixth day of the 13–day period beginning with 1–Ocelot. People born on this day tend to experience deep emotional conflicts in life. Their sex drives are very strong, yet they have equally strong urges to nurture others.

7–Rain
This is the seventh day of the 13–day period beginning with the day 1–Reed. People born on this day are natural teachers and healers. They tend to be over–confident, extremely communicative and cerebral, and often achieve success in writing and speaking.

8–Rain
This is the eighth day of the 13–day period beginning with the day 1–Grass. The urge to compromise and avoid conflict is so strong in those born on this day that they often find themselves victims in relationship matters. However, they are usually popular with others and excellent home–makers.

9–Rain
This is the ninth day of the 13–day period beginning with 1–Monkey. Public performers, including teachers and entertainers, seem to be born on this day. They are talkative, highly strung, multi–talented and have deep insights into human behavior.

10–Rain

This is the tenth day of the 13–day period beginning with 1–Dog. Consistency, loyalty and devotion to others and causes characterizes those born on this day. These people have strong group or association interests and often assume leadership roles.

11–Rain

This is the eleventh day of the 13–day period beginning with 1–Water. Positively, these are deeply emotional and extremely compassionate people who are often attracted to religion, spirituality and art. Many are intuitive and psychic, though some are emotionally unstable.

12–Rain

This is the twelfth day of the 13–day period beginning with 1–Rabbit. Cleverness and mental agility are characteristics of those born on this day. Many enjoy arguing or debating. They are fascinated by games and often take risks.

13–Rain

This is the thirteenth day of the 13–day period beginning with the day 1–Deer. Those born on this day are independent, somewhat nomadic and yet very attached to home and family. They have strong sexual appetites and are often connected in some way to the medical or healing professions.

Notables born under Rain

1 – John Wayne, Donny Osmond, Princess Diana

2 – Henry Fonda, Doc Watson, John Coltrane, Yoko Ono, Courteney Cox

3 – Jack LaLanne, Bob Seager, Sting, Isabella Rossellini

4 – Nathaniel Hawthorne, Dr. Seuss, Joe Frazier, Brad Pitt, Prince William

5 – Niels Bohr, Lawrence Ferlinghetti, Shirley Bassey, Roy Orbison

6 – Fats Waller, James Mason, Mitch Miller, Pete Seeger, Jim Carrey

7 – Anthony Perkins, Jerry Seinfeld, Kurt Cobain

8 – Sandra Day O'Conner, Wilt Chamberlain, Lenny Kravitz

9 – Andrew Wyeth, Sam Walton, Desmond Tutu, Ted Turner, Michael Richards

10 – Pierre Teilhard De Chardin, Jimmy Stewart, Tennessee Williams, Leonard Cohen, Al Gore

11 – Helena Blavatsky, Joseph Pulitzer, Joe DiMaggio, Dr. Ruth Westheimer

12 – Sybil Leek, Peter Sellers, Miles Davis, Gloria Steinem, Steve Martin, Prince

13 – Edgar Allan Poe, Kris Kristofferson, Annie Lennox, Janet Jackson

Flower

Indigenous Names
Maya: Ahau
Aztec: Xochitl

Direction: South

The Maya name for this day–sign translates as "lord" or "chief." It was considered by them to be the day–sign of the Sun. The glyph is that of a four–petaled flower, another symbol of the Sun. Some variants of the glyph show a face, presumably the solar deity. The Aztec word Xochitl translates as flower, a symbol of perfection and beauty. The day–sign was depicted by the image of a flower.

The Aztec goddess Xochiquetzal, which means "flower–feathered", was the ruling deity of this day–sign. She was the goddess of love, sexual desire and beauty, and also the patron deity of artists. Technically, she was a goddess of the underworld and was worshiped on the Day of the Dead. Her symbol was the flower, an image that symbolizes the temporary beauty of life.

Duran described this day–sign as one associated with painters, weavers, sculptors and other artists and artisans. He said that people born under it were clean and diligent and fond of beautiful clothing. Sahagun describes 1–Flower as a day of happiness and song, a day for jesters and entertainers to be born. 7 and 8–Flower were also good, but 9–Flower was a day of thieves and adulterers.

From the common sense perspective, flowers are beautiful, temporary, and they are the sex organs of the plant. They are used for decoration and beautification. These ideas may be relevant to the character of those born under this day–sign.

Experiential Observations

Key Meaning: Reaching for the ideal

Flower types are dreamers. They have ideals and strive, often stubbornly, to realize them. These are "nice" people, a bit awkward socially, but always well-intentioned. They are usually artistic, or have a great interest and respect for things that are aesthetically pleasing. Many Flower types have serious difficulties in close relationships because their expectations are unrealistic. They are stubborn and will not compromise their ideals easily. However, they are extremely devoted to others, including friends and lovers, and are hurt badly when left for another.

Those born under Flower are motivated by their ideals. They have a beautiful vision of what life, and most importantly life with another, can be. In many cases, this obsession with the future and perfection leads to illusions, unrealistic expectations and, ultimately, disappointments. In their effort to create a more perfect world, Flower types try to be as nice as possible to others. This approach is sometimes so much in contrast with the crude behaviors and attitudes of those around them that Flower types feel awkward and out-of-place. Others may regard them as spaced out, but certainly not a threat.

The world of art and beauty draws the interest of those born under this day-sign. Many become successful artists, or more usually craftspeople who produce decorative or aesthetically pleasing products. In many cases, jewelry is of special interest. Some appreciate man-made things, others the perfection of nature. The more intellectual types will be interested in the beauty of numbers or ideas. In all cases, Flower types have a need to come as close to a perfect universe as they possibly can. Unfortunately, for many this quest leads to unbalanced personal lives.

Relationships, particularly close, intimate relationships, are the greatest challenge for Flower types. Because they strive for perfection and hold onto unrealistic expectations, they tend to experience disappointment and disillusionment frequently in their lives. These are people who must be with others – at least that is what they think they must do. Ironically, many of them have so many problems with relationships that this doesn't happen. More often, they find themselves living alone at home and dreaming. One major problem is their unwillingness to compromise their ideals. These are very stubborn people who would rather die than accept a less than perfect situation. They will devote themselves to another with unbelievable intensity – and hold on for years after the relationship has ended. Such fanaticism often leads to an unbalanced life, exactly what they fear the most. These are people who should strive to become more well–rounded and flexible.

Of course there are many Flower types who do realize, to some extent, their dreams and ideals. Their devotion and dedication to another, or even to a cause or crusade, is considerable. These are people who take on the responsibilities and work involved in such a project, and they are rewarded accordingly. Some become extremely popular and successful, others find a comfortable niche in life that, to them, is perfection in and of itself. Others, especially writers and performers, will find success in communicating to others their experiences in love and life. Flower is a sign that needs to combine realism and idealism, and when this is done, the doors open to a more perfect world.

The Influence of the 13–Day Periods

1–Flower
This is the first day of the 13–day period beginning with the day 1–Flower. Those born on this day are great dreamers who open up new vistas for humanity. They are completely dedicated to their work and will stop at nothing to get it done.

2–Flower
This is the second day of the 13–day period beginning with 1–Rain. These are strong but compassionate people who can be extremely nurturing and protective. They are sincere, attempt to maintain high moral and ethical standards, and do well in the teaching and healing professions.

3–Flower
This is the third day of the 13–day period beginning with the day 1–Knife. People born on this day tend to be very idealistic about relationships and quick to make a personal sacrifice. They are often disappointed that this is not appreciated by the object of their affections.

4–Flower

This is the fourth day of the 13–day period beginning with the day 1–Earthquake. An unstable combination, those born on this day tend to experience serious adjustment crises in relationships. They often hold to a distorted view of life and may be regarded by others as somewhat off–beat.

5–Flower

This is the fifth day of the 13–day period beginning with the day 1–Vulture. Not much is perfect enough for those born on this day. They tend to be judgmental and status conscious, which keeps them working hard to improve what they do, which affects those close to them.

6–Flower

This is the sixth day of the 13–day period beginning with 1–Eagle. This is a combination that is independent and yet dependent on others for support. Those born on it are well–liked but are difficult to know really well.

7–Flower

This is the seventh day of the 13–day period beginning with 1–Ocelot. These are creative people who deeply understand the human condition. They explore human relationships with incisive intellect.

8–Flower

This is the eighth day of the 13–day period beginning with 1–Reed. Teachers and instructors are born on this day. However, their perspective on life tends to be somewhat authoritative or opinionated.

9–Flower

This is the ninth day of the 13–day period beginning with 1–Grass. These people don't want to hurt others, but often do so unintentionally. They tend to fall deeply in love but frequently suffer for it. They can be very artistic and popular, and very concerned with helping others.

10–Flower

This is the tenth day of the 13–day period beginning with the day 1–Monkey. Those born on this day are usually artistic and creative and will seek the limelight. They perform well, are charismatic, make excellent teachers, and generally tend to attract attention to themselves.

11–Flower
This is the eleventh day of the 13–day period beginning with 1–Dog. Loyalty and devotion to another or to a cause characterizes these sensitive and intelligent people. They strive to realize a collective ideal and generally see things in terms of the bigger picture.

12–Flower
This is the twelfth day of the 13–day period beginning with 1–Water. Over–emotional and idealistic, these people have serious difficulties in close relationships. Their drives are powerful and hard to repress.

13–Flower
This is the last day of the 13–day period beginning with 1–Rabbit. Those born on this day are very sociable and flirtatious but are also competitive. They have a strong political sense and make good entertainers and performers.

Notables born under Flower

1 – Mary Shelley, Alfred Kinsey, Jesse Owens, Roman Polanski, Calvin Klein

2 – William Blake, Hermann Hesse, Rachel Carson, Rosa Parks, Peter Fonda, Kenneth Starr, Mark Spitz, Jesse Ventura, Greg Louganis

3 – Victor Hugo, Mary Martin, Ariel Sharon, Fats Domino, Tonya Harding

4 – Norman Rockwell, Vicente Fox, James Taylor, Linda Hamilton, Sandra Bullock

5 – Max Weber, William Shatner, Abbie Hoffman, Bruce Springsteen

6 – Alfred Nobel, Octavio Paz, Groucho Marx, Gerald Ford, Dizzy Gillespie

7 – Ray Charles, Ken Kesey, Linda Schele, Leonardo DiCaprio

8 – Vincent Van Gogh, Frank Capra, Lloyd Bridges, Warren Beatty, Douglas Adams, Norah Jones

9 – C.S. Lewis, Ray Davies, Steve Jobs, Adam Carolla

10 – Maria Mitchell, Harold Urey, Pope John Paul II, Yogi Berra, Lynn Margulis

11 – Mary Baker Eddy, Albert Einstein, John Lee Hooker, Mikhail Gorbachev

12 – Albert Schweitzer, Tommy Chong, Patrick Swayze, Michelle Pfeiffer, Meg Ryan

13 – Helen Hayes, Bob Dole, Francis Crick, Bobby Darin, Ron Howard

The 13–Day Periods – Trecena

The day–sign itself seems to describe the most visible aspects of the personality. In some respects, it covers some of the same territory in the map of the self that the Sun and the Ascendant do in traditional Western astrology. It takes the Sun about 13 days to cover the same stretch of sky as the Moon does in only 1 day, an astronomical fact that links symbolically the 13–day period and the Moon. The 13–day period that a day–sign falls into does seem to have a lunar quality, that is, it describes some of the subconscious aspects of the personality.

Below are some delineations for the twenty 13–day periods that cover personal characteristics and also general social trends that may be observed during each trecena. The personal delineations should be used as a supplement to the comments made for each numbered day–sign that follow the main delineations of the day–signs. Keep in mind that a person's needs, interests, instinctive responses and general emotional patterns are probably indicated more accurately by the 13–day period they were born in than by their day–sign. The general trends of each 13–day period are often observable in the news, but also in the general social patterns of any large group. This suggests that the trecena are actually designating collective variations.

Notice that the order of the 13–day periods differs from that of the day–signs. The order below is the actual order of the periods beginning with the day 1–Crocodile. Remember that the last day of the 13–day period ruled by 1–Crocodile is 13–Reed, and the next day is 1–Ocelot, which occupies the second place in the list below. A glance at Table III will make this clear.

1–Crocodile
Beneath the surface personality is an emotional powerhouse. These people have strong creative urges and feel an instinctive need to nurture others. For many, this is a desire to have a family to protect, though this need can also be met through pets and friends. Those born during this period can be very dominating, in an unconscious way, and others may have problems with this. Collectively, this is a time when people struggle for security. Nationalism, schools, children, and family issues are often in

the news. Creativity is enhanced during this period which was ruled by the creator god/goddess of the ancient Mexicans.

1–Ocelot
Beneath the surface personality is an explorer of the human condition, a communicator, and a person who struggles with self–control. Critical events, such as deaths or other powerful transformations, may have caused them to turn inward and keep much to themselves. They need to be realistic about responsibilities because they tend to either shirk them or take on more than they can handle. Collectively, control over the passions seems to be the issue during this period. Reckless and prideful behaviors create problems, but psychological and technical insight finds solutions.

1–Deer
Beneath their surface personalities these people struggle with freedom versus security issues. Part of them wants to take off for parts unknown, but the rest of them wants the security of home and family. Because the struggle with this conflict leads them to unique solutions, they often become innovators of sorts, or at least creators of a somewhat unconventional lifestyle for themselves. Frequently, they have unusual interests that are of an investigative or searching nature. In ancient times, when might and power ruled, this 1–Deer was said to be a time of peaceful, even timid, behaviors. Today, it appears that sensitivity to others, and the equality of the sexes, are important themes for groups when this 13–day period is in effect.

1–Flower
Beneath the surface personality lies a self that is very romantic and attracted to a glamorous lifestyle. These people may find success in life as a performer, or as a "personality." Their greatest weakness is in matters of relationships. In this area they tend to be idealistic and often make poor choices that lead to many problems. Collectively, this is a time for demonstrating commitment to an ideal. It is a time of social progress and the settling of scores. People tend to respond to their feelings more during its influence making it a fine time for religion and the arts. This period was ruled by a coyote–like god known for wild dancing and irresponsible sexual activities.

1–Reed
Beneath the surface personality is a person who seeks to constantly improve themselves. They have a strong need to conquer their enemies and to achieve their objectives. While they make good teachers and role models, they also have a tendency to be somewhat self–righteous and overconfident of their own opinions. Strong–minded people are born under this period. Collectively, it is a time for rulings and decrees, treaties, judgments, promoting ideas, airing opinions, and debating policies. In ancient times it was considered an unfortunate period, probably because expressing your own ideas was not a good idea in a tightly controlled society. Its deity was a goddess of storms and chaos.

1–Death
Beneath the surface personality is a strong commitment to the community. These people will sacrifice time for others, though they are often not sure just why it is that they do this. They have an extremely strong sense of tradition and are attracted to history and antiquities. They are, ultimately, very down–to–earth people. This is one of the periods ruled by the Moon itself. Its patron deity was Teccizcatl, the self–sacrificer who actually became the Moon when the present age was created. Collectively, it is a time when people display devotion and dedication to collective causes and populist leaders. It is often a powerful time for the common people.

1–Rain
Beneath the surface personality lies a self that is very dependent on others. They have a strong need to feel that they belong – to feel part of a family. They also have an independent streak that often causes them to spend time alone, or apart from others. In this respect, they contain many internal contradictions. In ancient times this period was feared and considered very unfortunate. It was said to be the time when sorcerers were born and demons came to earth. Typically, crashes, bombings, and takeovers make the news during this period. Openness to nature and the universe is a more positive interpretation. Tlaloc, the great rain god, was its ruler.

1–Grass
Beneath their surface personalities these people have an interest in the deep, dark recesses of the world, the insides of people (medically and psychologically) and other such things that are private or hidden, and may do well in a career that allows them to legitimately explore such areas. Collectively, the settling of differences between individuals and nations, and also matters related to health and illness, often arise during this period. It is a time for healing and understanding in general. The ruler was the goddess Mayahuel and the general tendency during the period is for nurturing and healing to occur. Women or women's issues are prominent now also.

1–Serpent
Beneath the surface personality is a person who struggles with powerful inner conflicts. This internal wrestling often leads to taking some rather committed positions on issues. When these people get going, they play hardball, and others may think them a bit fanatical at times, or somewhat extremist. They seem to know intuitively what they have to do in life – even though they may not be able to express it logically. This period favors merchants and warriors and is a good time for traveling, for launching an expedition, or for going "boldly where none have gone before." In ancient Mexico soldiers marched to distant battles during this period. What we find today are confrontations, daring discoveries, and revelations of secrecy making the news.

1–Knife
Beneath the surface personality is a person seeking out powerful and transformative experiences. They are willing to go the distance in order to stimulate changes in themselves and in others. They are restless, and possibly a bit unstable in ways, but they are persistent and quite devoted to their calling in life. At times, they will take risks that may even be life–threatening – or they are attracted to others that do so. Collectively, demonstrations of competency often occur during this period. It was considered to be a time when skillful leaders emerged, or were born, and this still seems to be true. It is certainly a time for making choices and decisions. It was during this Trecena (August 15 – 28, 1998) that President Clinton made a public admission of his affair

with Monica Lewinsky. This was certainly a challenging time for him regarding leadership.

1–Monkey
Beneath the surface personality is a strong need to be in the limelight, or at least to gain the attention of the public. There is something of the politician in these people and they are instinctively attracted to activities like teaching, performance, and presentations of all kinds. They love to play and usually have several hobbies that keep them busy when they are not working. Collectively, this is a time favorable for artists, musicians, dancers, and other creative types. Likewise, it favors activities that involve good taste and innovation. It is also a time of posturing and drama in politics. Traditionally, a second theme has to do with the diagnosis of disease and healing.

1–Lizard
Beneath the surface personality are strong needs for attention and recognition. The reactive self is creatively alive and seeks outlets for this energy. These people are often leaders of sorts, and often with some charisma. Others admire them for their confidence and willingness to take a stand. According to ancient Mexican sources this was one of the more positive periods. Collectively, it does seem to favor youth and also great performances. People born now are said to be lucky and able to prosper without much effort. There is a premature side to its influence, however, and for all the show, strong actions taken during this period tend to fail.

1–Earthquake
Beneath the surface personality is a dreamer. These people have a fertile imagination and often find ways to make fantasy pay off for them. They may excel at one of the arts, or at least have a great appreciation for them. Their ability to find ways to practically apply their ideas, bridging the gap from fantasy to fact, is their greatest asset. Collectively, this is a serious time, said to be favorable only to those who did their penances. Tlazolteotl, a confession goddess, was the patron deity. Today it seems to be a time when political conditions become destabilized – reforms are in the works and boundaries are shifting and changing.

1–Dog
Beneath the surface personality is a person who is most consistent in belief and loyalty. They will continue with a program or activity for years and can be an inspiration to others – but they can also be extremely stubborn. No matter how unconventional their lifestyle, once committed to it, they are there for life. In ancient times this period was considered quite fortunate, a time when successful people were born. This seems to be (more or less) the case today, making it a good time for celebrations and cooperation on the collective level.

1–House
Beneath the surface personality is a deep need for very secure foundations. These security needs may be intellectual, as in science or religion, or they may be material, as in possession of valuables. Whether such people seek mental or economic security, they usually have high standards to meet and uphold. Collectively, this is a darker period, one said to be a time of trouble and vice. The patron deity was a goddess who haunted people in their sleep. Secret financial dealings, spy cases, group paranoia, and other such things may come to light during this time. It's probably a good time to come clean with the truth and not hide anything.

1–Vulture
Beneath the surface personality is a person of strong will, not easily convinced by others. They have high standards and tend to keep themselves above–it–all and beyond criticism. They have a deep fear of rejection and are often troubled by guilt, both of which have a strong effect on their sense of self–worth. Most are probably quite talented, or very knowledgeable, and have much to offer in the world. In some cases, however, they feel overshadowed in life by others. Collectively, this is a time of tough decisions and testing; easy for those who are realistic and self–controlled, not so good for the sensitive or weak. It is often a time of hard–ball politics. During this period we come to realize what is real and what is not. Some get depressed, others get to work.

1–Water
Beneath the surface personality is a strong will propelled by powerful, irrational urges. These people do things in life without a rational

explanation – just because they have to do them. They find it necessary to keep themselves under control much of the time, or they may risk offending others who don't understand them. They would be well advised to choose their friends very carefully for this reason. It seems that in ancient times this period was considered to be difficult, if not just plain unfortunate. It appears today, however, that this is a time when collectively we must deal with the messy aspects of life as well as our own negative emotions. Those who are unstable emotionally will be affected the most during this trecena, though it generally indicates a need for collective ventilation.

1–Wind
Beneath the surface personality are strong communication motivations. For some, this urge or interest may lead to a life of teaching or performing. Those born during this period are carriers of ideas, people with a message to get across. They will always be instinctively drawn to activities that will meet such needs. Collectively this can be a fickle and restless period, one during which spiritual, strange, and even unstable people make the news or influence events. It is also a time when control is weak, deviations occur, experiments are undertaken, and barriers are smashed.

1–Eagle
Beneath the surface personality is a person with powerful faculties of discrimination. They know how to express such distinctions and are often outstanding at articulating their feelings and emotions, or at least focusing them through a creative or artistic project. They are also somewhat psychic and find that their unconscious is their best friend, once they know how to listen to it. Collectively, it is a time that favors self–interest. Rash decisions and actions, usually proven later to be problematic, are often in the news. Everyone seems to do a lot of thinking and talking about details, though few see the big picture.

1–Rabbit
Beneath the surface personality is a competitor and fighter. This aspect of their character may not always be apparent to others – until they get to know them well. They secretly love a confrontation and will take risks in life to create them. These people prefer a life of excitement

rather than one of routine and they should try to meet these needs in a non–destructive way. This period was said to be ruled by Mayahuel, the Moon goddess. Collectively, it is a positive, productive period, a time when the public is moved or very enthusiastic about something. Popular heroes often make news at this time.

Day–Sign Ephemeris and Tables

The Ephemeris of the Day–Signs
Below are two sets of tables. Table I lists the dates for the beginning of each 13–day period from 1900 to 2029. First locate the nearest date preceding your birthday. If you were born on one of the dates listed, then you were born on a day linked with the number 1 and the sign listed is both your day–sign and the ruler of your 13–day period. For you, the calculations are over — just turn to the text description of that sign.

If you were not born on a day in the list, find the nearest date preceding your birthday and determine how many days later you were born. Count the first day as number one. Then turn to Table II. Find the column that begins with the sign that preceded your birthday and count the same number of days down the column to find your day–sign. Your 13–day period is ruled by the sign at the head of the column, the same one you found listed in Table I.

Example #1: For a person born on March 25th, 1900, we would first turn to Table I and locate the nearest previous date listed. The date is March 17th and the sign is 1–Reed. We now know that this person was born during the 13–day period ruled by 1–Reed and that this sign influences their personality. But to find their actual day–sign we must go 9 places ahead because March 25 is nine days ahead of March 17th, counting the 17th as number 1. We then turn to Table II and find the column beginning with 1–Reed. Counting down nine places we come to the day 9–Crocodile, the actual birthday. Our reading of the tables then indicates that this person was born under the day–sign Crocodile, in the 13–day period ruled by Reed.

Example #2: A person born on July 25, 1905 would be born during the 13–day period 1–House, which began on July 19th. Turning to Table II, finding 1–House and counting the 19th as 1, the 25th corresponds to 7–Water. The day–sign is Water, the 13–day period is 1–House.

An Important Note Regarding Birthtimes

For most people born in the continental USA, the ephemeris which forms the second half of this book needs no explanation. Those who were born in Europe or Asia, or close to midnight in the continental USA may want to convert their birth time to Central Standard Time, the time zone of Mexico. In some cases this will involve a change of day. For example, take someone born in Japan at 2 AM on January 1st. At that moment, it was 11 AM in Mexico, December 31st. Experience indicates that they are best described by the day–sign on the 31st. The following table, listing the necessary change from the birth time, will help you make this calculation.

Eastern Time: –1 hour
Central Time: no change
Mountain Time: +1 hour
Pacific Time: +2 hours
Greenwich Mean Time: –6 hours
Middle European Time: –7 hours
Time Zone 8 (China, Philippines): –14 hours
Time Zone 9 (Japan): –15 hours
Time Zone 10 (Eastern Australia): –16 hours

Another adjustment to the time of birth is necessary if Daylight Savings Time was in effect. If you were born during Daylight Savings Time subtract one hour from your recorded birth time. Daylight Savings Time has changed over the years but until 1988 began on the last Sunday of April and ended on the last Sunday of October. During World War I and II the entire country was on continuous daylight savings time. A few peculiarities about Daylight Savings Time are:

a. Most of the United States adopted it after WW II.
b. Prior to the late 1950s, it ran from the last Sunday in April to the last Sunday in September. Around 1955 many states added an extra month, ending it on the last Sunday in October.
c. One exception was made during the first energy crisis. In 1974 it began on January 6th, and in 1975 on February 23rd.
d. In 1988 a new law was passed having it begin on the first Sunday in April.

Table I – Ephemeris of the 13–Day Periods

Jan 11 1900   1 Rabbit
Jan 24 1900   1 Crocodile
Feb 6 1900   1 Ocelot
Feb 19 1900   1 Deer
Mar 4 1900   1 Flower
Mar 17 1900   1 Reed
Mar 30 1900   1 Death
Apr 12 1900   1 Rain
Apr 25 1900   1 Grass
May 8 1900   1 Serpent
May 21 1900   1 Knife
Jun 3 1900   1 Monkey
Jun 16 1900   1 Lizard
Jun 29 1900   1 Earthquake
Jul 12 1900   1 Dog
Jul 25 1900   1 House
Aug 7 1900   1 Vulture
Aug 20 1900   1 Water
Sep 2 1900   1 Wind
Sep 15 1900   1 Eagle
Sep 28 1900   1 Rabbit
Oct 11 1900   1 Crocodile
Oct 24 1900   1 Ocelot
Nov 6 1900   1 Deer
Nov 19 1900   1 Flower
Dec 2 1900   1 Reed
Dec 15 1900   1 Death
Dec 28 1900   1 Rain

Jan 10 1901   1 Grass
Jan 23 1901   1 Serpent
Feb 5 1901   1 Knife
Feb 18 1901   1 Monkey
Mar 3 1901   1 Lizard
Mar 16 1901   1 Earthquake
Mar 29 1901   1 Dog
Apr 11 1901   1 House
Apr 24 1901   1 Vulture
May 7 1901   1 Water
May 20 1901   1 Wind
Jun 2 1901   1 Eagle
Jun 15 1901   1 Rabbit
Jun 28 1901   1 Crocodile
Jul 11 1901   1 Ocelot
Jul 24 1901   1 Deer
Aug 6 1901   1 Flower
Aug 19 1901   1 Reed
Sep 1 1901   1 Death
Sep 14 1901   1 Rain
Sep 27 1901   1 Grass
Oct 10 1901   1 Serpent
Oct 23 1901   1 Knife
Nov 5 1901   1 Monkey
Nov 18 1901   1 Lizard
Dec 1 1901   1 Earthquake
Dec 14 1901   1 Dog
Dec 27 1901   1 House

Jan 9 1902   1 Vulture
Jan 22 1902   1 Water
Feb 4 1902   1 Wind
Feb 17 1902   1 Eagle
Mar 2 1902   1 Rabbit
Mar 15 1902   1 Crocodile
Mar 28 1902   1 Ocelot
Apr 10 1902   1 Deer
Apr 23 1902   1 Flower
May 6 1902   1 Reed
May 19 1902   1 Death
Jun 1 1902   1 Rain

Jun 14 1902   1 Grass
Jun 27 1902   1 Serpent
Jul 10 1902   1 Knife
Jul 23 1902   1 Monkey
Aug 5 1902   1 Lizard
Aug 18 1902   1 Earthquake
Aug 31 1902   1 Dog
Sep 13 1902   1 House
Sep 26 1902   1 Vulture
Oct 9 1902   1 Water
Oct 22 1902   1 Wind
Nov 4 1902   1 Eagle
Nov 17 1902   1 Rabbit
Nov 30 1902   1 Crocodile
Dec 13 1902   1 Ocelot
Dec 26 1902   1 Deer

Jan 8 1903   1 Flower
Jan 21 1903   1 Reed
Feb 3 1903   1 Death
Feb 16 1903   1 Rain
Mar 1 1903   1 Grass
Mar 14 1903   1 Serpent
Mar 27 1903   1 Knife
Apr 9 1903   1 Monkey
Apr 22 1903   1 Lizard
May 5 1903   1 Earthquake
May 18 1903   1 Dog
May 31 1903   1 House
Jun 13 1903   1 Vulture
Jun 26 1903   1 Water
Jul 9 1903   1 Wind
Jul 22 1903   1 Eagle
Aug 4 1903   1 Rabbit
Aug 17 1903   1 Crocodile

174 Day–Signs

Aug 30 1903 1 Ocelot	Dec 10 1904 1 Wind	Mar 10 1906 1 Earthquake
Sep 12 1903 1 Deer	Dec 23 1904 1 Eagle	Mar 23 1906 1 Dog
Sep 25 1903 1 Flower		Apr 5 1906 1 House
Oct 8 1903 1 Reed	Jan 5 1905 1 Rabbit	Apr 18 1906 1 Vulture
Oct 21 1903 1 Death	Jan 18 1905 1 Crocodile	May 1 1906 1 Water
Nov 3 1903 1 Rain	Jan 31 1905 1 Ocelot	May 14 1906 1 Wind
Nov 16 1903 1 Grass	Feb 13 1905 1 Deer	May 27 1906 1 Eagle
Nov 29 1903 1 Serpent	Feb 26 1905 1 Flower	Jun 9 1906 1 Rabbit
Dec 12 1903 1 Knife	Mar 11 1905 1 Reed	Jun 22 1906 1 Crocodile
Dec 25 1903 1 Monkey	Mar 24 1905 1 Death	Jul 5 1906 1 Ocelot
	Apr 6 1905 1 Rain	Jul 18 1906 1 Deer
Jan 7 1904 1 Lizard	Apr 19 1905 1 Grass	Jul 31 1906 1 Flower
Jan 20 1904 1 Earthquake	May 2 1905 1 Serpent	Aug 13 1906 1 Reed
Feb 2 1904 1 Dog	May 15 1905 1 Knife	Aug 26 1906 1 Death
Feb 15 1904 1 House	May 28 1905 1 Monkey	Sep 8 1906 1 Rain
Feb 28 1904 1 Vulture	Jun 10 1905 1 Lizard	Sep 21 1906 1 Grass
Mar 12 1904 1 Water	Jun 23 1905 1 Earthquake	Oct 4 1906 1 Serpent
Mar 25 1904 1 Wind	Jul 6 1905 1 Dog	Oct 17 1906 1 Knife
Apr 7 1904 1 Eagle	Jul 19 1905 1 House	Oct 30 1906 1 Monkey
Apr 20 1904 1 Rabbit	Aug 1 1905 1 Vulture	Nov 12 1906 1 Lizard
May 3 1904 1 Crocodile	Aug 14 1905 1 Water	Nov 25 1906 1 Earthquake
May 16 1904 1 Ocelot	Aug 27 1905 1 Wind	Dec 8 1906 1 Dog
May 29 1904 1 Deer	Sep 9 1905 1 Eagle	Dec 21 1906 1 House
Jun 11 1904 1 Flower	Sep 22 1905 1 Rabbit	
Jun 24 1904 1 Reed	Oct 5 1905 1 Crocodile	Jan 3 1907 1 Vulture
Jul 7 1904 1 Death	Oct 18 1905 1 Ocelot	Jan 16 1907 1 Water
Jul 20 1904 1 Rain	Oct 31 1905 1 Deer	Jan 29 1907 1 Wind
Aug 2 1904 1 Grass	Nov 13 1905 1 Flower	Feb 11 1907 1 Eagle
Aug 15 1904 1 Serpent	Nov 26 1905 1 Reed	Feb 24 1907 1 Rabbit
Aug 28 1904 1 Knife	Dec 9 1905 1 Death	Mar 9 1907 1 Crocodile
Sep 10 1904 1 Monkey	Dec 22 1905 1 Rain	Mar 22 1907 1 Ocelot
Sep 23 1904 1 Lizard		Apr 4 1907 1 Deer
Oct 6 1904 1 Earthquake	Jan 4 1906 1 Grass	Apr 17 1907 1 Flower
Oct 19 1904 1 Dog	Jan 17 1906 1 Serpent	Apr 30 1907 1 Reed
Nov 1 1904 1 House	Jan 30 1906 1 Knife	May 13 1907 1 Death
Nov 14 1904 1 Vulture	Feb 12 1906 1 Monkey	May 26 1907 1 Rain
Nov 27 1904 1 Water	Feb 25 1906 1 Lizard	Jun 8 1907 1 Grass

The Ephemeris of the Day–Signs 175

Jun 21 1907	1 Serpent	Oct 1 1908	1 Reed	Jan 12 1910	1 Crocodile
Jul 4 1907	1 Knife	Oct 14 1908	1 Death	Jan 25 1910	1 Ocelot
Jul 17 1907	1 Monkey	Oct 27 1908	1 Rain	Feb 7 1910	1 Deer
Jul 30 1907	1 Lizard	Nov 9 1908	1 Grass	Feb 20 1910	1 Flower
Aug 12 1907	1 Earthquake	Nov 22 1908	1 Serpent	Mar 5 1910	1 Reed
Aug 25 1907	1 Dog	Dec 5 1908	1 Knife	Mar 18 1910	1 Death
Sep 7 1907	1 House	Dec 18 1908	1 Monkey	Mar 31 1910	1 Rain
Sep 20 1907	1 Vulture	Dec 31 1908	1 Lizard	Apr 13 1910	1 Grass
Oct 3 1907	1 Water			Apr 26 1910	1 Serpent
Oct 16 1907	1 Wind	Jan 13 1909	1 Earthquake	May 9 1910	1 Knife
Oct 29 1907	1 Eagle	Jan 26 1909	1 Dog	May 22 1910	1 Monkey
Nov 11 1907	1 Rabbit	Feb 8 1909	1 House	Jun 4 1910	1 Lizard
Nov 24 1907	1 Crocodile	Feb 21 1909	1 Vulture	Jun 17 1910	1 Earthquake
Dec 7 1907	1 Ocelot	Mar 6 1909	1 Water	Jun 30 1910	1 Dog
Dec 20 1907	1 Deer	Mar 19 1909	1 Wind	Jul 13 1910	1 House
		Apr 1 1909	1 Eagle	Jul 26 1910	1 Vulture
Jan 2 1908	1 Flower	Apr 14 1909	1 Rabbit	Aug 8 1910	1 Water
Jan 15 1908	1 Reed	Apr 27 1909	1 Crocodile	Aug 21 1910	1 Wind
Jan 28 1908	1 Death	May 10 1909	1 Ocelot	Sep 3 1910	1 Eagle
Feb 10 1908	1 Rain	May 23 1909	1 Deer	Sep 16 1910	1 Rabbit
Feb 23 1908	1 Grass	Jun 5 1909	1 Flower	Sep 29 1910	1 Crocodile
Mar 7 1908	1 Serpent	Jun 18 1909	1 Reed	Oct 12 1910	1 Ocelot
Mar 20 1908	1 Knife	Jul 1 1909	1 Death	Oct 25 1910	1 Deer
Apr 2 1908	1 Monkey	Jul 14 1909	1 Rain	Nov 7 1910	1 Flower
Apr 15 1908	1 Lizard	Jul 27 1909	1 Grass	Nov 20 1910	1 Reed
Apr 28 1908	1 Earthquake	Aug 9 1909	1 Serpent	Dec 3 1910	1 Death
May 11 1908	1 Dog	Aug 22 1909	1 Knife	Dec 16 1910	1 Rain
May 24 1908	1 House	Sep 4 1909	1 Monkey	Dec 29 1910	1 Grass
Jun 6 1908	1 Vulture	Sep 17 1909	1 Lizard		
Jun 19 1908	1 Water	Sep 30 1909	1 Earthquake	Jan 11 1911	1 Serpent
Jul 2 1908	1 Wind	Oct 13 1909	1 Dog	Jan 24 1911	1 Knife
Jul 15 1908	1 Eagle	Oct 26 1909	1 House	Feb 6 1911	1 Monkey
Jul 28 1908	1 Rabbit	Nov 8 1909	1 Vulture	Feb 19 1911	1 Lizard
Aug 10 1908	1 Crocodile	Nov 21 1909	1 Water	Mar 4 1911	1 Earthquake
Aug 23 1908	1 Ocelot	Dec 4 1909	1 Wind	Mar 17 1911	1 Dog
Sep 5 1908	1 Deer	Dec 17 1909	1 Eagle	Mar 30 1911	1 House
Sep 18 1908	1 Flower	Dec 30 1909	1 Rabbit	Apr 12 1911	1 Vulture

176   Day–Signs

Apr 25 1911 1 Water	Aug 5 1912 1 Earthquake	Nov 16 1913 1 Serpent
May 8 1911 1 Wind	Aug 18 1912 1 Dog	Nov 29 1913 1 Knife
May 21 1911 1 Eagle	Aug 31 1912 1 House	Dec 12 1913 1 Monkey
Jun 3 1911 1 Rabbit	Sep 13 1912 1 Vulture	Dec 25 1913 1 Lizard
Jun 16 1911 1 Crocodile	Sep 26 1912 1 Water	
Jun 29 1911 1 Ocelot	Oct 9 1912 1 Wind	Jan 7 1914 1 Earthquake
Jul 12 1911 1 Deer	Oct 22 1912 1 Eagle	Jan 20 1914 1 Dog
Jul 25 1911 1 Flower	Nov 4 1912 1 Rabbit	Feb 2 1914 1 House
Aug 7 1911 1 Reed	Nov 17 1912 1 Crocodile	Feb 15 1914 1 Vulture
Aug 20 1911 1 Death	Nov 30 1912 1 Ocelot	Feb 28 1914 1 Water
Sep 2 1911 1 Rain	Dec 13 1912 1 Deer	Mar 13 1914 1 Wind
Sep 15 1911 1 Grass	Dec 26 1912 1 Flower	Mar 26 1914 1 Eagle
Sep 28 1911 1 Serpent		Apr 8 1914 1 Rabbit
Oct 11 1911 1 Knife	Jan 8 1913 1 Reed	Apr 21 1914 1 Crocodile
Oct 24 1911 1 Monkey	Jan 21 1913 1 Death	May 4 1914 1 Ocelot
Nov 6 1911 1 Lizard	Feb 3 1913 1 Rain	May 17 1914 1 Deer
Nov 19 1911 1 Earthquake	Feb 16 1913 1 Grass	May 30 1914 1 Flower
Dec 2 1911 1 Dog	Mar 1 1913 1 Serpent	Jun 12 1914 1 Reed
Dec 15 1911 1 House	Mar 14 1913 1 Knife	Jun 25 1914 1 Death
Dec 28 1911 1 Vulture	Mar 27 1913 1 Monkey	Jul 8 1914 1 Rain
	Apr 9 1913 1 Lizard	Jul 21 1914 1 Grass
Jan 10 1912 1 Water	Apr 22 1913 1 Earthquake	Aug 3 1914 1 Serpent
Jan 23 1912 1 Wind	May 5 1913 1 Dog	Aug 16 1914 1 Knife
Feb 5 1912 1 Eagle	May 18 1913 1 House	Aug 29 1914 1 Monkey
Feb 18 1912 1 Rabbit	May 31 1913 1 Vulture	Sep 11 1914 1 Lizard
Mar 2 1912 1 Crocodile	Jun 13 1913 1 Water	Sep 24 1914 1 Earthquake
Mar 15 1912 1 Ocelot	Jun 26 1913 1 Wind	Oct 7 1914 1 Dog
Mar 28 1912 1 Deer	Jul 9 1913 1 Eagle	Oct 20 1914 1 House
Apr 10 1912 1 Flower	Jul 22 1913 1 Rabbit	Nov 2 1914 1 Vulture
Apr 23 1912 1 Reed	Aug 4 1913 1 Crocodile	Nov 15 1914 1 Water
May 6 1912 1 Death	Aug 17 1913 1 Ocelot	Nov 28 1914 1 Wind
May 19 1912 1 Rain	Aug 30 1913 1 Deer	Dec 11 1914 1 Eagle
Jun 1 1912 1 Grass	Sep 12 1913 1 Flower	Dec 24 1914 1 Rabbit
Jun 14 1912 1 Serpent	Sep 25 1913 1 Reed	
Jun 27 1912 1 Knife	Oct 8 1913 1 Death	Jan 6 1915 1 Crocodile
Jul 10 1912 1 Monkey	Oct 21 1913 1 Rain	Jan 19 1915 1 Ocelot
Jul 23 1912 1 Lizard	Nov 3 1913 1 Grass	Feb 1 1915 1 Deer

The Ephemeris of the Day–Signs   177

Feb 14 1915 1 Flower	Jun 9 1916 1 Crocodile	Sep 20 1917 1 Water
Feb 27 1915 1 Reed	Jun 22 1916 1 Ocelot	Oct 3 1917 1 Wind
Mar 12 1915 1 Death	Jul 5 1916 1 Deer	Oct 16 1917 1 Eagle
Mar 25 1915 1 Rain	Jul 18 1916 1 Flower	Oct 29 1917 1 Rabbit
Apr 7 1915 1 Grass	Jul 31 1916 1 Reed	Nov 11 1917 1 Crocodile
Apr 20 1915 1 Serpent	Aug 13 1916 1 Death	Nov 24 1917 1 Ocelot
May 3 1915 1 Knife	Aug 26 1916 1 Rain	Dec 7 1917 1 Deer
May 16 1915 1 Monkey	Sep 8 1916 1 Grass	Dec 20 1917 1 Flower
May 29 1915 1 Lizard	Sep 21 1916 1 Serpent	
Jun 11 1915 1 Earthquake	Oct 4 1916 1 Knife	Jan 2 1918 1 Reed
Jul 7 1915 1 House	Oct 17 1916 1 Monkey	Jan 15 1918 1 Death
Jul 20 1915 1 Vulture	Oct 30 1916 1 Lizard	Jan 28 1918 1 Rain
Aug 2 1915 1 Water	Nov 12 1916 1 Earthquake	Feb 10 1918 1 Grass
Aug 15 1915 1 Wind	Nov 25 1916 1 Dog	Feb 23 1918 1 Serpent
Aug 28 1915 1 Eagle	Dec 8 1916 1 House	Mar 8 1918 1 Knife
Sep 10 1915 1 Rabbit	Dec 21 1916 1 Vulture	Mar 21 1918 1 Monkey
Sep 23 1915 1 Crocodile		Apr 3 1918 1 Lizard
Oct 6 1915 1 Ocelot	Jan 3 1917 1 Water	Apr 16 1918 1 Earthquake
Oct 19 1915 1 Deer	Jan 16 1917 1 Wind	Apr 29 1918 1 Dog
Nov 1 1915 1 Flower	Jan 29 1917 1 Eagle	May 12 1918 1 House
Nov 14 1915 1 Reed	Feb 11 1917 1 Rabbit	May 25 1918 1 Vulture
Nov 27 1915 1 Death	Feb 24 1917 1 Crocodile	Jun 7 1918 1 Water
Dec 10 1915 1 Rain	Mar 9 1917 1 Ocelot	Jun 20 1918 1 Wind
Dec 23 1915 1 Grass	Mar 22 1917 1 Deer	Jul 3 1918 1 Eagle
	Apr 4 1917 1 Flower	Jul 16 1918 1 Rabbit
Jan 5 1916 1 Serpent	Apr 17 1917 1 Reed	Jul 29 1918 1 Crocodile
Jan 18 1916 1 Knife	Apr 30 1917 1 Death	Aug 11 1918 1 Ocelot
Jan 31 1916 1 Monkey	May 13 1917 1 Rain	Aug 24 1918 1 Deer
Feb 13 1916 1 Lizard	May 26 1917 1 Grass	Sep 6 1918 1 Flower
Feb 26 1916 1 Earthquake	Jun 8 1917 1 Serpent	Sep 19 1918 1 Reed
Mar 10 1916 1 Dog	Jun 21 1917 1 Knife	Oct 2 1918 1 Death
Mar 23 1916 1 House	Jul 4 1917 1 Monkey	Oct 15 1918 1 Rain
Apr 5 1916 1 Vulture	Jul 17 1917 1 Lizard	Oct 28 1918 1 Grass
Apr 18 1916 1 Water	Jul 30 1917 1 Earthquake	Nov 10 1918 1 Serpent
May 1 1916 1 Wind	Aug 12 1917 1 Dog	Nov 23 1918 1 Knife
May 14 1916 1 Eagle	Aug 25 1917 1 House	Dec 6 1918 1 Monkey
May 27 1916 1 Rabbit	Sep 7 1917 1 Vulture	Dec 19 1918 1 Lizard

Day–Signs

Jan 1 1919 1 Earthquake	Apr 13 1920 1 Serpent	Jul 25 1921 1 Reed
Jan 14 1919 1 Dog	Apr 26 1920 1 Knife	Aug 7 1921 1 Death
Jan 27 1919 1 House	May 9 1920 1 Monkey	Aug 20 1921 1 Rain
Feb 9 1919 1 Vulture	May 22 1920 1 Lizard	Sep 2 1921 1 Grass
Feb 22 1919 1 Water	Jun 4 1920 1 Earthquake	Sep 15 1921 1 Serpent
Mar 7 1919 1 Wind	Jun 17 1920 1 Dog	Sep 28 1921 1 Knife
Mar 20 1919 1 Eagle	Jun 30 1920 1 House	Oct 11 1921 1 Monkey
Apr 2 1919 1 Rabbit	Jul 13 1920 1 Vulture	Oct 24 1921 1 Lizard
Apr 15 1919 1 Crocodile	Jul 26 1920 1 Water	Nov 6 1921 1 Earthquake
Apr 28 1919 1 Ocelot	Aug 8 1920 1 Wind	Nov 19 1921 1 Dog
May 11 1919 1 Deer	Aug 21 1920 1 Eagle	Dec 2 1921 1 House
May 24 1919 1 Flower	Sep 3 1920 1 Rabbit	Dec 15 1921 1 Vulture
Jun 6 1919 1 Reed	Sep 16 1920 1 Crocodile	Dec 28 1921 1 Water
Jun 19 1919 1 Death	Sep 29 1920 1 Ocelot	
Jul 2 1919 1 Rain	Oct 12 1920 1 Deer	Jan 10 1922 1 Wind
Jul 15 1919 1 Grass	Oct 25 1920 1 Flower	Jan 23 1922 1 Eagle
Jul 28 1919 1 Serpent	Nov 7 1920 1 Reed	Feb 5 1922 1 Rabbit
Aug 10 1919 1 Knife	Nov 20 1920 1 Death	Feb 18 1922 1 Crocodile
Aug 23 1919 1 Monkey	Dec 3 1920 1 Rain	Mar 3 1922 1 Ocelot
Sep 5 1919 1 Lizard	Dec 16 1920 1 Grass	Mar 16 1922 1 Deer
Sep 18 1919 1 Earthquake	Dec 29 1920 1 Serpent	Mar 29 1922 1 Flower
Oct 1 1919 1 Dog		Apr 11 1922 1 Reed
Oct 14 1919 1 House	Jan 11 1921 1 Knife	Apr 24 1922 1 Death
Oct 27 1919 1 Vulture	Jan 24 1921 1 Monkey	May 7 1922 1 Rain
Nov 9 1919 1 Water	Feb 6 1921 1 Lizard	May 20 1922 1 Grass
Nov 22 1919 1 Wind	Feb 19 1921 1 Earthquake	Jun 2 1922 1 Serpent
Dec 5 1919 1 Eagle	Mar 4 1921 1 Dog	Jun 15 1922 1 Knife
Dec 18 1919 1 Rabbit	Mar 17 1921 1 House	Jun 28 1922 1 Monkey
Dec 31 1919 1 Crocodile	Mar 30 1921 1 Vulture	Jul 11 1922 1 Lizard
	Apr 12 1921 1 Water	Jul 24 1922 1 Earthquake
Jan 13 1920 1 Ocelot	Apr 25 1921 1 Wind	Aug 6 1922 1 Dog
Jan 26 1920 1 Deer	May 8 1921 1 Eagle	Aug 19 1922 1 House
Feb 8 1920 1 Flower	May 21 1921 1 Rabbit	Sep 1 1922 1 Vulture
Feb 21 1920 1 Reed	Jun 3 1921 1 Crocodile	Sep 14 1922 1 Water
Mar 5 1920 1 Death	Jun 16 1921 1 Ocelot	Sep 27 1922 1 Wind
Mar 18 1920 1 Rain	Jun 29 1921 1 Deer	Oct 10 1922 1 Eagle
Mar 31 1920 1 Grass	Jul 12 1921 1 Flower	Oct 23 1922 1 Rabbit

The Ephemeris of the Day–Signs

Nov 5 1922 1 Crocodile	Feb 3 1924 1 Vulture	May 16 1925 1 Lizard
Nov 18 1922 1 Ocelot	Feb 16 1924 1 Water	May 29 1925 1 Earthquake
Dec 1 1922 1 Deer	Feb 29 1924 1 Wind	Jun 11 1925 1 Dog
Dec 14 1922 1 Flower	Mar 13 1924 1 Eagle	Jun 24 1925 1 House
Dec 27 1922 1 Reed	Mar 26 1924 1 Rabbit	Jul 7 1925 1 Vulture
	Apr 8 1924 1 Crocodile	Jul 20 1925 1 Water
Jan 9 1923 1 Death	Apr 21 1924 1 Ocelot	Aug 2 1925 1 Wind
Jan 22 1923 1 Rain	May 4 1924 1 Deer	Aug 15 1925 1 Eagle
Feb 4 1923 1 Grass	May 17 1924 1 Flower	Aug 28 1925 1 Rabbit
Feb 17 1923 1 Serpent	May 30 1924 1 Reed	Sep 10 1925 1 Crocodile
Mar 2 1923 1 Knife	Jun 12 1924 1 Death	Sep 23 1925 1 Ocelot
Mar 15 1923 1 Monkey	Jun 25 1924 1 Rain	Oct 6 1925 1 Deer
Mar 28 1923 1 Lizard	Jul 8 1924 1 Grass	Oct 19 1925 1 Flower
Apr 10 1923 1 Earthquake	Jul 21 1924 1 Serpent	Nov 1 1925 1 Reed
Apr 23 1923 1 Dog	Aug 3 1924 1 Knife	Nov 14 1925 1 Death
May 6 1923 1 House	Aug 16 1924 1 Monkey	Nov 27 1925 1 Rain
May 19 1923 1 Vulture	Aug 29 1924 1 Lizard	Dec 10 1925 1 Grass
Jun 1 1923 1 Water	Sep 11 1924 1 Earthquake	Dec 23 1925 1 Serpent
Jun 14 1923 1 Wind	Sep 24 1924 1 Dog	
Jun 27 1923 1 Eagle	Oct 7 1924 1 House	Jan 5 1926 1 Knife
Jul 10 1923 1 Rabbit	Oct 20 1924 1 Vulture	Jan 18 1926 1 Monkey
Jul 23 1923 1 Crocodile	Nov 2 1924 1 Water	Jan 31 1926 1 Lizard
Aug 5 1923 1 Ocelot	Nov 15 1924 1 Wind	Feb 13 1926 1 Earthquake
Aug 18 1923 1 Deer	Nov 28 1924 1 Eagle	Feb 26 1926 1 Dog
Aug 31 1923 1 Flower	Dec 11 1924 1 Rabbit	Mar 11 1926 1 House
Sep 13 1923 1 Reed	Dec 24 1924 1 Crocodile	Mar 24 1926 1 Vulture
Sep 26 1923 1 Death		Apr 6 1926 1 Water
Oct 9 1923 1 Rain	Jan 6 1925 1 Ocelot	Apr 19 1926 1 Wind
Oct 22 1923 1 Grass	Jan 19 1925 1 Deer	May 2 1926 1 Eagle
Nov 4 1923 1 Serpent	Feb 1 1925 1 Flower	May 15 1926 1 Rabbit
Nov 17 1923 1 Knife	Feb 14 1925 1 Reed	May 28 1926 1 Crocodile
Nov 30 1923 1 Monkey	Feb 27 1925 1 Death	Jun 10 1926 1 Ocelot
Dec 13 1923 1 Lizard	Mar 12 1925 1 Rain	Jun 23 1926 1 Deer
Dec 26 1923 1 Earthquake	Mar 25 1925 1 Grass	Jul 6 1926 1 Flower
	Apr 7 1925 1 Serpent	Jul 19 1926 1 Reed
Jan 8 1924 1 Dog	Apr 20 1925 1 Knife	Aug 1 1926 1 Death
Jan 21 1924 1 House	May 3 1925 1 Monkey	Aug 14 1926 1 Rain

180 Day–Signs

Aug 27 1926 1 Grass	Dec 8 1927 1 Flower	Mar 7 1929 1 Eagle
Sep 9 1926 1 Serpent	Dec 21 1927 1 Reed	Mar 20 1929 1 Rabbit
Sep 22 1926 1 Knife		Apr 2 1929 1 Crocodile
Oct 5 1926 1 Monkey	Jan 3 1928 1 Death	Apr 15 1929 1 Ocelot
Oct 18 1926 1 Lizard	Jan 16 1928 1 Rain	Apr 28 1929 1 Deer
Oct 31 1926 1 Earthquake	Jan 29 1928 1 Grass	May 11 1929 1 Flower
Nov 13 1926 1 Dog	Feb 11 1928 1 Serpent	May 24 1929 1 Reed
Nov 26 1926 1 House	Feb 24 1928 1 Knife	Jun 6 1929 1 Death
Dec 9 1926 1 Vulture	Mar 8 1928 1 Monkey	Jun 19 1929 1 Rain
Dec 22 1926 1 Water	Mar 21 1928 1 Lizard	Jul 2 1929 1 Grass
	Apr 3 1928 1 Earthquake	Jul 15 1929 1 Serpent
Jan 4 1927 1 Wind	Apr 16 1928 1 Dog	Jul 28 1929 1 Knife
Jan 17 1927 1 Eagle	Apr 29 1928 1 House	Aug 10 1929 1 Monkey
Jan 30 1927 1 Rabbit	May 12 1928 1 Vulture	Aug 23 1929 1 Lizard
Feb 12 1927 1 Crocodile	May 25 1928 1 Water	Sep 5 1929 1 Earthquake
Feb 25 1927 1 Ocelot	Jun 7 1928 1 Wind	Sep 18 1929 1 Dog
Mar 10 1927 1 Deer	Jun 20 1928 1 Eagle	Oct 1 1929 1 House
Mar 23 1927 1 Flower	Jul 3 1928 1 Rabbit	Oct 14 1929 1 Vulture
Apr 5 1927 1 Reed	Jul 16 1928 1 Crocodile	Oct 27 1929 1 Water
Apr 18 1927 1 Death	Jul 29 1928 1 Ocelot	Nov 9 1929 1 Wind
May 1 1927 1 Rain	Aug 11 1928 1 Deer	Nov 22 1929 1 Eagle
May 14 1927 1 Grass	Aug 24 1928 1 Flower	Dec 5 1929 1 Rabbit
May 27 1927 1 Serpent	Sep 6 1928 1 Reed	Dec 18 1929 1 Crocodile
Jun 9 1927 1 Knife	Sep 19 1928 1 Death	Dec 31 1929 1 Ocelot
Jun 22 1927 1 Monkey	Oct 2 1928 1 Rain	
Jul 5 1927 1 Lizard	Oct 15 1928 1 Grass	Jan 13 1930 1 Deer
Jul 18 1927 1 Earthquake	Oct 28 1928 1 Serpent	Jan 26 1930 1 Flower
Jul 31 1927 1 Dog	Nov 10 1928 1 Knife	Feb 8 1930 1 Reed
Aug 13 1927 1 House	Nov 23 1928 1 Monkey	Feb 21 1930 1 Death
Aug 26 1927 1 Vulture	Dec 6 1928 1 Lizard	Mar 6 1930 1 Rain
Sep 8 1927 1 Water	Dec 19 1928 1 Earthquake	Mar 19 1930 1 Grass
Sep 21 1927 1 Wind		Apr 1 1930 1 Serpent
Oct 4 1927 1 Eagle	Jan 1 1929 1 Dog	Apr 14 1930 1 Knife
Oct 17 1927 1 Rabbit	Jan 14 1929 1 House	Apr 27 1930 1 Monkey
Oct 30 1927 1 Crocodile	Jan 27 1929 1 Vulture	May 10 1930 1 Lizard
Nov 12 1927 1 Ocelot	Feb 9 1929 1 Water	May 23 1930 1 Earthquake
Nov 25 1927 1 Deer	Feb 22 1929 1 Wind	Jun 5 1930 1 Dog

The Ephemeris of the Day–Signs 181

Jun 18 1930	1 House	Sep 29 1931	1 Monkey	Jan 9 1933	1 Rain
Jul 1 1930	1 Vulture	Oct 12 1931	1 Lizard	Jan 22 1933	1 Grass
Jul 14 1930	1 Water	Oct 25 1931	1 Earthquake	Feb 4 1933	1 Serpent
Jul 27 1930	1 Wind	Nov 7 1931	1 Dog	Feb 17 1933	1 Knife
Aug 9 1930	1 Eagle	Nov 20 1931	1 House	Mar 2 1933	1 Monkey
Aug 22 1930	1 Rabbit	Dec 3 1931	1 Vulture	Mar 15 1933	1 Lizard
Sep 4 1930	1 Crocodile	Dec 16 1931	1 Water	Mar 28 1933	1 Earthquake
Sep 17 1930	1 Ocelot	Dec 29 1931	1 Wind	Apr 10 1933	1 Dog
Sep 30 1930	1 Deer			Apr 23 1933	1 House
Oct 13 1930	1 Flower	Jan 11 1932	1 Eagle	May 6 1933	1 Vulture
Oct 26 1930	1 Reed	Jan 24 1932	1 Rabbit	May 19 1933	1 Water
Nov 8 1930	1 Death	Feb 6 1932	1 Crocodile	Jun 1 1933	1 Wind
Nov 21 1930	1 Rain	Feb 19 1932	1 Ocelot	Jun 14 1933	1 Eagle
Dec 4 1930	1 Grass	Mar 3 1932	1 Deer	Jun 27 1933	1 Rabbit
Dec 17 1930	1 Serpent	Mar 16 1932	1 Flower	Jul 10 1933	1 Crocodile
Dec 30 1930	1 Knife	Mar 29 1932	1 Reed	Jul 23 1933	1 Ocelot
		Apr 11 1932	1 Death	Aug 5 1933	1 Deer
Jan 12 1931	1 Monkey	Apr 24 1932	1 Rain	Aug 18 1933	1 Flower
Jan 25 1931	1 Lizard	May 7 1932	1 Grass	Aug 31 1933	1 Reed
Feb 7 1931	1 Earthquake	May 20 1932	1 Serpent	Sep 13 1933	1 Death
Feb 20 1931	1 Dog	Jun 2 1932	1 Knife	Sep 26 1933	1 Rain
Mar 5 1931	1 House	Jun 15 1932	1 Monkey	Oct 9 1933	1 Grass
Mar 18 1931	1 Vulture	Jun 28 1932	1 Lizard	Oct 22 1933	1 Serpent
Mar 31 1931	1 Water	Jul 11 1932	1 Earthquake	Nov 4 1933	1 Knife
Apr 13 1931	1 Wind	Jul 24 1932	1 Dog	Nov 17 1933	1 Monkey
Apr 26 1931	1 Eagle	Aug 6 1932	1 House	Nov 30 1933	1 Lizard
May 9 1931	1 Rabbit	Aug 19 1932	1 Vulture	Dec 13 1933	1 Earthquake
May 22 1931	1 Crocodile	Sep 1 1932	1 Water	Dec 26 1933	1 Dog
Jun 4 1931	1 Ocelot	Sep 14 1932	1 Wind		
Jun 17 1931	1 Deer	Sep 27 1932	1 Eagle	Jan 8 1934	1 House
Jun 30 1931	1 Flower	Oct 10 1932	1 Rabbit	Jan 21 1934	1 Vulture
Jul 13 1931	1 Reed	Oct 23 1932	1 Crocodile	Feb 3 1934	1 Water
Jul 26 1931	1 Death	Nov 5 1932	1 Ocelot	Feb 16 1934	1 Wind
Aug 8 1931	1 Rain	Nov 18 1932	1 Deer	Mar 1 1934	1 Eagle
Aug 21 1931	1 Grass	Dec 1 1932	1 Flower	Mar 14 1934	1 Rabbit
Sep 3 1931	1 Serpent	Dec 14 1932	1 Reed	Mar 27 1934	1 Crocodile
Sep 16 1931	1 Knife	Dec 27 1932	1 Death	Apr 9 1934	1 Ocelot

182 Day–Signs

Apr 22 1934 1 Deer	Aug 3 1935 1 Eagle	Nov 13 1936 1 House
May 5 1934 1 Flower	Aug 16 1935 1 Rabbit	Nov 26 1936 1 Vulture
May 18 1934 1 Reed	Aug 29 1935 1 Crocodile	Dec 9 1936 1 Water
May 31 1934 1 Death	Sep 11 1935 1 Ocelot	Dec 22 1936 1 Wind
Jun 13 1934 1 Rain	Sep 24 1935 1 Deer	
Jun 26 1934 1 Grass	Oct 7 1935 1 Flower	Jan 4 1937 1 Eagle
Jul 9 1934 1 Serpent	Oct 20 1935 1 Reed	Jan 17 1937 1 Rabbit
Jul 22 1934 1 Knife	Nov 2 1935 1 Death	Jan 30 1937 1 Crocodile
Aug 4 1934 1 Monkey	Nov 15 1935 1 Rain	Feb 12 1937 1 Ocelot
Aug 17 1934 1 Lizard	Nov 28 1935 1 Grass	Feb 25 1937 1 Deer
Aug 30 1934 1 Earthquake	Dec 11 1935 1 Serpent	Mar 10 1937 1 Flower
Sep 12 1934 1 Dog	Dec 24 1935 1 Knife	Mar 23 1937 1 Reed
Sep 25 1934 1 House		Apr 5 1937 1 Death
Oct 8 1934 1 Vulture	Jan 6 1936 1 Monkey	Apr 18 1937 1 Rain
Oct 21 1934 1 Water	Jan 19 1936 1 Lizard	May 1 1937 1 Grass
Nov 3 1934 1 Wind	Feb 1 1936 1 Earthquake	May 14 1937 1 Serpent
Nov 16 1934 1 Eagle	Feb 14 1936 1 Dog	May 27 1937 1 Knife
Nov 29 1934 1 Rabbit	Feb 27 1936 1 House	Jun 9 1937 1 Monkey
Dec 12 1934 1 Crocodile	Mar 11 1936 1 Vulture	Jun 22 1937 1 Lizard
Dec 25 1934 1 Ocelot	Mar 24 1936 1 Water	Jul 5 1937 1 Earthquake
	Apr 6 1936 1 Wind	Jul 18 1937 1 Dog
Jan 7 1935 1 Deer	Apr 19 1936 1 Eagle	Jul 31 1937 1 House
Jan 20 1935 1 Flower	May 2 1936 1 Rabbit	Aug 13 1937 1 Vulture
Feb 2 1935 1 Reed	May 15 1936 1 Crocodile	Aug 26 1937 1 Water
Feb 15 1935 1 Death	May 28 1936 1 Ocelot	Sep 8 1937 1 Wind
Feb 28 1935 1 Rain	Jun 10 1936 1 Deer	Sep 21 1937 1 Eagle
Mar 13 1935 1 Grass	Jun 23 1936 1 Flower	Oct 4 1937 1 Rabbit
Mar 26 1935 1 Serpent	Jul 6 1936 1 Reed	Oct 17 1937 1 Crocodile
Apr 8 1935 1 Knife	Jul 19 1936 1 Death	Oct 30 1937 1 Ocelot
Apr 21 1935 1 Monkey	Aug 1 1936 1 Rain	Nov 12 1937 1 Deer
May 4 1935 1 Lizard	Aug 14 1936 1 Grass	Nov 25 1937 1 Flower
May 17 1935 1 Earthquake	Aug 27 1936 1 Serpent	Dec 8 1937 1 Reed
May 30 1935 1 Dog	Sep 9 1936 1 Knife	Dec 21 1937 1 Death
Jun 12 1935 1 House	Sep 22 1936 1 Monkey	
Jun 25 1935 1 Vulture	Oct 5 1936 1 Lizard	Jan 3 1938 1 Rain
Jul 8 1935 1 Water	Oct 18 1936 1 Earthquake	Jan 16 1938 1 Grass
Jul 21 1935 1 Wind	Oct 31 1936 1 Dog	Jan 29 1938 1 Serpent

The Ephemeris of the Day–Signs

Feb 11 1938 1 Knife	May 25 1939 1 Death	Sep 4 1940 1 Ocelot
Feb 24 1938 1 Monkey	Jun 7 1939 1 Rain	Sep 17 1940 1 Deer
Mar 9 1938 1 Lizard	Jun 20 1939 1 Grass	Sep 30 1940 1 Flower
Mar 22 1938 1 Earthquake	Jul 3 1939 1 Serpent	Oct 13 1940 1 Reed
Apr 4 1938 1 Dog	Jul 16 1939 1 Knife	Oct 26 1940 1 Death
Apr 17 1938 1 House	Jul 29 1939 1 Monkey	Nov 8 1940 1 Rain
Apr 30 1938 1 Vulture	Aug 11 1939 1 Lizard	Nov 21 1940 1 Grass
May 13 1938 1 Water	Aug 24 1939 1 Earthquake	Dec 4 1940 1 Serpent
May 26 1938 1 Wind	Sep 6 1939 1 Dog	Dec 17 1940 1 Knife
Jun 8 1938 1 Eagle	Sep 19 1939 1 House	Dec 30 1940 1 Monkey
Jun 21 1938 1 Rabbit	Oct 2 1939 1 Vulture	
Jul 4 1938 1 Crocodile	Oct 15 1939 1 Water	Jan 12 1941 1 Lizard
Jul 17 1938 1 Ocelot	Oct 28 1939 1 Wind	Jan 25 1941 1 Earthquake
Jul 30 1938 1 Deer	Nov 10 1939 1 Eagle	Feb 7 1941 1 Dog
Aug 12 1938 1 Flower	Nov 23 1939 1 Rabbit	Feb 20 1941 1 House
Aug 25 1938 1 Reed	Dec 6 1939 1 Crocodile	Mar 5 1941 1 Vulture
Sep 7 1938 1 Death	Dec 19 1939 1 Ocelot	Mar 18 1941 1 Water
Sep 20 1938 1 Rain		Mar 31 1941 1 Wind
Oct 3 1938 1 Grass	Jan 1 1940 1 Deer	Apr 13 1941 1 Eagle
Oct 16 1938 1 Serpent	Jan 14 1940 1 Flower	Apr 26 1941 1 Rabbit
Oct 29 1938 1 Knife	Jan 27 1940 1 Reed	May 9 1941 1 Crocodile
Nov 11 1938 1 Monkey	Feb 9 1940 1 Death	May 22 1941 1 Ocelot
Nov 24 1938 1 Lizard	Feb 22 1940 1 Rain	Jun 4 1941 1 Deer
Dec 7 1938 1 Earthquake	Mar 6 1940 1 Grass	Jun 17 1941 1 Flower
Dec 20 1938 1 Dog	Mar 19 1940 1 Serpent	Jun 30 1941 1 Reed
	Apr 1 1940 1 Knife	Jul 13 1941 1 Death
Jan 2 1939 1 House	Apr 14 1940 1 Monkey	Jul 26 1941 1 Rain
Jan 15 1939 1 Vulture	Apr 27 1940 1 Lizard	Aug 8 1941 1 Grass
Jan 28 1939 1 Water	May 10 1940 1 Earthquake	Aug 21 1941 1 Serpent
Feb 10 1939 1 Wind	May 23 1940 1 Dog	Sep 3 1941 1 Knife
Feb 23 1939 1 Eagle	Jun 5 1940 1 House	Sep 16 1941 1 Monkey
Mar 8 1939 1 Rabbit	Jun 18 1940 1 Vulture	Sep 29 1941 1 Lizard
Mar 21 1939 1 Crocodile	Jul 1 1940 1 Water	Oct 12 1941 1 Earthquake
Apr 3 1939 1 Ocelot	Jul 14 1940 1 Wind	Oct 25 1941 1 Dog
Apr 16 1939 1 Deer	Jul 27 1940 1 Eagle	Nov 7 1941 1 House
Apr 29 1939 1 Flower	Aug 9 1940 1 Rabbit	Nov 20 1941 1 Vulture
May 12 1939 1 Reed	Aug 22 1940 1 Crocodile	Dec 3 1941 1 Water

184 Day–Signs

Dec 16 1941 1 Wind	Mar 16 1943 1 Earthquake	Jun 26 1944 1 Serpent
Dec 29 1941 1 Eagle	Mar 29 1943 1 Dog	Jul 9 1944 1 Knife
	Apr 11 1943 1 House	Jul 22 1944 1 Monkey
Jan 11 1942 1 Rabbit	Apr 24 1943 1 Vulture	Aug 4 1944 1 Lizard
Jan 24 1942 1 Crocodile	May 7 1943 1 Water	Aug 17 1944 1 Earthquake
Feb 6 1942 1 Ocelot	May 20 1943 1 Wind	Aug 30 1944 1 Dog
Feb 19 1942 1 Deer	Jun 2 1943 1 Eagle	Sep 12 1944 1 House
Mar 4 1942 1 Flower	Jun 15 1943 1 Rabbit	Sep 25 1944 1 Vulture
Mar 17 1942 1 Reed	Jun 28 1943 1 Crocodile	Oct 8 1944 1 Water
Mar 30 1942 1 Death	Jul 11 1943 1 Ocelot	Oct 21 1944 1 Wind
Apr 12 1942 1 Rain	Jul 24 1943 1 Deer	Nov 3 1944 1 Eagle
Apr 25 1942 1 Grass	Aug 6 1943 1 Flower	Nov 16 1944 1 Rabbit
May 8 1942 1 Serpent	Aug 19 1943 1 Reed	Nov 29 1944 1 Crocodile
May 21 1942 1 Knife	Sep 1 1943 1 Death	Dec 12 1944 1 Ocelot
Jun 3 1942 1 Monkey	Sep 14 1943 1 Rain	Dec 25 1944 1 Deer
Jun 16 1942 1 Lizard	Sep 27 1943 1 Grass	
Jun 29 1942 1 Earthquake	Oct 10 1943 1 Serpent	Jan 7 1945 1 Flower
Jul 12 1942 1 Dog	Oct 23 1943 1 Knife	Jan 20 1945 1 Reed
Jul 25 1942 1 House	Nov 5 1943 1 Monkey	Feb 2 1945 1 Death
Aug 7 1942 1 Vulture	Nov 18 1943 1 Lizard	Feb 15 1945 1 Rain
Aug 20 1942 1 Water	Dec 1 1943 1 Earthquake	Feb 28 1945 1 Grass
Sep 2 1942 1 Wind	Dec 14 1943 1 Dog	Mar 13 1945 1 Serpent
Sep 15 1942 1 Eagle	Dec 27 1943 1 House	Mar 26 1945 1 Knife
Sep 28 1942 1 Rabbit		Apr 8 1945 1 Monkey
Oct 11 1942 1 Crocodile	Jan 10 1944 1 Earthquake	Apr 21 1945 1 Lizard
Oct 24 1942 1 Ocelot	Jan 22 1944 1 Water	May 4 1945 1 Earthquake
Nov 6 1942 1 Deer	Feb 4 1944 1 Wind	May 17 1945 1 Dog
Nov 19 1942 1 Flower	Feb 17 1944 1 Eagle	May 30 1945 1 House
Dec 2 1942 1 Reed	Mar 1 1944 1 Rabbit	Jun 12 1945 1 Vulture
Dec 15 1942 1 Death	Mar 14 1944 1 Crocodile	Jun 25 1945 1 Water
Dec 28 1942 1 Rain	Mar 27 1944 1 Ocelot	Jul 8 1945 1 Wind
	Apr 9 1944 1 Deer	Jul 21 1945 1 Eagle
Jan 10 1943 1 Grass	Apr 22 1944 1 Flower	Aug 3 1945 1 Rabbit
Jan 23 1943 1 Serpent	May 5 1944 1 Reed	Aug 16 1945 1 Crocodile
Feb 5 1943 1 Knife	May 18 1944 1 Death	Aug 29 1945 1 Ocelot
Feb 18 1943 1 Monkey	May 31 1944 1 Rain	Sep 11 1945 1 Deer
Mar 3 1943 1 Lizard	Jun 13 1944 1 Grass	Sep 24 1945 1 Flower

The Ephemeris of the Day–Signs   185

Oct 7 1945 1 Reed	Jan 5 1947 1 Rabbit	Apr 17 1948 1 Vulture
Oct 20 1945 1 Death	Jan 18 1947 1 Crocodile	Apr 30 1948 1 Water
Nov 2 1945 1 Rain	Jan 31 1947 1 Ocelot	May 13 1948 1 Wind
Nov 15 1945 1 Grass	Feb 13 1947 1 Deer	May 26 1948 1 Eagle
Nov 28 1945 1 Serpent	Feb 26 1947 1 Flower	Jun 8 1948 1 Rabbit
Dec 11 1945 1 Knife	Mar 11 1947 1 Reed	Jun 21 1948 1 Crocodile
Dec 24 1945 1 Monkey	Mar 24 1947 1 Death	Jul 4 1948 1 Ocelot
	Apr 6 1947 1 Rain	Jul 17 1948 1 Deer
Jan 6 1946 1 Lizard	Apr 19 1947 1 Grass	Jul 30 1948 1 Flower
Jan 19 1946 1 Earthquake	May 2 1947 1 Serpent	Aug 12 1948 1 Reed
Feb 1 1946 1 Dog	May 15 1947 1 Knife	Aug 25 1948 1 Death
Feb 14 1946 1 House	May 28 1947 1 Monkey	Sep 7 1948 1 Rain
Feb 27 1946 1 Vulture	Jun 10 1947 1 Lizard	Sep 20 1948 1 Grass
Mar 12 1946 1 Water	Jun 23 1947 1 Earthquake	Oct 3 1948 1 Serpent
Mar 25 1946 1 Wind	Jul 6 1947 1 Dog	Oct 16 1948 1 Knife
Apr 7 1946 1 Eagle	Jul 19 1947 1 House	Oct 29 1948 1 Monkey
Apr 20 1946 1 Rabbit	Aug 1 1947 1 Vulture	Nov 11 1948 1 Lizard
May 3 1946 1 Crocodile	Aug 14 1947 1 Water	Nov 24 1948 1 Earthquake
May 16 1946 1 Ocelot	Aug 27 1947 1 Wind	Dec 7 1948 1 Dog
May 29 1946 1 Deer	Sep 9 1947 1 Eagle	Dec 20 1948 1 House
Jun 11 1946 1 Flower	Sep 22 1947 1 Rabbit	
Jun 24 1946 1 Reed	Oct 5 1947 1 Crocodile	Jan 2 1949 1 Vulture
Jul 7 1946 1 Death	Oct 18 1947 1 Ocelot	Jan 15 1949 1 Water
Jul 20 1946 1 Rain	Oct 31 1947 1 Deer	Jan 28 1949 1 Wind
Aug 2 1946 1 Grass	Nov 13 1947 1 Flower	Feb 10 1949 1 Eagle
Aug 15 1946 1 Serpent	Nov 26 1947 1 Reed	Feb 23 1949 1 Rabbit
Aug 28 1946 1 Knife	Dec 9 1947 1 Death	Mar 8 1949 1 Crocodile
Sep 10 1946 1 Monkey	Dec 22 1947 1 Rain	Mar 21 1949 1 Ocelot
Sep 23 1946 1 Lizard		Apr 3 1949 1 Deer
Oct 6 1946 1 Earthquake	Jan 4 1948 1 Grass	Apr 16 1949 1 Flower
Oct 19 1946 1 Dog	Jan 17 1948 1 Serpent	Apr 29 1949 1 Reed
Nov 1 1946 1 House	Jan 30 1948 1 Knife	May 12 1949 1 Death
Nov 14 1946 1 Vulture	Feb 12 1948 1 Monkey	May 25 1949 1 Rain
Nov 27 1946 1 Water	Feb 25 1948 1 Lizard	Jun 7 1949 1 Grass
Dec 10 1946 1 Wind	Mar 9 1948 1 Earthquake	Jun 20 1949 1 Serpent
Dec 23 1946 1 Eagle	Mar 22 1948 1 Dog	Jul 3 1949 1 Knife
	Apr 4 1948 1 House	Jul 16 1949 1 Monkey

Jul 29 1949   1 Lizard
Aug 11 1949 1 Earthquake
Aug 24 1949 1 Dog
Sep 6 1949   1 House
Sep 19 1949 1 Vulture
Oct 2 1949   1 Water
Oct 15 1949 1 Wind
Oct 28 1949 1 Eagle
Nov 10 1949 1 Rabbit
Nov 23 1949 1 Crocodile
Dec 6 1949   1 Ocelot
Dec 19 1949 1 Deer

Jan 1 1950   1 Flower
Jan 14 1950 1 Reed
Jan 27 1950 1 Death
Feb 9 1950   1 Rain
Feb 22 1950 1 Grass
Mar 7 1950   1 Serpent
Mar 20 1950 1 Knife
Apr 2 1950   1 Monkey
Apr 15 1950 1 Lizard
Apr 28 1950 1 Earthquake
May 11 1950 1 Dog
May 24 1950 1 House
Jun 6 1950   1 Vulture
Jun 19 1950 1 Water
Jul 2 1950   1 Wind
Jul 15 1950 1 Eagle
Jul 28 1950 1 Rabbit
Aug 10 1950 1 Crocodile
Aug 23 1950 1 Ocelot
Sep 5 1950   1 Deer
Sep 18 1950 1 Flower
Oct 1 1950   1 Reed
Oct 14 1950 1 Death
Oct 27 1950 1 Rain

Nov 9 1950   1 Grass
Nov 22 1950 1 Serpent
Dec 5 1950   1 Knife
Dec 18 1950 1 Monkey
Dec 31 1950 1 Lizard

Jan 13 1951 1 Earthquake
Jan 26 1951 1 Dog
Feb 8 1951   1 House
Feb 21 1951 1 Vulture
Mar 6 1951   1 Water
Mar 19 1951 1 Wind
Apr 1 1951   1 Eagle
Apr 14 1951 1 Rabbit
Apr 27 1951 1 Crocodile
May 10 1951 1 Ocelot
May 23 1951 1 Deer
Jun 5 1951   1 Flower
Jun 18 1951 1 Reed
Jul 1 1951   1 Death
Jul 14 1951 1 Rain
Jul 27 1951 1 Grass
Aug 9 1951   1 Serpent
Aug 22 1951 1 Knife
Sep 4 1951   1 Monkey
Sep 17 1951 1 Lizard
Sep 30 1951 1 Earthquake
Oct 13 1951 1 Dog
Oct 26 1951 1 House
Nov 8 1951   1 Vulture
Nov 21 1951 1 Water
Dec 4 1951   1 Wind
Dec 17 1951 1 Eagle
Dec 30 1951 1 Rabbit

Jan 12 1952 1 Crocodile
Jan 25 1952 1 Ocelot

Feb 7 1952   1 Deer
Feb 20 1952 1 Flower
Mar 4 1952   1 Reed
Mar 17 1952 1 Death
Mar 30 1952 1 Rain
Apr 12 1952 1 Grass
Apr 25 1952 1 Serpent
May 8 1952   1 Knife
May 21 1952 1 Monkey
Jun 3 1952   1 Lizard
Jun 16 1952 1 Earthquake
Jun 29 1952 1 Dog
Jul 12 1952 1 House
Jul 25 1952 1 Vulture
Aug 7 1952   1 Water
Aug 20 1952 1 Wind
Sep 2 1952   1 Eagle
Sep 15 1952 1 Rabbit
Sep 28 1952 1 Crocodile
Oct 11 1952 1 Ocelot
Oct 24 1952 1 Deer
Nov 6 1952   1 Flower
Nov 19 1952 1 Reed
Dec 2 1952   1 Death
Dec 15 1952 1 Rain
Dec 28 1952 1 Grass

Jan 10 1953 1 Serpent
Jan 23 1953 1 Knife
Feb 5 1953   1 Monkey
Feb 18 1953 1 Lizard
Mar 3 1953   1 Earthquake
Mar 16 1953 1 Dog
Mar 29 1953 1 House
Apr 11 1953 1 Vulture
Apr 24 1953 1 Water
May 7 1953   1 Wind

The Ephemeris of the Day–Signs

May 20 1953 1 Eagle	Aug 31 1954 1 House	Dec 12 1955 1 Monkey
Jun 2 1953 1 Rabbit	Sep 13 1954 1 Vulture	Dec 25 1955 1 Lizard
Jun 15 1953 1 Crocodile	Sep 26 1954 1 Water	
Jun 28 1953 1 Ocelot	Oct 9 1954 1 Wind	Jan 7 1956 1 Earthquake
Jul 11 1953 1 Deer	Oct 22 1954 1 Eagle	Jan 20 1956 1 Dog
Jul 24 1953 1 Flower	Nov 4 1954 1 Rabbit	Feb 2 1956 1 House
Aug 6 1953 1 Reed	Nov 17 1954 1 Crocodile	Feb 15 1956 1 Vulture
Aug 19 1953 1 Death	Nov 30 1954 1 Ocelot	Feb 28 1956 1 Water
Sep 1 1953 1 Rain	Dec 13 1954 1 Deer	Mar 12 1956 1 Wind
Sep 14 1953 1 Grass	Dec 26 1954 1 Flower	Mar 25 1956 1 Eagle
Sep 27 1953 1 Serpent		Apr 7 1956 1 Rabbit
Oct 10 1953 1 Knife	Jan 8 1955 1 Reed	Apr 20 1956 1 Crocodile
Oct 23 1953 1 Monkey	Jan 21 1955 1 Death	May 3 1956 1 Ocelot
Nov 5 1953 1 Lizard	Feb 3 1955 1 Rain	May 16 1956 1 Deer
Nov 18 1953 1 Earthquake	Feb 16 1955 1 Grass	May 29 1956 1 Flower
Dec 1 1953 1 Dog	Mar 1 1955 1 Serpent	Jun 11 1956 1 Reed
Dec 14 1953 1 House	Mar 14 1955 1 Knife	Jun 24 1956 1 Death
Dec 27 1953 1 Vulture	Mar 27 1955 1 Monkey	Jul 7 1956 1 Rain
	Apr 9 1955 1 Lizard	Jul 20 1956 1 Grass
Jan 9 1954 1 Water	Apr 22 1955 1 Earthquake	Aug 2 1956 1 Serpent
Jan 22 1954 1 Wind	May 5 1955 1 Dog	Aug 15 1956 1 Knife
Feb 4 1954 1 Eagle	May 18 1955 1 House	Aug 28 1956 1 Monkey
Feb 17 1954 1 Rabbit	May 31 1955 1 Vulture	Sep 10 1956 1 Lizard
Mar 2 1954 1 Crocodile	Jun 13 1955 1 Water	Sep 23 1956 1 Earthquake
Mar 15 1954 1 Ocelot	Jun 26 1955 1 Wind	Oct 6 1956 1 Dog
Mar 28 1954 1 Deer	Jul 9 1955 1 Eagle	Oct 19 1956 1 House
Apr 10 1954 1 Flower	Jul 22 1955 1 Rabbit	Nov 1 1956 1 Vulture
Apr 23 1954 1 Reed	Aug 4 1955 1 Crocodile	Nov 14 1956 1 Water
May 6 1954 1 Death	Aug 17 1955 1 Ocelot	Nov 27 1956 1 Wind
May 19 1954 1 Rain	Aug 30 1955 1 Deer	Dec 10 1956 1 Eagle
Jun 1 1954 1 Grass	Sep 12 1955 1 Flower	Dec 23 1956 1 Rabbit
Jun 14 1954 1 Serpent	Sep 25 1955 1 Reed	
Jun 27 1954 1 Knife	Oct 8 1955 1 Death	Jan 5 1957 1 Crocodile
Jul 10 1954 1 Monkey	Oct 21 1955 1 Rain	Jan 18 1957 1 Ocelot
Jul 23 1954 1 Lizard	Nov 3 1955 1 Grass	Jan 31 1957 1 Deer
Aug 5 1954 1 Earthquake	Nov 16 1955 1 Serpent	Feb 13 1957 1 Flower
Aug 18 1954 1 Dog	Nov 29 1955 1 Knife	Feb 26 1957 1 Reed

188   Day–Signs

Mar 11 1957 1 Death	Jul 5 1958 1 Deer	Oct 16 1959 1 Eagle
Apr 6 1957 1 Grass	Jul 18 1958 1 Flower	Oct 29 1959 1 Rabbit
Apr 19 1957 1 Serpent	Jul 31 1958 1 Reed	Nov 11 1959 1 Crocodile
May 2 1957 1 Knife	Aug 13 1958 1 Death	Nov 24 1959 1 Ocelot
May 15 1957 1 Monkey	Aug 26 1958 1 Rain	Dec 7 1959 1 Deer
May 28 1957 1 Lizard	Sep 8 1958 1 Grass	Dec 20 1959 1 Flower
Jun 10 1957 1 Earthquake	Sep 21 1958 1 Serpent	
Jun 23 1957 1 Dog	Oct 4 1958 1 Knife	Jan 2 1960 1 Reed
Jul 6 1957 1 House	Oct 17 1958 1 Monkey	Jan 15 1960 1 Death
Jul 19 1957 1 Vulture	Oct 30 1958 1 Lizard	Jan 28 1960 1 Rain
Aug 1 1957 1 Water	Nov 12 1958 1 Earthquake	Feb 10 1960 1 Grass
Aug 14 1957 1 Wind	Nov 25 1958 1 Dog	Feb 23 1960 1 Serpent
Aug 27 1957 1 Eagle	Dec 8 1958 1 House	Mar 7 1960 1 Knife
Sep 9 1957 1 Rabbit	Dec 21 1958 1 Vulture	Mar 20 1960 1 Monkey
Sep 22 1957 1 Crocodile		Apr 2 1960 1 Lizard
Oct 5 1957 1 Ocelot	Jan 3 1959 1 Water	Apr 15 1960 1 Earthquake
Oct 18 1957 1 Deer	Jan 16 1959 1 Wind	Apr 28 1960 1 Dog
Oct 31 1957 1 Flower	Jan 29 1959 1 Eagle	May 11 1960 1 House
Nov 13 1957 1 Reed	Feb 11 1959 1 Rabbit	May 24 1960 1 Vulture
Nov 26 1957 1 Death	Feb 24 1959 1 Crocodile	Jun 6 1960 1 Water
Dec 9 1957 1 Rain	Mar 9 1959 1 Ocelot	Jun 19 1960 1 Wind
Dec 22 1957 1 Grass	Mar 22 1959 1 Deer	Jul 2 1960 1 Eagle
	Apr 4 1959 1 Flower	Jul 15 1960 1 Rabbit
Jan 4 1958 1 Serpent	Apr 17 1959 1 Reed	Jul 28 1960 1 Crocodile
Jan 17 1958 1 Knife	Apr 30 1959 1 Death	Aug 10 1960 1 Ocelot
Jan 30 1958 1 Monkey	May 13 1959 1 Rain	Aug 23 1960 1 Deer
Feb 12 1958 1 Lizard	May 26 1959 1 Grass	Sep 5 1960 1 Flower
Feb 25 1958 1 Earthquake	Jun 8 1959 1 Serpent	Sep 18 1960 1 Reed
Mar 10 1958 1 Dog	Jun 21 1959 1 Knife	Oct 1 1960 1 Death
Mar 23 1958 1 House	Jul 4 1959 1 Monkey	Oct 14 1960 1 Rain
Apr 5 1958 1 Vulture	Jul 17 1959 1 Lizard	Oct 27 1960 1 Grass
Apr 18 1958 1 Water	Jul 30 1959 1 Earthquake	Nov 9 1960 1 Serpent
May 1 1958 1 Wind	Aug 12 1959 1 Dog	Nov 22 1960 1 Knife
May 14 1958 1 Eagle	Aug 25 1959 1 House	Dec 5 1960 1 Monkey
May 27 1958 1 Rabbit	Sep 7 1959 1 Vulture	Dec 18 1960 1 Lizard
Jun 9 1958 1 Crocodile	Sep 20 1959 1 Water	Dec 31 1960 1 Earthquake
Jun 22 1958 1 Ocelot	Oct 3 1959 1 Wind	

The Ephemeris of the Day–Signs   189

Jan 13 1961 1 Dog	Apr 26 1962 1 Knife	Aug 7 1963 1 Death
Jan 26 1961 1 House	May 9 1962 1 Monkey	Aug 20 1963 1 Rain
Feb 8 1961 1 Vulture	May 22 1962 1 Lizard	Sep 2 1963 1 Grass
Feb 21 1961 1 Water	Jun 4 1962 1 Earthquake	Sep 15 1963 1 Serpent
Mar 6 1961 1 Wind	Jun 17 1962 1 Dog	Sep 28 1963 1 Knife
Mar 19 1961 1 Eagle	Jun 30 1962 1 House	Oct 11 1963 1 Monkey
Apr 1 1961 1 Rabbit	Jul 13 1962 1 Vulture	Oct 24 1963 1 Lizard
Apr 14 1961 1 Crocodile	Jul 26 1962 1 Water	Nov 6 1963 1 Earthquake
Apr 27 1961 1 Ocelot	Aug 8 1962 1 Wind	Nov 19 1963 1 Dog
May 10 1961 1 Deer	Aug 21 1962 1 Eagle	Dec 2 1963 1 House
May 23 1961 1 Flower	Sep 3 1962 1 Rabbit	Dec 15 1963 1 Vulture
Jun 5 1961 1 Reed	Sep 16 1962 1 Crocodile	Dec 28 1963 1 Water
Jun 18 1961 1 Death	Sep 29 1962 1 Ocelot	
Jul 1 1961 1 Rain	Oct 12 1962 1 Deer	Jan 10 1964 1 Wind
Jul 14 1961 1 Grass	Oct 25 1962 1 Flower	Jan 23 1964 1 Eagle
Jul 27 1961 1 Serpent	Nov 7 1962 1 Reed	Feb 5 1964 1 Rabbit
Aug 9 1961 1 Knife	Nov 20 1962 1 Death	Feb 18 1964 1 Crocodile
Aug 22 1961 1 Monkey	Dec 3 1962 1 Rain	Mar 2 1964 1 Ocelot
Sep 4 1961 1 Lizard	Dec 16 1962 1 Grass	Mar 15 1964 1 Deer
Sep 17 1961 1 Earthquake	Dec 29 1962 1 Serpent	Mar 28 1964 1 Flower
Sep 30 1961 1 Dog		Apr 10 1964 1 Reed
Oct 13 1961 1 House	Jan 11 1963 1 Knife	Apr 23 1964 1 Death
Oct 26 1961 1 Vulture	Jan 24 1963 1 Monkey	May 6 1964 1 Rain
Nov 8 1961 1 Water	Feb 6 1963 1 Lizard	May 19 1964 1 Grass
Nov 21 1961 1 Wind	Feb 19 1963 1 Earthquake	Jun 1 1964 1 Serpent
Dec 4 1961 1 Eagle	Mar 4 1963 1 Dog	Jun 14 1964 1 Knife
Dec 17 1961 1 Rabbit	Mar 17 1963 1 House	Jun 27 1964 1 Monkey
Dec 30 1961 1 Crocodile	Mar 30 1963 1 Vulture	Jul 10 1964 1 Lizard
	Apr 12 1963 1 Water	Jul 23 1964 1 Earthquake
Jan 12 1962 1 Ocelot	Apr 25 1963 1 Wind	Aug 5 1964 1 Dog
Jan 25 1962 1 Deer	May 8 1963 1 Eagle	Aug 18 1964 1 House
Feb 7 1962 1 Flower	May 21 1963 1 Rabbit	Aug 31 1964 1 Vulture
Feb 20 1962 1 Reed	Jun 3 1963 1 Crocodile	Sep 13 1964 1 Water
Mar 5 1962 1 Death	Jun 16 1963 1 Ocelot	Sep 26 1964 1 Wind
Mar 18 1962 1 Rain	Jun 29 1963 1 Deer	Oct 9 1964 1 Eagle
Mar 31 1962 1 Grass	Jul 12 1963 1 Flower	Oct 22 1964 1 Rabbit
Apr 13 1962 1 Serpent	Jul 25 1963 1 Reed	Nov 4 1964 1 Crocodile

190 Day–Signs

Nov 17 1964 1 Ocelot	Feb 15 1966 1 Water	May 29 1967 1 Earthquake
Nov 30 1964 1 Deer	Feb 28 1966 1 Wind	Jun 11 1967 1 Dog
Dec 13 1964 1 Flower	Mar 13 1966 1 Eagle	Jun 24 1967 1 House
Dec 26 1964 1 Reed	Mar 26 1966 1 Rabbit	Jul 7 1967 1 Vulture
	Apr 8 1966 1 Crocodile	Jul 20 1967 1 Water
Jan 8 1965 1 Death	Apr 21 1966 1 Ocelot	Aug 2 1967 1 Wind
Jan 21 1965 1 Rain	May 4 1966 1 Deer	Aug 15 1967 1 Eagle
Feb 3 1965 1 Grass	May 17 1966 1 Flower	Aug 28 1967 1 Rabbit
Feb 16 1965 1 Serpent	May 30 1966 1 Reed	Sep 10 1967 1 Crocodile
Mar 1 1965 1 Knife	Jun 12 1966 1 Death	Sep 23 1967 1 Ocelot
Mar 14 1965 1 Monkey	Jun 25 1966 1 Rain	Oct 6 1967 1 Deer
Mar 27 1965 1 Lizard	Jul 8 1966 1 Grass	Oct 19 1967 1 Flower
Apr 9 1965 1 Earthquake	Jul 21 1966 1 Serpent	Nov 1 1967 1 Reed
Apr 22 1965 1 Dog	Aug 3 1966 1 Knife	Nov 14 1967 1 Death
May 5 1965 1 House	Aug 16 1966 1 Monkey	Nov 27 1967 1 Rain
May 18 1965 1 Vulture	Aug 29 1966 1 Lizard	Dec 10 1967 1 Grass
May 31 1965 1 Water	Sep 11 1966 1 Earthquake	Dec 23 1967 1 Serpent
Jun 13 1965 1 Wind	Sep 24 1966 1 Dog	
Jun 26 1965 1 Eagle	Oct 7 1966 1 House	Jan 5 1968 1 Knife
Jul 9 1965 1 Rabbit	Oct 20 1966 1 Vulture	Jan 18 1968 1 Monkey
Jul 22 1965 1 Crocodile	Nov 2 1966 1 Water	Jan 31 1968 1 Lizard
Aug 4 1965 1 Ocelot	Nov 15 1966 1 Wind	Feb 13 1968 1 Earthquake
Aug 17 1965 1 Deer	Nov 28 1966 1 Eagle	Feb 26 1968 1 Dog
Aug 30 1965 1 Flower	Dec 11 1966 1 Rabbit	Mar 10 1968 1 House
Sep 12 1965 1 Reed	Dec 24 1966 1 Crocodile	Mar 23 1968 1 Vulture
Sep 25 1965 1 Death		Apr 5 1968 1 Water
Oct 8 1965 1 Rain	Jan 6 1967 1 Ocelot	Apr 18 1968 1 Wind
Oct 21 1965 1 Grass	Jan 19 1967 1 Deer	May 1 1968 1 Eagle
Nov 3 1965 1 Serpent	Feb 1 1967 1 Flower	May 14 1968 1 Rabbit
Nov 16 1965 1 Knife	Feb 14 1967 1 Reed	May 27 1968 1 Crocodile
Nov 29 1965 1 Monkey	Feb 27 1967 1 Death	Jun 9 1968 1 Ocelot
Dec 12 1965 1 Lizard	Mar 12 1967 1 Rain	Jun 22 1968 1 Deer
Dec 25 1965 1 Earthquake	Mar 25 1967 1 Grass	Jul 5 1968 1 Flower
	Apr 7 1967 1 Serpent	Jul 18 1968 1 Reed
Jan 7 1966 1 Dog	Apr 20 1967 1 Knife	Jul 31 1968 1 Death
Jan 20 1966 1 House	May 3 1967 1 Monkey	Aug 13 1968 1 Rain
Feb 2 1966 1 Vulture	May 16 1967 1 Lizard	Aug 26 1968 1 Grass

The Ephemeris of the Day–Signs 191

Sep 8 1968	1 Serpent	Dec 20 1969	1 Reed	Mar 20 1971	1 Rabbit
Sep 21 1968	1 Knife			Apr 2 1971	1 Crocodile
Oct 4 1968	1 Monkey	Jan 2 1970	1 Death	Apr 15 1971	1 Ocelot
Oct 17 1968	1 Lizard	Jan 15 1970	1 Rain	Apr 28 1971	1 Deer
Oct 30 1968	1 Earthquake	Jan 28 1970	1 Grass	May 11 1971	1 Flower
Nov 12 1968	1 Dog	Feb 10 1970	1 Serpent	May 24 1971	1 Reed
Nov 25 1968	1 House	Feb 23 1970	1 Knife	Jun 6 1971	1 Death
Dec 8 1968	1 Vulture	Mar 8 1970	1 Monkey	Jun 19 1971	1 Rain
Dec 21 1968	1 Water	Mar 21 1970	1 Lizard	Jul 2 1971	1 Grass
		Apr 3 1970	1 Earthquake	Jul 15 1971	1 Serpent
Jan 3 1969	1 Wind	Apr 16 1970	1 Dog	Jul 28 1971	1 Knife
Jan 16 1969	1 Eagle	Apr 29 1970	1 House	Aug 10 1971	1 Monkey
Jan 29 1969	1 Rabbit	May 12 1970	1 Vulture	Aug 23 1971	1 Lizard
Feb 11 1969	1 Crocodile	May 25 1970	1 Water	Sep 5 1971	1 Earthquake
Feb 24 1969	1 Ocelot	Jun 7 1970	1 Wind	Sep 18 1971	1 Dog
Mar 9 1969	1 Deer	Jun 20 1970	1 Eagle	Oct 1 1971	1 House
Mar 22 1969	1 Flower	Jul 3 1970	1 Rabbit	Oct 14 1971	1 Vulture
Apr 4 1969	1 Reed	Jul 16 1970	1 Crocodile	Oct 27 1971	1 Water
Apr 17 1969	1 Death	Jul 29 1970	1 Ocelot	Nov 9 1971	1 Wind
Apr 30 1969	1 Rain	Aug 11 1970	1 Deer	Nov 22 1971	1 Eagle
May 13 1969	1 Grass	Aug 24 1970	1 Flower	Dec 5 1971	1 Rabbit
May 26 1969	1 Serpent	Sep 6 1970	1 Reed	Dec 18 1971	1 Crocodile
Jun 8 1969	1 Knife	Sep 19 1970	1 Death	Dec 31 1971	1 Ocelot
Jun 21 1969	1 Monkey	Oct 2 1970	1 Rain		
Jul 4 1969	1 Lizard	Oct 15 1970	1 Grass	Jan 13 1972	1 Deer
Jul 17 1969	1 Earthquake	Oct 28 1970	1 Serpent	Jan 26 1972	1 Flower
Jul 30 1969	1 Dog	Nov 10 1970	1 Knife	Feb 8 1972	1 Reed
Aug 12 1969	1 House	Nov 23 1970	1 Monkey	Feb 21 1972	1 Death
Aug 25 1969	1 Vulture	Dec 6 1970	1 Lizard	Mar 5 1972	1 Rain
Sep 7 1969	1 Water	Dec 19 1970	1 Earthquake	Mar 18 1972	1 Grass
Sep 20 1969	1 Wind			Mar 31 1972	1 Serpent
Oct 3 1969	1 Eagle	Jan 1 1971	1 Dog	Apr 13 1972	1 Knife
Oct 16 1969	1 Rabbit	Jan 14 1971	1 House	Apr 26 1972	1 Monkey
Oct 29 1969	1 Crocodile	Jan 27 1971	1 Vulture	May 9 1972	1 Lizard
Nov 11 1969	1 Ocelot	Feb 9 1971	1 Water	May 22 1972	1 Earthquake
Nov 24 1969	1 Deer	Feb 22 1971	1 Wind	Jun 4 1972	1 Dog
Dec 7 1969	1 Flower	Mar 7 1971	1 Eagle	Jun 17 1972	1 House

192 Day–Signs

Jun 30 1972 1 Vulture	Oct 11 1973 1 Lizard	Jan 9 1975 1 Rain
Jul 13 1972 1 Water	Oct 24 1973 1 Earthquake	Jan 22 1975 1 Grass
Jul 26 1972 1 Wind	Nov 6 1973 1 Dog	Feb 4 1975 1 Serpent
Aug 8 1972 1 Eagle	Nov 19 1973 1 House	Feb 17 1975 1 Knife
Aug 21 1972 1 Rabbit	Dec 2 1973 1 Vulture	Mar 2 1975 1 Monkey
Sep 3 1972 1 Crocodile	Dec 15 1973 1 Water	Mar 15 1975 1 Lizard
Sep 16 1972 1 Ocelot	Dec 28 1973 1 Wind	Mar 28 1975 1 Earthquake
Sep 29 1972 1 Deer		Apr 10 1975 1 Dog
Oct 12 1972 1 Flower	Jan 10 1974 1 Eagle	Apr 23 1975 1 House
Oct 25 1972 1 Reed	Jan 23 1974 1 Rabbit	May 6 1975 1 Vulture
Nov 7 1972 1 Death	Feb 5 1974 1 Crocodile	May 19 1975 1 Water
Nov 20 1972 1 Rain	Feb 18 1974 1 Ocelot	Jun 1 1975 1 Wind
Dec 3 1972 1 Grass	Mar 3 1974 1 Deer	Jun 14 1975 1 Eagle
Dec 16 1972 1 Serpent	Mar 16 1974 1 Flower	Jun 27 1975 1 Rabbit
Dec 29 1972 1 Knife	Mar 29 1974 1 Reed	Jul 10 1975 1 Crocodile
	Apr 11 1974 1 Death	Jul 23 1975 1 Ocelot
Jan 11 1973 1 Monkey	Apr 23 1974 1 Rain	Aug 5 1975 1 Deer
Jan 24 1973 1 Lizard	May 7 1974 1 Grass	Aug 18 1975 1 Flower
Feb 6 1973 1 Earthquake	May 20 1974 1 Serpent	Aug 31 1975 1 Reed
Feb 19 1973 1 Dog	Jun 2 1974 1 Knife	Sep 13 1975 1 Death
Mar 4 1973 1 House	Jun 15 1974 1 Monkey	Sep 26 1975 1 Rain
Mar 17 1973 1 Vulture	Jun 28 1974 1 Lizard	Oct 9 1975 1 Grass
Mar 30 1973 1 Water	Jul 11 1974 1 Earthquake	Oct 22 1975 1 Serpent
Apr 12 1973 1 Wind	Jul 24 1974 1 Dog	Nov 4 1975 1 Knife
Apr 25 1973 1 Eagle	Aug 6 1974 1 House	Nov 17 1975 1 Monkey
May 8 1973 1 Rabbit	Aug 19 1974 1 Vulture	Nov 30 1975 1 Lizard
May 21 1973 1 Crocodile	Sep 1 1974 1 Water	Dec 13 1975 1 Earthquake
Jun 3 1973 1 Ocelot	Sep 14 1974 1 Wind	Dec 26 1975 1 Dog
Jun 16 1973 1 Deer	Sep 27 1974 1 Eagle	
Jun 29 1973 1 Flower	Oct 10 1974 1 Rabbit	Jan 8 1976 1 House
Jul 12 1973 1 Reed	Oct 23 1974 1 Crocodile	Jan 21 1976 1 Vulture
Jul 25 1973 1 Death	Nov 5 1974 1 Ocelot	Feb 3 1976 1 Water
Aug 7 1973 1 Rain	Nov 18 1974 1 Deer	Feb 16 1976 1 Wind
Aug 20 1973 1 Grass	Dec 1 1974 1 Flower	Feb 29 1976 1 Eagle
Sep 2 1973 1 Serpent	Dec 14 1974 1 Reed	Mar 13 1976 1 Rabbit
Sep 15 1973 1 Knife	Dec 27 1974 1 Death	Mar 26 1976 1 Crocodile
Sep 28 1973 1 Monkey		Apr 8 1976 1 Ocelot

The Ephemeris of the Day–Signs 193

Apr 21 1976 1 Deer	Aug 2 1977 1 Eagle	Nov 13 1978 1 House
May 4 1976 1 Flower	Aug 15 1977 1 Rabbit	Nov 26 1978 1 Vulture
May 17 1976 1 Reed	Aug 28 1977 1 Crocodile	Dec 9 1978 1 Water
May 30 1976 1 Death	Sep 10 1977 1 Ocelot	Dec 22 1978 1 Wind
Jun 12 1976 1 Rain	Sep 23 1977 1 Deer	
Jun 25 1976 1 Grass	Oct 6 1977 1 Flower	Jan 4 1979 1 Eagle
Jul 8 1976 1 Serpent	Oct 19 1977 1 Reed	Jan 17 1979 1 Rabbit
Jul 21 1976 1 Knife	Nov 1 1977 1 Death	Jan 30 1979 1 Crocodile
Aug 3 1976 1 Monkey	Nov 14 1977 1 Rain	Feb 12 1979 1 Ocelot
Aug 16 1976 1 Lizard	Nov 27 1977 1 Grass	Feb 25 1979 1 Deer
Aug 29 1976 1 Earthquake	Dec 10 1977 1 Serpent	Mar 10 1979 1 Flower
Sep 11 1976 1 Dog	Dec 23 1977 1 Knife	Mar 23 1979 1 Reed
Sep 24 1976 1 House		Apr 5 1979 1 Death
Oct 7 1976 1 Vulture	Jan 5 1978 1 Monkey	Apr 18 1979 1 Rain
Oct 20 1976 1 Water	Jan 18 1978 1 Lizard	May 1 1979 1 Grass
Nov 2 1976 1 Wind	Jan 31 1978 1 Earthquake	May 14 1979 1 Serpent
Nov 15 1976 1 Eagle	Feb 13 1978 1 Dog	May 27 1979 1 Knife
Nov 28 1976 1 Rabbit	Feb 26 1978 1 House	Jun 9 1979 1 Monkey
Dec 11 1976 1 Crocodile	Mar 11 1978 1 Vulture	Jun 22 1979 1 Lizard
Dec 24 1976 1 Ocelot	Mar 24 1978 1 Water	Jul 5 1979 1 Earthquake
	Apr 6 1978 1 Wind	Jul 18 1979 1 Dog
Jan 6 1977 1 Deer	Apr 19 1978 1 Eagle	Jul 31 1979 1 House
Jan 19 1977 1 Flower	May 2 1978 1 Rabbit	Aug 13 1979 1 Vulture
Feb 1 1977 1 Reed	May 15 1978 1 Crocodile	Aug 26 1979 1 Water
Feb 14 1977 1 Death	May 28 1978 1 Ocelot	Sep 8 1979 1 Wind
Feb 27 1977 1 Rain	Jun 10 1978 1 Deer	Sep 21 1979 1 Eagle
Mar 12 1977 1 Grass	Jun 23 1978 1 Flower	Oct 4 1979 1 Rabbit
Mar 25 1977 1 Serpent	Jul 6 1978 1 Reed	Oct 17 1979 1 Crocodile
Apr 7 1977 1 Knife	Jul 19 1978 1 Death	Oct 30 1979 1 Ocelot
Apr 20 1977 1 Monkey	Aug 1 1978 1 Rain	Nov 12 1979 1 Deer
May 3 1977 1 Lizard	Aug 14 1978 1 Grass	Nov 25 1979 1 Flower
May 16 1977 1 Earthquake	Aug 27 1978 1 Serpent	Dec 8 1979 1 Reed
May 29 1977 1 Dog	Sep 9 1978 1 Knife	Dec 21 1979 1 Death
Jun 11 1977 1 House	Sep 22 1978 1 Monkey	
Jun 24 1977 1 Vulture	Oct 5 1978 1 Lizard	Jan 3 1980 1 Rain
Jul 7 1977 1 Water	Oct 18 1978 1 Earthquake	Jan 16 1980 1 Grass
Jul 20 1977 1 Wind	Oct 31 1978 1 Dog	Jan 29 1980 1 Serpent

194 Day–Signs

Feb 11 1980 1 Knife	May 24 1981 1 Death	Sep 4 1982 1 Ocelot
Feb 24 1980 1 Monkey	Jun 6 1981 1 Rain	Sep 17 1982 1 Deer
Mar 8 1980 1 Lizard	Jun 19 1981 1 Grass	Sep 30 1982 1 Flower
Mar 21 1980 1 Earthquake	Jul 2 1981 1 Serpent	Oct 13 1982 1 Reed
Apr 3 1980 1 Dog	Jul 15 1981 1 Knife	Oct 26 1982 1 Death
Apr 16 1980 1 House	Jul 28 1981 1 Monkey	Nov 8 1982 1 Rain
Apr 29 1980 1 Vulture	Aug 10 1981 1 Lizard	Nov 21 1982 1 Grass
May 12 1980 1 Water	Aug 23 1981 1 Earthquake	Dec 4 1982 1 Serpent
May 25 1980 1 Wind	Sep 5 1981 1 Dog	Dec 17 1982 1 Knife
Jun 7 1980 1 Eagle	Sep 18 1981 1 House	Dec 30 1982 1 Monkey
Jun 20 1980 1 Rabbit	Oct 1 1981 1 Vulture	
Jul 3 1980 1 Crocodile	Oct 14 1981 1 Water	Jan 12 1983 1 Lizard
Jul 16 1980 1 Ocelot	Oct 27 1981 1 Wind	Jan 25 1983 1 Earthquake
Jul 29 1980 1 Deer	Nov 9 1981 1 Eagle	Feb 7 1983 1 Dog
Aug 11 1980 1 Flower	Nov 22 1981 1 Rabbit	Feb 20 1983 1 House
Aug 24 1980 1 Reed	Dec 5 1981 1 Crocodile	Mar 5 1983 1 Vulture
Sep 6 1980 1 Death	Dec 18 1981 1 Ocelot	Mar 18 1983 1 Water
Sep 19 1980 1 Rain	Dec 31 1981 1 Deer	Mar 31 1983 1 Wind
Oct 2 1980 1 Grass		Apr 13 1983 1 Eagle
Oct 15 1980 1 Serpent	Jan 13 1982 1 Flower	Apr 26 1983 1 Rabbit
Oct 28 1980 1 Knife	Jan 26 1982 1 Reed	May 9 1983 1 Crocodile
Nov 10 1980 1 Monkey	Feb 8 1982 1 Death	May 22 1983 1 Ocelot
Nov 23 1980 1 Lizard	Feb 21 1982 1 Rain	Jun 4 1983 1 Deer
Dec 6 1980 1 Earthquake	Mar 6 1982 1 Grass	Jun 17 1983 1 Flower
Dec 19 1980 1 Dog	Mar 19 1982 1 Serpent	Jun 30 1983 1 Reed
	Apr 1 1982 1 Knife	Jul 13 1983 1 Death
Jan 1 1981 1 House	Apr 14 1982 1 Monkey	Jul 26 1983 1 Rain
Jan 14 1981 1 Vulture	Apr 27 1982 1 Lizard	Aug 8 1983 1 Grass
Jan 27 1981 1 Water	May 10 1982 1 Earthquake	Aug 21 1983 1 Serpent
Feb 9 1981 1 Wind	May 23 1982 1 Dog	Sep 3 1983 1 Knife
Feb 22 1981 1 Eagle	Jun 5 1982 1 House	Sep 16 1983 1 Monkey
Mar 7 1981 1 Rabbit	Jun 18 1982 1 Vulture	Sep 29 1983 1 Lizard
Mar 20 1981 1 Crocodile	Jul 1 1982 1 Water	Oct 12 1983 1 Earthquake
Apr 2 1981 1 Ocelot	Jul 14 1982 1 Wind	Oct 25 1983 1 Dog
Apr 15 1981 1 Deer	Jul 27 1982 1 Eagle	Nov 7 1983 1 House
Apr 28 1981 1 Flower	Aug 9 1982 1 Rabbit	Nov 20 1983 1 Vulture
May 11 1981 1 Reed	Aug 22 1982 1 Crocodile	Dec 3 1983 1 Water

The Ephemeris of the Day–Signs

Dec 16 1983 1 Wind	Mar 15 1985 1 Earthquake	Jun 26 1986 1 Serpent
Dec 29 1983 1 Eagle	Mar 28 1985 1 Dog	Jul 9 1986 1 Knife
	Apr 10 1985 1 House	Jul 22 1986 1 Monkey
Jan 11 1984 1 Rabbit	Apr 23 1985 1 Vulture	Aug 4 1986 1 Lizard
Jan 24 1984 1 Crocodile	May 6 1985 1 Water	Aug 17 1986 1 Earthquake
Feb 6 1984 1 Ocelot	May 19 1985 1 Wind	Aug 30 1986 1 Dog
Feb 19 1984 1 Deer	Jun 1 1985 1 Eagle	Sep 12 1986 1 House
Mar 3 1984 1 Flower	Jun 14 1985 1 Rabbit	Sep 25 1986 1 Vulture
Mar 16 1984 1 Reed	Jun 27 1985 1 Crocodile	Oct 8 1986 1 Water
Mar 29 1984 1 Death	Jul 10 1985 1 Ocelot	Oct 21 1986 1 Wind
Apr 11 1984 1 Rain	Jul 23 1985 1 Deer	Nov 3 1986 1 Eagle
Apr 24 1984 1 Grass	Aug 5 1985 1 Flower	Nov 16 1986 1 Rabbit
May 7 1984 1 Serpent	Aug 18 1985 1 Reed	Nov 29 1986 1 Crocodile
May 20 1984 1 Knife	Aug 31 1985 1 Death	Dec 12 1986 1 Ocelot
Jun 2 1984 1 Monkey	Sep 13 1985 1 Rain	Dec 25 1986 1 Deer
Jun 15 1984 1 Lizard	Sep 26 1985 1 Grass	
Jun 28 1984 1 Earthquake	Oct 9 1985 1 Serpent	Jan 7 1987 1 Flower
Jul 11 1984 1 Dog	Oct 22 1985 1 Knife	Jan 20 1987 1 Reed
Jul 24 1984 1 House	Nov 4 1985 1 Monkey	Feb 2 1987 1 Death
Aug 6 1984 1 Vulture	Nov 17 1985 1 Lizard	Feb 15 1987 1 Rain
Aug 19 1984 1 Water	Nov 30 1985 1 Earthquake	Feb 28 1987 1 Grass
Sep 1 1984 1 Wind	Dec 13 1985 1 Dog	Mar 13 1987 1 Serpent
Sep 14 1984 1 Eagle	Dec 26 1985 1 House	Mar 26 1987 1 Knife
Sep 27 1984 1 Rabbit		Apr 8 1987 1 Monkey
Oct 10 1984 1 Crocodile	Jan 8 1986 1 Vulture	Apr 21 1987 1 Lizard
Oct 23 1984 1 Ocelot	Jan 21 1986 1 Water	May 4 1987 1 Earthquake
Nov 5 1984 1 Deer	Feb 3 1986 1 Wind	May 17 1987 1 Dog
Nov 18 1984 1 Flower	Feb 16 1986 1 Eagle	May 30 1987 1 House
Dec 1 1984 1 Reed	Mar 1 1986 1 Rabbit	Jun 12 1987 1 Vulture
Dec 14 1984 1 Death	Mar 14 1986 1 Crocodile	Jun 25 1987 1 Water
Dec 27 1984 1 Rain	Mar 27 1986 1 Ocelot	Jul 8 1987 1 Wind
	Apr 9 1986 1 Deer	Jul 21 1987 1 Eagle
Jan 9 1985 1 Grass	Apr 22 1986 1 Flower	Aug 3 1987 1 Rabbit
Jan 22 1985 1 Serpent	May 5 1986 1 Reed	Aug 16 1987 1 Crocodile
Feb 4 1985 1 Knife	May 18 1986 1 Death	Aug 29 1987 1 Ocelot
Feb 17 1985 1 Monkey	May 31 1986 1 Rain	Sep 11 1987 1 Deer
Mar 2 1985 1 Lizard	Jun 13 1986 1 Grass	Sep 24 1987 1 Flower

196 Day–Signs

Oct 7 1987 1 Reed	Jan 4 1989 1 Rabbit	Apr 17 1990 1 Vulture
Oct 20 1987 1 Death	Jan 17 1989 1 Crocodile	Apr 30 1990 1 Water
Nov 2 1987 1 Rain	Jan 30 1989 1 Ocelot	May 13 1990 1 Wind
Nov 15 1987 1 Grass	Feb 12 1989 1 Deer	May 26 1990 1 Eagle
Nov 28 1987 1 Serpent	Feb 25 1989 1 Flower	Jun 8 1990 1 Rabbit
Dec 11 1987 1 Knife	Mar 10 1989 1 Reed	Jun 21 1990 1 Crocodile
Dec 24 1987 1 Monkey	Mar 23 1989 1 Death	Jul 4 1990 1 Ocelot
	Apr 5 1989 1 Rain	Jul 17 1990 1 Deer
Jan 6 1988 1 Lizard	Apr 18 1989 1 Grass	Jul 30 1990 1 Flower
Jan 19 1988 1 Earthquake	May 1 1989 1 Serpent	Aug 12 1990 1 Reed
Feb 1 1988 1 Dog	May 14 1989 1 Knife	Aug 25 1990 1 Death
Feb 14 1988 1 House	May 27 1989 1 Monkey	Sep 7 1990 1 Rain
Feb 27 1988 1 Vulture	Jun 9 1989 1 Lizard	Sep 20 1990 1 Grass
Mar 11 1988 1 Water	Jun 22 1989 1 Earthquake	Oct 3 1990 1 Serpent
Mar 24 1988 1 Wind	Jul 5 1989 1 Dog	Oct 16 1990 1 Knife
Apr 6 1988 1 Eagle	Jul 18 1989 1 House	Oct 29 1990 1 Monkey
Apr 19 1988 1 Rabbit	Jul 31 1989 1 Vulture	Nov 11 1990 1 Lizard
May 2 1988 1 Crocodile	Aug 13 1989 1 Water	Nov 24 1990 1 Earthquake
May 15 1988 1 Ocelot	Aug 26 1989 1 Wind	Dec 7 1990 1 Dog
May 28 1988 1 Deer	Sep 8 1989 1 Eagle	Dec 20 1990 1 House
Jun 10 1988 1 Flower	Sep 21 1989 1 Rabbit	
Jun 23 1988 1 Reed	Oct 4 1989 1 Crocodile	Jan 2 1991 1 Vulture
Jul 6 1988 1 Death	Oct 17 1989 1 Ocelot	Jan 15 1991 1 Water
Jul 19 1988 1 Rain	Oct 30 1989 1 Deer	Jan 28 1991 1 Wind
Aug 1 1988 1 Grass	Nov 12 1989 1 Flower	Feb 10 1991 1 Eagle
Aug 14 1988 1 Serpent	Nov 25 1989 1 Reed	Feb 23 1991 1 Rabbit
Aug 27 1988 1 Knife	Dec 8 1989 1 Death	Mar 8 1991 1 Crocodile
Sep 9 1988 1 Monkey	Dec 21 1989 1 Rain	Mar 21 1991 1 Ocelot
Sep 22 1988 1 Lizard		Apr 3 1991 1 Deer
Oct 5 1988 1 Earthquake	Jan 3 1990 1 Grass	Apr 16 1991 1 Flower
Oct 18 1988 1 Dog	Jan 16 1990 1 Serpent	Apr 29 1991 1 Reed
Oct 31 1988 1 House	Jan 29 1990 1 Knife	May 12 1991 1 Death
Nov 13 1988 1 Vulture	Feb 11 1990 1 Monkey	May 25 1991 1 Rain
Nov 26 1988 1 Water	Feb 24 1990 1 Lizard	Jun 7 1991 1 Grass
Dec 9 1988 1 Wind	Mar 9 1990 1 Earthquake	Jun 20 1991 1 Serpent
Dec 22 1988 1 Eagle	Mar 22 1990 1 Dog	Jul 3 1991 1 Knife
	Apr 4 1990 1 House	Jul 16 1991 1 Monkey

The Ephemeris of the Day–Signs

Jul 29 1991	1 Lizard	Nov 8 1992	1 Grass	Feb 6 1994	1 Deer
Aug 11 1991	1 Earthquake	Nov 21 1992	1 Serpent	Feb 19 1994	1 Flower
Aug 24 1991	1 Dog	Dec 4 1992	1 Knife	Mar 4 1994	1 Reed
Sep 6 1991	1 House	Dec 17 1992	1 Monkey	Mar 17 1994	1 Death
Sep 19 1991	1 Vulture	Dec 30 1992	1 Lizard	Mar 30 1994	1 Rain
Oct 2 1991	1 Water			Apr 12 1994	1 Grass
Oct 15 1991	1 Wind	Jan 12 1993	1 Earthquake	Apr 25 1994	1 Serpent
Oct 28 1991	1 Eagle	Jan 25 1993	1 Dog	May 8 1994	1 Knife
Nov 10 1991	1 Rabbit	Feb 7 1993	1 House	May 21 1994	1 Monkey
Nov 23 1991	1 Crocodile	Feb 20 1993	1 Vulture	Jun 3 1994	1 Lizard
Dec 6 1991	1 Ocelot	Mar 5 1993	1 Water	Jun 16 1994	1 Earthquake
Dec 19 1991	1 Deer	Mar 18 1993	1 Wind	Jun 29 1994	1 Dog
		Mar 31 1993	1 Eagle	Jul 12 1994	1 House
Jan 1 1992	1 Flower	Apr 13 1993	1 Rabbit	Jul 25 1994	1 Vulture
Jan 14 1992	1 Reed	Apr 26 1993	1 Crocodile	Aug 7 1994	1 Water
Jan 27 1992	1 Death	May 9 1993	1 Ocelot	Aug 20 1994	1 Wind
Feb 9 1992	1 Rain	May 22 1993	1 Deer	Sep 2 1994	1 Eagle
Feb 22 1992	1 Grass	Jun 4 1993	1 Flower	Sep 15 1994	1 Rabbit
Mar 6 1992	1 Serpent	Jun 17 1993	1 Reed	Sep 28 1994	1 Crocodile
Mar 19 1992	1 Knife	Jun 30 1993	1 Death	Oct 11 1994	1 Ocelot
Apr 1 1992	1 Monkey	Jul 13 1993	1 Rain	Oct 24 1994	1 Deer
Apr 14 1992	1 Lizard	Jul 26 1993	1 Grass	Nov 6 1994	1 Flower
Apr 27 1992	1 Earthquake	Aug 8 1993	1 Serpent	Nov 19 1994	1 Reed
May 10 1992	1 Dog	Aug 21 1993	1 Knife	Dec 2 1994	1 Death
May 23 1992	1 House	Sep 3 1993	1 Monkey	Dec 15 1994	1 Rain
Jun 5 1992	1 Vulture	Sep 16 1993	1 Lizard	Dec 28 1994	1 Grass
Jun 18 1992	1 Water	Sep 29 1993	1 Earthquake		
Jul 1 1992	1 Wind	Oct 12 1993	1 Dog	Jan 10 1995	1 Serpent
Jul 14 1992	1 Eagle	Oct 25 1993	1 House	Jan 23 1995	1 Knife
Jul 27 1992	1 Rabbit	Nov 7 1993	1 Vulture	Feb 5 1995	1 Monkey
Aug 9 1992	1 Crocodile	Nov 20 1993	1 Water	Feb 18 1995	1 Lizard
Aug 22 1992	1 Ocelot	Dec 3 1993	1 Wind	Mar 3 1995	1 Earthquake
Sep 4 1992	1 Deer	Dec 16 1993	1 Eagle	Mar 16 1995	1 Dog
Sep 17 1992	1 Flower	Dec 29 1993	1 Rabbit	Mar 29 1995	1 House
Sep 30 1992	1 Reed			Apr 11 1995	1 Vulture
Oct 13 1992	1 Death	Jan 11 1994	1 Crocodile	Apr 24 1995	1 Water
Oct 26 1992	1 Rain	Jan 24 1994	1 Ocelot	May 7 1995	1 Wind

198 Day–Signs

May 20 1995 1 Eagle	Aug 30 1996 1 House	Dec 11 1997 1 Monkey
Jun 2 1995 1 Rabbit	Sep 12 1996 1 Vulture	Dec 24 1997 1 Lizard
Jun 15 1995 1 Crocodile	Sep 25 1996 1 Water	
Jun 28 1995 1 Ocelot	Oct 8 1996 1 Wind	Jan 6 1998 1 Earthquake
Jul 11 1995 1 Deer	Oct 21 1996 1 Eagle	Jan 19 1998 1 Dog
Jul 24 1995 1 Flower	Nov 3 1996 1 Rabbit	Feb 1 1998 1 House
Aug 6 1995 1 Reed	Nov 16 1996 1 Crocodile	Feb 14 1998 1 Vulture
Aug 19 1995 1 Death	Nov 29 1996 1 Ocelot	Feb 27 1998 1 Water
Sep 1 1995 1 Rain	Dec 12 1996 1 Deer	Mar 12 1998 1 Wind
Sep 14 1995 1 Grass	Dec 25 1996 1 Flower	Mar 25 1998 1 Eagle
Sep 27 1995 1 Serpent		Apr 7 1998 1 Rabbit
Oct 10 1995 1 Knife	Jan 7 1997 1 Reed	Apr 20 1998 1 Crocodile
Oct 23 1995 1 Monkey	Jan 20 1997 1 Death	May 3 1998 1 Ocelot
Nov 5 1995 1 Lizard	Feb 2 1997 1 Rain	May 16 1998 1 Deer
Nov 18 1995 1 Earthquake	Feb 15 1997 1 Grass	May 29 1998 1 Flower
Dec 1 1995 1 Dog	Feb 28 1997 1 Serpent	Jun 11 1998 1 Reed
Dec 14 1995 1 House	Mar 13 1997 1 Knife	Jun 24 1998 1 Death
Dec 27 1995 1 Vulture	Mar 26 1997 1 Monkey	Jul 7 1998 1 Rain
	Apr 8 1997 1 Lizard	Jul 20 1998 1 Grass
Jan 9 1996 1 Water	Apr 21 1997 1 Earthquake	Aug 2 1998 1 Serpent
Jan 22 1996 1 Wind	May 4 1997 1 Dog	Aug 15 1998 1 Knife
Feb 4 1996 1 Eagle	May 17 1997 1 House	Aug 28 1998 1 Monkey
Feb 17 1996 1 Rabbit	May 30 1997 1 Vulture	Sep 10 1998 1 Lizard
Mar 1 1996 1 Crocodile	Jun 12 1997 1 Water	Sep 23 1998 1 Earthquake
Mar 14 1996 1 Ocelot	Jun 25 1997 1 Wind	Oct 6 1998 1 Dog
Mar 27 1996 1 Deer	Jul 8 1997 1 Eagle	Oct 19 1998 1 House
Apr 9 1996 1 Flower	Jul 21 1997 1 Rabbit	Nov 1 1998 1 Vulture
Apr 22 1996 1 Reed	Aug 3 1997 1 Crocodile	Nov 14 1998 1 Water
May 5 1996 1 Death	Aug 16 1997 1 Ocelot	Nov 27 1998 1 Wind
May 18 1996 1 Rain	Aug 29 1997 1 Deer	Dec 10 1998 1 Eagle
May 31 1996 1 Grass	Sep 11 1997 1 Flower	Dec 23 1998 1 Rabbit
Jun 13 1996 1 Serpent	Sep 24 1997 1 Reed	
Jun 26 1996 1 Knife	Oct 7 1997 1 Death	Jan 5 1999 1 Crocodile
Jul 9 1996 1 Monkey	Oct 20 1997 1 Rain	Jan 18 1999 1 Ocelot
Jul 22 1996 1 Lizard	Nov 2 1997 1 Grass	Jan 31 1999 1 Deer
Aug 4 1996 1 Earthquake	Nov 15 1997 1 Serpent	Feb 13 1999 1 Flower
Aug 17 1996 1 Dog	Nov 28 1997 1 Knife	Feb 26 1999 1 Reed

The Ephemeris of the Day–Signs

Mar 11 1999 1 Death	Jun 21 2000 1 Ocelot	Oct 15 2001 1 Eagle
Mar 24 1999 1 Rain	Jul 4 2000 1 Deer	Oct 28 2001 1 Rabbit
Apr 6 1999 1 Grass	Jul 17 2000 1 Flower	Nov 10 2001 1 Crocodile
Apr 19 1999 1 Serpent	Jul 30 2000 1 Reed	Nov 23 2001 1 Ocelot
May 2 1999 1 Knife	Aug 12 2000 1 Death	Dec 6 2001 1 Deer
May 15 1999 1 Monkey	Aug 25 2000 1 Rain	Dec 19 2001 1 Flower
May 28 1999 1 Lizard	Sep 7 2000 1 Grass	
Jun 10 1999 1 Earthquake	Sep 20 2000 1 Serpent	Jan 1 2002 1 Reed
Jun 23 1999 1 Dog	Oct 3 2000 1 Knife	Jan 14 2002 1 Death
Jul 6 1999 1 House	Oct 16 2000 1 Monkey	Jan 27 2002 1 Rain
Jul 19 1999 1 Vulture	Oct 29 2000 1 Lizard	Feb 9 2002 1 Grass
Aug 1 1999 1 Water	Nov 11 2000 1 Earthquake	Feb 22 2002 1 Serpent
Aug 14 1999 1 Wind	Nov 24 2000 1 Dog	Mar 7 2002 1 Knife
Aug 27 1999 1 Eagle	Dec 7 2000 1 House	Mar 20 2002 1 Monkey
Sep 9 1999 1 Rabbit	Dec 20 2000 1 Vulture	Apr 2 2002 1 Lizard
Sep 22 1999 1 Crocodile		Apr 15 2002 1 Earthquake
Oct 5 1999 1 Ocelot	Jan 2 2001 1 Water	Apr 28 2002 1 Dog
Oct 18 1999 1 Deer	Jan 15 2001 1 Wind	May 11 2002 1 House
Oct 31 1999 1 Flower	Jan 28 2001 1 Eagle	May 24 2002 1 Vulture
Nov 13 1999 1 Reed	Feb 10 2001 1 Rabbit	Jun 6 2002 1 Water
Nov 26 1999 1 Death	Feb 23 2001 1 Crocodile	Jun 19 2002 1 Wind
Dec 9 1999 1 Rain	Mar 8 2001 1 Ocelot	Jul 2 2002 1 Eagle
Dec 22 1999 1 Grass	Mar 21 2001 1 Deer	Jul 15 2002 1 Rabbit
	Apr 3 2001 1 Flower	Jul 28 2002 1 Crocodile
Jan 4 2000 1 Serpent	Apr 16 2001 1 Reed	Aug 10 2002 1 Ocelot
Jan 17 2000 1 Knife	Apr 29 2001 1 Death	Aug 23 2002 1 Deer
Jan 30 2000 1 Monkey	May 12 2001 1 Rain	Sep 5 2002 1 Flower
Feb 12 2000 1 Lizard	May 25 2001 1 Grass	Sep 18 2002 1 Reed
Feb 25 2000 1 Earthquake	Jun 7 2001 1 Serpent	Oct 1 2002 1 Death
Mar 9 2000 1 Dog	Jun 20 2001 1 Knife	Oct 14 2002 1 Rain
Mar 22 2000 1 House	Jul 3 2001 1 Monkey	Oct 27 2002 1 Grass
Apr 4 2000 1 Vulture	Jul 16 2001 1 Lizard	Nov 9 2002 1 Serpent
Apr 17 2000 1 Water	Jul 29 2001 1 Earthquake	Nov 22 2002 1 Knife
Apr 30 2000 1 Wind	Aug 11 2001 1 Dog	Dec 5 2002 1 Monkey
May 13 2000 1 Eagle	Aug 24 2001 1 House	Dec 18 2002 1 Lizard
May 26 2000 1 Rabbit	Sep 19 2001 1 Water	Dec 31 2002 1 Earthquake
Jun 8 2000 1 Crocodile	Oct 2 2001 1 Wind	

200 Day–Signs

Jan 13 2003 1 Dog	Apr 25 2004 1 Knife	Aug 19 2005 1 Rain
Jan 26 2003 1 House	May 8 2004 1 Monkey	Sep 1 2005 1 Grass
Feb 8 2003 1 Vulture	May 21 2004 1 Lizard	Sep 14 2005 1 Serpent
Feb 21 2003 1 Water	Jun 3 2004 1 Earthquake	Sep 27 2005 1 Knife
Mar 6 2003 1 Wind	Jun 16 2004 1 Dog	Oct 10 2005 1 Monkey
Mar 19 2003 1 Eagle	Jun 29 2004 1 House	Oct 23 2005 1 Lizard
Apr 1 2003 1 Rabbit	Jul 12 2004 1 Vulture	Nov 5 2005 1 Earthquake
Apr 14 2003 1 Crocodile	Jul 25 2004 1 Water	Nov 18 2005 1 Dog
Apr 27 2003 1 Ocelot	Aug 7 2004 1 Wind	Dec 1 2005 1 House
May 10 2003 1 Deer	Aug 20 2004 1 Eagle	Dec 14 2005 1 Vulture
May 23 2003 1 Flower	Sep 2 2004 1 Rabbit	Dec 27 2005 1 Water
Jun 5 2003 1 Reed	Sep 15 2004 1 Crocodile	
Jun 18 2003 1 Death	Sep 28 2004 1 Ocelot	Jan 9 2006 1 Wind
Jul 1 2003 1 Rain	Oct 11 2004 1 Deer	Jan 22 2006 1 Eagle
Jul 14 2003 1 Grass	Oct 24 2004 1 Flower	Feb 4 2006 1 Rabbit
Jul 27 2003 1 Serpent	Nov 6 2004 1 Reed	Feb 17 2006 1 Crocodile
Aug 9 2003 1 Knife	Nov 19 2004 1 Death	Mar 2 2006 1 Ocelot
Aug 22 2003 1 Monkey	Dec 2 2004 1 Rain	Mar 15 2006 1 Deer
Sep 4 2003 1 Lizard	Dec 15 2004 1 Grass	Mar 28 2006 1 Flower
Sep 17 2003 1 Earthquake	Dec 28 2004 1 Serpent	Apr 10 2006 1 Reed
Sep 30 2003 1 Dog		Apr 23 2006 1 Death
Oct 13 2003 1 House	Jan 10 2005 1 Knife	May 6 2006 1 Rain
Oct 26 2003 1 Vulture	Jan 23 2005 1 Monkey	May 19 2006 1 Grass
Nov 8 2003 1 Water	Feb 5 2005 1 Lizard	Jun 1 2006 1 Serpent
Nov 21 2003 1 Wind	Feb 18 2005 1 Earthquake	Jun 14 2006 1 Knife
Dec 4 2003 1 Eagle	Mar 3 2005 1 Dog	Jun 27 2006 1 Monkey
Dec 17 2003 1 Rabbit	Mar 16 2005 1 House	Jul 10 2006 1 Lizard
Dec 30 2003 1 Crocodile	Mar 29 2005 1 Vulture	Jul 23 2006 1 Earthquake
	Apr 11 2005 1 Water	Aug 5 2006 1 Dog
Jan 12 2004 1 Ocelot	Apr 24 2005 1 Wind	Aug 18 2006 1 House
Jan 25 2004 1 Deer	May 7 2005 1 Eagle	Aug 31 2006 1 Vulture
Feb 7 2004 1 Flower	May 20 2005 1 Rabbit	Sep 13 2006 1 Water
Feb 20 2004 1 Reed	Jun 15 2005 1 Ocelot	Sep 26 2006 1 Wind
Mar 4 2004 1 Death	Jun 28 2005 1 Deer	Oct 9 2006 1 Eagle
Mar 17 2004 1 Rain	Jul 11 2005 1 Flower	Oct 22 2006 1 Rabbit
Mar 30 2004 1 Grass	Jul 24 2005 1 Reed	Nov 4 2006 1 Crocodile
Apr 12 2004 1 Serpent	Aug 6 2005 1 Death	Nov 17 2006 1 Ocelot

The Ephemeris of the Day–Signs   201

Nov 30 2006 1 Deer	Feb 28 2008 1 Wind	Jun 10 2009 1 Dog
Dec 13 2006 1 Flower	Mar 12 2008 1 Eagle	Jun 23 2009 1 House
Dec 26 2006 1 Reed	Mar 25 2008 1 Rabbit	Jul 6 2009 1 Vulture
	Apr 7 2008 1 Crocodile	Jul 19 2009 1 Water
Jan 8 2007 1 Death	Apr 20 2008 1 Ocelot	Aug 1 2009 1 Wind
Jan 21 2007 1 Rain	May 3 2008 1 Deer	Aug 14 2009 1 Eagle
Feb 3 2007 1 Grass	May 16 2008 1 Flower	Aug 27 2009 1 Rabbit
Feb 16 2007 1 Serpent	May 29 2008 1 Reed	Sep 9 2009 1 Crocodile
Mar 1 2007 1 Knife	Jun 11 2008 1 Death	Sep 22 2009 1 Ocelot
Mar 14 2007 1 Monkey	Jun 24 2008 1 Rain	Oct 5 2009 1 Deer
Mar 27 2007 1 Lizard	Jul 7 2008 1 Grass	Oct 18 2009 1 Flower
Apr 9 2007 1 Earthquake	Jul 20 2008 1 Serpent	Oct 31 2009 1 Reed
Apr 22 2007 1 Dog	Aug 2 2008 1 Knife	Nov 13 2009 1 Death
May 5 2007 1 House	Aug 15 2008 1 Monkey	Nov 26 2009 1 Rain
May 18 2007 1 Vulture	Aug 28 2008 1 Lizard	Dec 9 2009 1 Grass
May 31 2007 1 Water	Sep 10 2008 1 Earthquake	Dec 22 2009 1 Serpent
Jun 13 2007 1 Wind	Sep 23 2008 1 Dog	
Jun 26 2007 1 Eagle	Oct 6 2008 1 House	Jan 4 2010 1 Knife
Jul 9 2007 1 Rabbit	Oct 19 2008 1 Vulture	Jan 17 2010 1 Monkey
Jul 22 2007 1 Crocodile	Nov 1 2008 1 Water	Jan 30 2010 1 Lizard
Aug 4 2007 1 Ocelot	Nov 14 2008 1 Wind	Feb 12 2010 1 Earthquake
Aug 17 2007 1 Deer	Nov 27 2008 1 Eagle	Feb 25 2010 1 Dog
Aug 30 2007 1 Flower	Dec 10 2008 1 Rabbit	Mar 10 2010 1 House
Sep 12 2007 1 Reed	Dec 23 2008 1 Crocodile	Mar 23 2010 1 Vulture
Sep 25 2007 1 Death		Apr 5 2010 1 Water
Oct 8 2007 1 Rain	Jan 5 2009 1 Ocelot	Apr 18 2010 1 Wind
Oct 21 2007 1 Grass	Jan 18 2009 1 Deer	May 1 2010 1 Eagle
Nov 3 2007 1 Serpent	Jan 31 2009 1 Flower	May 14 2010 1 Rabbit
Nov 16 2007 1 Knife	Feb 13 2009 1 Reed	May 27 2010 1 Crocodile
Nov 29 2007 1 Monkey	Feb 26 2009 1 Death	Jun 9 2010 1 Ocelot
Dec 12 2007 1 Lizard	Mar 11 2009 1 Rain	Jun 22 2010 1 Deer
Dec 25 2007 1 Earthquake	Mar 24 2009 1 Grass	Jul 5 2010 1 Flower
	Apr 6 2009 1 Serpent	Jul 18 2010 1 Reed
Jan 7 2008 1 Dog	Apr 19 2009 1 Knife	Jul 31 2010 1 Death
Jan 20 2008 1 House	May 2 2009 1 Monkey	Aug 13 2010 1 Rain
Feb 2 2008 1 Vulture	May 15 2009 1 Lizard	Aug 26 2010 1 Grass
Feb 15 2008 1 Water	May 28 2009 1 Earthquake	Sep 8 2010 1 Serpent

Sep 21 2010 1 Knife
Oct 4 2010 1 Monkey
Oct 17 2010 1 Lizard
Oct 30 2010 1 Earthquake
Nov 12 2010 1 Dog
Nov 25 2010 1 House
Dec 8 2010 1 Vulture
Dec 21 2010 1 Water

Jan 3 2011 1 Wind
Jan 16 2011 1 Eagle
Jan 29 2011 1 Rabbit
Feb 11 2011 1 Crocodile
Feb 24 2011 1 Ocelot
Mar 9 2011 1 Deer
Mar 22 2011 1 Flower
Apr 4 2011 1 Reed
Apr 17 2011 1 Death
Apr 30 2011 1 Rain
May 13 2011 1 Grass
May 26 2011 1 Serpent
Jun 8 2011 1 Knife
Jun 21 2011 1 Monkey
Jul 4 2011 1 Lizard
Jul 17 2011 1 Earthquake
Jul 30 2011 1 Dog
Aug 12 2011 1 House
Aug 25 2011 1 Vulture
Sep 7 2011 1 Water
Sep 20 2011 1 Wind
Oct 3 2011 1 Eagle
Oct 16 2011 1 Rabbit
Oct 29 2011 1 Crocodile
Nov 11 2011 1 Ocelot
Nov 24 2011 1 Deer
Dec 7 2011 1 Flower
Dec 20 2011 1 Reed

Jan 2 2012 1 Death
Jan 15 2012 1 Rain
Jan 28 2012 1 Grass
Feb 10 2012 1 Serpent
Feb 23 2012 1 Knife
Mar 7 2012 1 Monkey
Mar 20 2012 1 Lizard
Apr 2 2012 1 Earthquake
Apr 15 2012 1 Dog
Apr 28 2012 1 House
May 11 2012 1 Vulture
May 24 2012 1 Water
Jun 6 2012 1 Wind
Jun 19 2012 1 Eagle
Jul 2 2012 1 Rabbit
Jul 15 2012 1 Crocodile
Jul 28 2012 1 Ocelot
Aug 10 2012 1 Deer
Aug 23 2012 1 Flower
Sep 5 2012 1 Reed
Sep 18 2012 1 Death
Oct 1 2012 1 Rain
Oct 14 2012 1 Grass
Oct 27 2012 1 Serpent
Nov 9 2012 1 Knife
Nov 22 2012 1 Monkey
Dec 5 2012 1 Lizard
Dec 18 2012 1 Earthquake
Dec 31 2012 1 Dog

Jan 13 2013 1 House
Jan 26 2013 1 Vulture
Feb 8 2013 1 Water
Feb 21 2013 1 Wind
Mar 6 2013 1 Eagle
Mar 19 2013 1 Rabbit
Apr 1 2013 1 Crocodile

Apr 14 2013 1 Ocelot
Apr 27 2013 1 Deer
May 10 2013 1 Flower
May 23 2013 1 Reed
Jun 5 2013 1 Death
Jun 18 2013 1 Rain
Jul 1 2013 1 Grass
Jul 14 2013 1 Serpent
Jul 27 2013 1 Knife
Aug 9 2013 1 Monkey
Aug 22 2013 1 Lizard
Sep 4 2013 1 Earthquake
Sep 17 2013 1 Dog
Sep 30 2013 1 House
Oct 13 2013 1 Vulture
Oct 26 2013 1 Water
Nov 8 2013 1 Wind
Nov 21 2013 1 Eagle
Dec 4 2013 1 Rabbit
Dec 17 2013 1 Crocodile
Dec 30 2013 1 Ocelot

Jan 12 2014 1 Deer
Jan 25 2014 1 Flower
Feb 7 2014 1 Reed
Feb 20 2014 1 Death
Mar 5 2014 1 Rain
Mar 18 2014 1 Grass
Mar 31 2014 1 Serpent
Apr 13 2014 1 Knife
Apr 26 2014 1 Monkey
May 9 2014 1 Lizard
May 22 2014 1 Earthquake
Jun 4 2014 1 Dog
Jun 17 2014 1 House
Jun 30 2014 1 Vulture
Jul 13 2014 1 Water

The Ephemeris of the Day–Signs

Jul 26 2014 1 Wind	Nov 19 2015 1 House	Feb 16 2017 1 Knife
Aug 8 2014 1 Eagle	Dec 2 2015 1 Vulture	Mar 1 2017 1 Monkey
Aug 21 2014 1 Rabbit	Dec 15 2015 1 Water	Mar 14 2017 1 Lizard
Sep 3 2014 1 Crocodile	Dec 28 2015 1 Wind	Mar 27 2017 1 Earthquake
Sep 16 2014 1 Ocelot		Apr 9 2017 1 Dog
Sep 29 2014 1 Deer	Jan 10 2016 1 Eagle	Apr 22 2017 1 House
Oct 12 2014 1 Flower	Jan 23 2016 1 Rabbit	May 5 2017 1 Vulture
Oct 25 2014 1 Reed	Feb 5 2016 1 Crocodile	May 18 2017 1 Water
Nov 7 2014 1 Death	Feb 18 2016 1 Ocelot	May 31 2017 1 Wind
Nov 20 2014 1 Rain	Mar 2 2016 1 Deer	Jun 13 2017 1 Eagle
Dec 3 2014 1 Grass	Mar 15 2016 1 Flower	Jun 26 2017 1 Rabbit
Dec 16 2014 1 Serpent	Mar 28 2016 1 Reed	Jul 9 2017 1 Crocodile
Dec 29 2014 1 Knife	Apr 10 2016 1 Death	Jul 22 2017 1 Ocelot
	Apr 23 2016 1 Rain	Aug 4 2017 1 Deer
Jan 11 2015 1 Monkey	May 6 2016 1 Grass	Aug 17 2017 1 Flower
Jan 24 2015 1 Lizard	May 19 2016 1 Serpent	Aug 30 2017 1 Reed
Feb 6 2015 1 Earthquake	Jun 1 2016 1 Knife	Sep 12 2017 1 Death
Feb 19 2015 1 Dog	Jun 14 2016 1 Monkey	Sep 25 2017 1 Rain
Mar 4 2015 1 House	Jun 27 2016 1 Lizard	Oct 8 2017 1 Grass
Mar 30 2015 1 Water	Jul 10 2016 1 Earthquake	Oct 21 2017 1 Serpent
Apr 12 2015 1 Wind	Jul 23 2016 1 Dog	Nov 3 2017 1 Knife
Apr 25 2015 1 Eagle	Aug 5 2016 1 House	Nov 16 2017 1 Monkey
May 8 2015 1 Rabbit	Aug 18 2016 1 Vulture	Nov 29 2017 1 Lizard
May 21 2015 1 Crocodile	Aug 31 2016 1 Water	Dec 12 2017 1 Earthquake
Jun 3 2015 1 Ocelot	Sep 13 2016 1 Wind	Dec 25 2017 1 Dog
Jun 16 2015 1 Deer	Sep 26 2016 1 Eagle	
Jun 29 2015 1 Flower	Oct 9 2016 1 Rabbit	Jan 7 2018 1 House
Jul 12 2015 1 Reed	Oct 22 2016 1 Crocodile	Jan 20 2018 1 Vulture
Jul 25 2015 1 Death	Nov 4 2016 1 Ocelot	Feb 2 2018 1 Water
Aug 7 2015 1 Rain	Nov 17 2016 1 Deer	Feb 15 2018 1 Wind
Aug 20 2015 1 Grass	Nov 30 2016 1 Flower	Feb 28 2018 1 Eagle
Sep 2 2015 1 Serpent	Dec 13 2016 1 Reed	Mar 13 2018 1 Rabbit
Sep 15 2015 1 Knife	Dec 26 2016 1 Death	Mar 26 2018 1 Crocodile
Sep 28 2015 1 Monkey		Apr 8 2018 1 Ocelot
Oct 11 2015 1 Lizard	Jan 8 2017 1 Rain	Apr 21 2018 1 Deer
Oct 24 2015 1 Earthquake	Jan 21 2017 1 Grass	May 4 2018 1 Flower
Nov 6 2015 1 Dog	Feb 3 2017 1 Serpent	May 17 2018 1 Reed

May 30 2018 1 Death
Jun 12 2018 1 Rain
Jun 25 2018 1 Grass
Jul 8 2018 1 Serpent
Jul 21 2018 1 Knife
Aug 3 2018 1 Monkey
Aug 16 2018 1 Lizard
Aug 29 2018 1 Earthquake
Sep 11 2018 1 Dog
Sep 24 2018 1 House
Oct 7 2018 1 Vulture
Oct 20 2018 1 Water
Nov 2 2018 1 Wind
Nov 15 2018 1 Eagle
Nov 28 2018 1 Rabbit
Dec 11 2018 1 Crocodile
Dec 24 2018 1 Ocelot

Jan 6 2019 1 Deer
Jan 19 2019 1 Flower
Feb 1 2019 1 Reed
Feb 14 2019 1 Death
Feb 27 2019 1 Rain
Mar 12 2019 1 Grass
Mar 25 2019 1 Serpent
Apr 7 2019 1 Knife
Apr 20 2019 1 Monkey
May 3 2019 1 Lizard
May 16 2019 1 Earthquake
May 29 2019 1 Dog
Jun 11 2019 1 House
Jun 24 2019 1 Vulture
Jul 7 2019 1 Water
Jul 20 2019 1 Wind
Aug 2 2019 1 Eagle
Aug 15 2019 1 Rabbit
Sep 10 2019 1 Ocelot

Sep 23 2019 1 Deer
Oct 6 2019 1 Flower
Oct 19 2019 1 Reed
Nov 1 2019 1 Death
Nov 14 2019 1 Rain
Nov 27 2019 1 Grass
Dec 10 2019 1 Serpent
Dec 23 2019 1 Knife

Jan 5 2020 1 Monkey
Jan 18 2020 1 Lizard
Jan 31 2020 1 Earthquake
Feb 13 2020 1 Dog
Feb 26 2020 1 House
Mar 10 2020 1 Vulture
Mar 23 2020 1 Water
Apr 5 2020 1 Wind
Apr 18 2020 1 Eagle
May 1 2020 1 Rabbit
May 14 2020 1 Crocodile
May 27 2020 1 Ocelot
Jun 9 2020 1 Deer
Jun 22 2020 1 Flower
Jul 5 2020 1 Reed
Jul 18 2020 1 Death
Jul 31 2020 1 Rain
Aug 13 2020 1 Grass
Aug 26 2020 1 Serpent
Sep 8 2020 1 Knife
Sep 21 2020 1 Monkey
Oct 4 2020 1 Lizard
Oct 17 2020 1 Earthquake
Oct 30 2020 1 Dog
Nov 12 2020 1 House
Nov 25 2020 1 Vulture
Dec 8 2020 1 Water
Dec 21 2020 1 Wind

Jan 3 2021 1 Eagle
Jan 16 2021 1 Rabbit
Jan 29 2021 1 Crocodile
Feb 11 2021 1 Ocelot
Feb 24 2021 1 Deer
Mar 9 2021 1 Flower
Mar 22 2021 1 Reed
Apr 4 2021 1 Death
Apr 17 2021 1 Rain
Apr 30 2021 1 Grass
May 13 2021 1 Serpent
May 26 2021 1 Knife
Jun 8 2021 1 Monkey
Jun 21 2021 1 Lizard
Jul 4 2021 1 Earthquake
Jul 17 2021 1 Dog
Jul 30 2021 1 House
Aug 12 2021 1 Vulture
Aug 25 2021 1 Water
Sep 7 2021 1 Wind
Sep 20 2021 1 Eagle
Oct 3 2021 1 Rabbit
Oct 16 2021 1 Crocodile
Oct 29 2021 1 Ocelot
Nov 11 2021 1 Deer
Nov 24 2021 1 Flower
Dec 7 2021 1 Reed
Dec 20 2021 1 Death

Jan 2 2022 1 Rain
Jan 15 2022 1 Grass
Jan 28 2022 1 Serpent
Feb 10 2022 1 Knife
Feb 23 2022 1 Monkey
Mar 8 2022 1 Lizard
Mar 21 2022 1 Earthquake
Apr 3 2022 1 Dog

The Ephemeris of the Day–Signs

Apr 16 2022 1 House	Jul 28 2023 1 Monkey	Nov 7 2024 1 Rain
Apr 29 2022 1 Vulture	Aug 10 2023 1 Lizard	Nov 20 2024 1 Grass
May 12 2022 1 Water	Aug 23 2023 1 Earthquake	Dec 3 2024 1 Serpent
May 25 2022 1 Wind	Sep 5 2023 1 Dog	Dec 16 2024 1 Knife
Jun 7 2022 1 Eagle	Sep 18 2023 1 House	Dec 29 2024 1 Monkey
Jun 20 2022 1 Rabbit	Oct 1 2023 1 Vulture	
Jul 3 2022 1 Crocodile	Oct 14 2023 1 Water	Jan 11 2025 1 Lizard
Jul 16 2022 1 Ocelot	Oct 27 2023 1 Wind	Jan 24 2025 1 Earthquake
Jul 29 2022 1 Deer	Nov 9 2023 1 Eagle	Feb 6 2025 1 Dog
Aug 11 2022 1 Flower	Nov 22 2023 1 Rabbit	Feb 19 2025 1 House
Aug 24 2022 1 Reed	Dec 5 2023 1 Crocodile	Mar 4 2025 1 Vulture
Sep 6 2022 1 Death	Dec 18 2023 1 Ocelot	Mar 17 2025 1 Water
Sep 19 2022 1 Rain	Dec 31 2023 1 Deer	Mar 30 2025 1 Wind
Oct 2 2022 1 Grass		Apr 12 2025 1 Eagle
Oct 15 2022 1 Serpent	Jan 13 2024 1 Flower	Apr 25 2025 1 Rabbit
Oct 28 2022 1 Knife	Jan 26 2024 1 Reed	May 8 2025 1 Crocodile
Nov 10 2022 1 Monkey	Feb 8 2024 1 Death	May 21 2025 1 Ocelot
Nov 23 2022 1 Lizard	Feb 21 2024 1 Rain	Jun 3 2025 1 Deer
Dec 6 2022 1 Earthquake	Mar 5 2024 1 Grass	Jun 16 2025 1 Flower
Dec 19 2022 1 Dog	Mar 18 2024 1 Serpent	Jun 29 2025 1 Reed
	Mar 31 2024 1 Knife	Jul 12 2025 1 Death
Jan 1 2023 1 House	Apr 13 2024 1 Monkey	Jul 25 2025 1 Rain
Jan 14 2023 1 Vulture	Apr 26 2024 1 Lizard	Aug 7 2025 1 Grass
Jan 27 2023 1 Water	May 9 2024 1 Earthquake	Aug 20 2025 1 Serpent
Feb 9 2023 1 Wind	May 22 2024 1 Dog	Sep 2 2025 1 Knife
Feb 22 2023 1 Eagle	Jun 4 2024 1 House	Sep 15 2025 1 Monkey
Mar 7 2023 1 Rabbit	Jun 17 2024 1 Vulture	Sep 28 2025 1 Lizard
Mar 20 2023 1 Crocodile	Jun 30 2024 1 Water	Oct 11 2025 1 Earthquake
Apr 2 2023 1 Ocelot	Jul 13 2024 1 Wind	Oct 24 2025 1 Dog
Apr 15 2023 1 Deer	Jul 26 2024 1 Eagle	Nov 6 2025 1 House
Apr 28 2023 1 Flower	Aug 8 2024 1 Rabbit	Nov 19 2025 1 Vulture
May 11 2023 1 Reed	Aug 21 2024 1 Crocodile	Dec 2 2025 1 Water
May 24 2023 1 Death	Sep 3 2024 1 Ocelot	Dec 15 2025 1 Wind
Jun 6 2023 1 Rain	Sep 16 2024 1 Deer	Dec 28 2025 1 Eagle
Jun 19 2023 1 Grass	Sep 29 2024 1 Flower	
Jul 2 2023 1 Serpent	Oct 12 2024 1 Reed	Jan 10 2026 1 Rabbit
Jul 15 2023 1 Knife	Oct 25 2024 1 Death	Jan 23 2026 1 Crocodile

Feb 5 2026 1 Ocelot
Feb 18 2026 1 Deer
Mar 3 2026 1 Flower
Mar 16 2026 1 Reed
Mar 29 2026 1 Death
Apr 11 2026 1 Rain
Apr 24 2026 1 Grass
May 7 2026 1 Serpent
May 20 2026 1 Knife
Jun 2 2026 1 Monkey
Jun 15 2026 1 Lizard
Jun 28 2026 1 Earthquake
Jul 11 2026 1 Dog
Jul 24 2026 1 House
Aug 6 2026 1 Vulture
Aug 19 2026 1 Water
Sep 1 2026 1 Wind
Sep 14 2026 1 Eagle
Sep 27 2026 1 Rabbit
Oct 10 2026 1 Crocodile
Oct 23 2026 1 Ocelot
Nov 5 2026 1 Deer
Nov 18 2026 1 Flower
Dec 1 2026 1 Reed
Dec 14 2026 1 Death
Dec 27 2026 1 Rain

Jan 9 2027 1 Grass
Jan 22 2027 1 Serpent
Feb 4 2027 1 Knife
Feb 17 2027 1 Monkey
Mar 2 2027 1 Lizard
Mar 15 2027 1 Earthquake
Mar 28 2027 1 Dog
Apr 10 2027 1 House
Apr 23 2027 1 Vulture
May 6 2027 1 Water
May 19 2027 1 Wind
Jun 1 2027 1 Eagle
Jun 14 2027 1 Rabbit
Jun 27 2027 1 Crocodile
Jul 10 2027 1 Ocelot
Jul 23 2027 1 Deer
Aug 5 2027 1 Flower
Aug 18 2027 1 Reed
Aug 31 2027 1 Death
Sep 13 2027 1 Rain
Sep 26 2027 1 Grass
Oct 9 2027 1 Serpent
Oct 22 2027 1 Knife
Nov 4 2027 1 Monkey
Nov 17 2027 1 Lizard
Nov 30 2027 1 Earthquake
Dec 13 2027 1 Dog
Dec 26 2027 1 House

Jan 8 2028 1 Vulture
Jan 21 2028 1 Water
Feb 3 2028 1 Wind
Feb 16 2028 1 Eagle
Feb 29 2028 1 Rabbit
Mar 13 2028 1 Crocodile
Mar 26 2028 1 Ocelot
Apr 8 2028 1 Deer
Apr 21 2028 1 Flower
May 4 2028 1 Reed
May 17 2028 1 Death
May 30 2028 1 Rain
Jun 12 2028 1 Grass
Jun 25 2028 1 Serpent
Jul 8 2028 1 Knife
Jul 21 2028 1 Monkey
Aug 3 2028 1 Lizard
Aug 16 2028 1 Earthquake
Aug 29 2028 1 Dog
Sep 11 2028 1 House
Sep 24 2028 1 Vulture
Oct 7 2028 1 Water
Oct 20 2028 1 Wind
Nov 2 2028 1 Eagle
Nov 15 2028 1 Rabbit
Nov 28 2028 1 Crocodile
Dec 11 2028 1 Ocelot
Dec 24 2028 1 Deer

Table II – The Order of the Day–Signs

1	**Crocodile**	8	Ocelot	1	**Death**
2	Wind	9	Eagle	2	Deer
3	House	10	Vulture	3	Rabbit
4	Lizard	11	Earthquake	4	Water
5	Serpent	12	Knife	5	Dog
6	Death	13	Rain	6	Monkey
7	Deer			7	Grass
8	Rabbit	1	**Flower**	8	Reed
9	Water	2	Crocodile	9	Ocelot
10	Dog	3	Wind	10	Eagle
11	Monkey	4	House	11	Vulture
12	Grass	5	Lizard	12	Earthquake
13	Reed	6	Serpent	13	Knife
		7	Death		
1	**Ocelot**	8	Deer	1	**Rain**
2	Eagle	9	Rabbit	2	Flower
3	Vulture	10	Water	3	Crocodile
4	Earthquake	11	Dog	4	Wind
5	Knife	12	Monkey	5	House
6	Rain	13	Grass	6	Lizard
7	Flower			7	Serpent
8	Crocodile	1	**Reed**	8	Death
9	Wind	2	Ocelot	9	Deer
10	House	3	Eagle	10	Rabbit
11	Lizard	4	Vulture	11	Water
12	Serpent	5	Earthquake	12	Dog
13	Death	6	Knife	13	Monkey
		7	Rain		
1	**Deer**	8	Flower	1	**Grass**
2	Rabbit	9	Crocodile	2	Reed
3	Water	10	Wind	3	Oclelot
4	Dog	11	House	4	Eagle
5	Monkey	12	Lizard	5	Vulture
6	Grass	13	Serpent	6	Earthquake
7	Reed			7	Knife

Day–Signs

8 Rain
9 Flower
10 Crocodile
11 Wind
12 House
13 Lizard

1 Serpent
2 Death
3 Deer
4 Rabbit
5 Water
6 Dog
7 Monkey
8 Grass
9 Reed
10 Ocelot
11 Eagle
12 Vulture
13 Earthquake

1 Knife
2 Rain
3 Flower
4 Crocodile
5 Wind
6 House
7 Lizard
8 Serpent
9 Death
10 Deer
11 Rabbit
12 Water
13 Dog

1 Monkey
2 Grass

3 Reed
4 Ocelot
5 Eagle
6 Vulture
7 Earthquake
8 Knife
9 Rain
10 Flower
11 Crocodile
12 Wind
13 House

1 Lizard
2 Serpent
3 Death
4 Deer
5 Rabbit
6 Water
7 Dog
8 Monkey
9 Grass
10 Reed
11 Ocelot
12 Eagle
13 Vulture

1 Earthquake
2 Knife
3 Rain
4 Flower
5 Crocodile
6 Wind
7 House
8 Lizard
9 Serpent
10 Death
11 Deer

12 Rabbit
13 Water

1 Dog
2 Monkey
3 Grass
4 Reed
5 Ocelot
6 Eagle
7 Vulture
8 Earthquake
9 Knife
10 Rain
11 Flower
12 Crocodile
13 Wind

1 House
2 Lizard
3 Serpent
4 Death
5 Deer
6 Rabbit
7 Water
8 Dog
9 Monkey
10 Grass
11 Reed
12 Ocelot
13 Eagle

1 Vulture
2 Earthquake
3 Knife
4 Rain
5 Flower
6 Crocodile

7	Wind	1	**Eagle**
8	House	2	Vulture
9	Lizard	3	Earthquake
10	Serpent	4	Knife
11	Death	5	Rain
12	Deer	6	Flower
13	Rabbit	7	Crocodile
		8	Wind
1	**Water**	9	House
2	Dog	10	Lizard
3	Monkey	11	Serpent
4	Grass	12	Death
5	Reed	13	Deer
6	Ocelot		
7	Eagle	1	**Rabbit**
8	Vulture	2	Water
9	Earthquake	3	Dog
10	Knife	4	Monkey
11	Rain	5	Grass
12	Flower	6	Reed
13	Crocodile	7	Ocelot
		8	Eagle
1	**Wind**	9	Vulture
2	House	10	Earthquake
3	Lizard	11	Knife
4	Serpent	12	Rain
5	Death	13	Flower
6	Deer		
7	Rabbit		
8	Water		
9	Dog		
10	Monkey		
11	Grass		
12	Reed		
13	Ocelot		

References

Arguelles, Jose A. *The Mayan Factor*, Santa Fe: Bear and Co., 1987

Aveni, Anthony F. *Skywatchers of Ancient Mexico*, Austin: University of Texas Press, 1980.

Aveni, Anthony F. *Empires of Time*, New York: Basic Books, 1989.

Barrios, Carlos. *The Book of Destiny*, NY: Harper Collins, 2009.

Burland, C.A. *The Gods of Mexico*, New York: G.P. Putnam's Sons, 1967.

Codex Perez and the Book of Chilam Balam of Mani, Translation by Eugene R. Craine and Reginal C. Reindorp, Norman: University of Oklahoma Press, 1979.

Coe, Michael D. *Mexico*, Mexico, D.F.: Ediciones Lara, 1962.

Duran, Fray Diego, *The Book of the Gods and the Rites and the Ancient Calendar*, Trans. and ed. by F. Horcasitas and D. Heyden, Norman: University of Oklahoma Press, 1971.

Edmonson, Munro S. *The Book of the Year*, Salt Lake City: University of Utah Press, 1988.

Johnson, Kenneth. *Jaguar Wisdom: Mayan Calendar Wisdom*, St. Paul, MN: Llewellyn Publications, 1997.

Krupp, Dr. E.C. *Echoes of the Ancient Skies*, New York: Harper and Row, 1983.

Landa, Friar Diego de. *Yucatan Before and After the Conquest*, Translated by William Gates, New York: Dover Publications, 1978.

Morley, Sylvanus Griswold. *The Ancient Maya*, Stanford: Stanford University Press, 1956.

Roys, R.L. *The Book of Chilam Balam of Chumayel*, Norman: University of Oklahoma Press, 1967.

Sahagun, Fray Bernardino de. *Florentine Codex: General History of the the Things of New Spain, Books 4 and 5*, Trans. C.E. Dibble and A.J.O. Anderson, Ogden: University of Utah Press, 1957.

Scofield, Bruce and Angela Cordova. *The Aztec Circle of Destiny*, St. Paul: Llewellyn Publications, 1988.

Scofield, Bruce. *Signs of Time: An Introduction to Mesoamerican Astrology*, Amherst, MA: One Reed Publications, 1994.

Scofield, Bruce and Barry Orr. *How to Practice Mayan Astrology*. Rochester, VT: Bear & Company. 2007.

Seler, Eduard. *The Tonalamatl of the Aubin Collection*, Berlin and London, 1901.

Tedlock, Barbara. *Time and the Highland Maya*, Albuquerque: University of New Mexico Press, 1982.

Thompson, J. Eric S. *Maya Hieroglyphic Writing: An Introduction*, Norman: University of Oklahoma Press, 1960.

Other Titles from The Wessex Astrologer
www.wessexastrologer.com

Martin Davis
Astrolocality Astrology: A Guide to What it is and How to Use it
From Here to There: An Astrologer's Guide to Astromapping

Wanda Sellar
The Consultation Chart
An Introduction to Medical Astrology
An Introduction to Decumbiture

Geoffrey Cornelius
The Moment of Astrology

Darrelyn Gunzburg
Life After Grief: An Astrological Guide to Dealing with Grief
AstroGraphology: The Hidden Link between your Horoscope and your Handwriting

Paul F. Newman
Declination: The Steps of the Sun
Luna: The Book of the Moon

Deborah Houlding
The Houses: Temples of the Sky

Dorian Geiseler Greenbaum
Temperament: Astrology's Forgotten Key

Howard Sasportas
The Gods of Change

Patricia L. Walsh
Understanding Karmic Complexes

M. Kelly Hunter
Living Lilith: the Four Dimensions of the Cosmic Feminine

Barbara Dunn
Horary Astrology Re-Examined

Deva Green
Evolutionary Astrology

Jeff Green
Pluto Volume 1: The Evolutionary Journey of the Soul
Pluto Volume 2: The Evolutionary Journey of the Soul Through Relationships
Essays on Evolutionary Astrology (ed. by Deva Green)

Dolores Ashcroft-Nowicki and Stephanie V. Norris
The Door Unlocked: An Astrological Insight into Initiation

Greg Bogart
Astrology and Meditation: The Fearless Contemplation of Change

Henry Seltzer
The Tenth Planet: Revelations from the Astrological Eris

Ray Grasse
Under a Sacred Sky: Essays on the Practice and Philosophy of Astrology

Martin Gansten
Primary Directions

Joseph Crane
Astrological Roots: The Hellenistic Legacy
Between Fortune and Providence

John Gadbury
The Nativity of the Late King Charles

Komilla Sutton
The Essentials of Vedic Astrology
The Lunar Nodes: Crisis and Redemption
Personal Panchanga: The Five Sources of Light
The Nakshatras: the Stars Beyond the Zodiac

Anthony Louis
The Art of Forecasting using Solar Returns

Reina James
All the Sun Goes Round: Tales from the Zodiac

Oscar Hofman
Classical Medical Astrology

Bernadette Brady
Astrology, A Place in Chaos
Star and Planet Combinations

Richard Idemon
The Magic Thread
Through the Looking Glass

Nick Campion
The Book of World Horoscopes

Judy Hall
Patterns of the Past
Karmic Connections
Good Vibrations
The Soulmate Myth: A Dream Come True or Your Worst Nightmare?
The Book of Why: Understanding your Soul's Journey
Book of Psychic Development

Neil D. Paris
Surfing your Solar Cycles

Michele Finey
The Sacred Dance of Venus and Mars

David Hamblin
The Spirit of Numbers

Dennis Elwell
Cosmic Loom

Gillian Helfgott
The Insightful Turtle

Bob Makransky
Planetary Strength
Planetary Hours
Planetary Combination

www.ingramcontent.com/pod-product-compliance
Lightning Source LLC
Chambersburg PA
CBHW062022220426
43662CB00010B/1435